Darkest England

Idries Shah

As I mentally review the many grim episodes and reflect on the marvellously narrow escapes from utter destruction to which we have been subjected during our various journeys to and fro through that immense and gloomy extent of primeval forest, I feel utterly unable to attribute our salvation to any other cause than to a gracious Providence who for some purpose of His own preserved us.

H. M. Stanley: *Darkest Africa,* London 1890

What should they know of England
Who only England know?

Kipling: *The English Flag*

Books by Idries Shah

Sufi Studies and Middle Eastern Literature
The Sufis
Caravan of Dreams
The Way of the Sufi
Tales of the Dervishes: *Teaching-stories Over a Thousand Years*
Sufi Thought and Action

**Traditional Psychology,
Teaching Encounters and Narratives**
Thinkers of the East: *Studies in Experientialism*
Wisdom of the Idiots
The Dermis Probe
Learning How to Learn: *Psychology and Spirituality in the Sufi Way*
Knowing How to Know
The Magic Monastery: *Analogical and Action Philosophy*
Seeker After Truth
Observations
Evenings with Idries Shah
The Commanding Self

University Lectures
A Perfumed Scorpion (Institute for the Study of Human Knowledge and California University)
Special Problems in the Study of Sufi Ideas (Sussex University)
The Elephant in the Dark: *Christianity, Islam and the Sufis* (Geneva University)
Neglected Aspects of Sufi Study: *Beginning to Begin* (The New School for Social Research)
Letters and Lectures of Idries Shah

Current and Traditional Ideas
Reflections
The Book of the Book
A Veiled Gazelle: *Seeing How to See*
Special Illumination: *The Sufi Use of Humor*

The Mulla Nasrudin Corpus
The Pleasantries of the Incredible Mulla Nasrudin
The Subtleties of the Inimitable Mulla Nasrudin
The Exploits of the Incomparable Mulla Nasrudin
The World of Nasrudin

Travel and Exploration
Destination Mecca

Studies in Minority Beliefs
The Secret Lore of Magic
Oriental Magic

Selected Folktales and Their Background
World Tales

A Novel
Kara Kush

Sociological Works
Darkest England
The Natives Are Restless
The Englishman's Handbook

Translated by Idries Shah
The Hundred Tales of Wisdom (Aflaki's *Munaqib*)

DARKEST ENGLAND

Adventures, Facts and Fantasy in

by

Idries Shah

ISF PUBLISHING

Copyright © The Estate of Idries Shah

The right of the Estate of Idries Shah to be identified as the owner of this work has been asserted by them in accordance with the Copyright, Designs and Patents Act 1988.

All rights reserved
Copyright throughout the world

ISBN 978-1-78479-171-1

First published 1987
Published in this edition 2020

No part of this publication may be reproduced or transmitted in any form or by any means, electronic, mechanical or photographic, by recording or any information storage or retrieval system or method now known or to be invented or adapted, without prior permission obtained in writing from the publisher, ISF Publishing, except by a reviewer quoting brief passages in a review written for inclusion in a journal, magazine, newspaper, blog or broadcast.

Requests for permission to reprint, reproduce etc., to:
The Permissions Department
ISF Publishing
The Idries Shah Foundation
P. O. Box 71911
London NW2 9QA
United Kingdom
permissions@isf-publishing.org

In association with The Idries Shah Foundation

The Idries Shah Foundation is a registered charity in the United Kingdom
Charity No. 1150876

Contents

Foreword	ix
Roots and Anglekins	1
Cruel Lords	18
Damage Control	24
Certainly Not From Trinidad	34
Angles Down the Road	47
Pliny Rules in Badgersden	59
The Cipher	75
Gy-i Fee-a	87
The Dear Martian	101
Wise Men Never Tell	116
Tribal Rituals	136
Unsuitable for Antarctica	156
All Very Well in Nairobi	168
Woadlore	178
Carriemoss	186
Pirates and Admirals	195
Xavier Turlough is My Name	206
Stands to Reason	217
Smoke and Frozen Tiger	222
Demons of the Upper Air	233
Just Before Albania	242
Mouse in Milk	255
Government by Astonishment	260
Guerrilla at the Palace	271
Security, and So On	279
The Secret System of the Angleans	291

What He's Really Like	303
Thrakintwist and Ciclaton	312
Watching Them	327
Heisenberg Wasn't So Original	335
Secret Rituals	348
The Hidden Teaching Method	355
Where IS Everybody?	365
Going Native	379
New English Bottles	392
The Solution	398
Nothing of Significance to Say	405

Foreword

> Some enthusiasts have even gone so far as to write "foreword" for "preface" at the beginning of their books... to write "foreword" is a piece of mere sentimental perversity.
> Austin K. Gray, BA:
> *A Dictionary of Synonyms*

SPEND TIME IN England, and look at its people; and even without the insights of anthropology you'll notice that your experiences are strangely like those which the English themselves used to report from their far-flung Empire. You'll not get malaria or easily Go Native: but you may well contract bronchitis and learn to Muddle Through.

A hundred kinds of social maneuvring replace ritual dances, found elsewhere: though totemism is rife. There is no broiling sun, but I can guarantee wind and rain aplenty. Magical potions, whether offered for alcoholic forgetfulness or instant beauty, are not lacking, either. Today, indigent beggars are uncommon: but a thousand importuning salespeople besiege you at the door, through the media, even on the telephone. Local and national chiefs? A myriad of them, in tax offices, companies, town halls, public utilities, vicarages or manors, answer well enough.

Tribal organization, native chants and war-cries, exotic regalia, strange attire: they have them all. The darkness of England is filled with superstition. On unlucky Friday the

Thirteenth, millions feel the hair rising on the backs of their necks. Ladders are avoided as assiduously as any taboo objects anywhere; black cats, rabbits' feet and newspaper astrology all have their devotees. And as for cults...

The magnificent dignity of a proud and remote people, cut off as surely as any Himalayan community or long-house settlement, excites our admiration, as such survivals must. Some, at least, of the amazing delicacies of the table would intrigue anyone: pie and mash, cows' heel jelly, bubble and squeak, to name but a few.

The English, like all isolated peoples with archaic ways, are splendid. And they have produced endless numbers of dauntless explorers of other peoples' countries. Names like Rhodes, Thesiger and Newby and hundreds more, testify to the record.

This book, however, is not written by one of their disciples, respected though these pioneers may be.

I take my inspiration from such as Ibn Battutah of Tangier, the extraordinary fourteenth-century globetrotter who still holds the record as the greatest traveler of all time. And from Ibn Khaldun of Tunisia; accepted, even in the West, as the first theoretician of human historical development – the founder of sociology, in fact.

Springing from a family settled since the ninth century in the folds of the Hindu-Kush, though myself born in the Himalayas, I have trodden many a lonely path, faced many hazards, noted many a confidence, to assemble these impressions of Darkest England.

Providing you're tough, there are adequate rewards in this endeavor; as the English say, "It's a Great Life if you Don't Weaken."

Idries Shah
London 1987

1

Roots and Anglekins

> *Englisc*
> No one spoke of Saxon or Sexisc, not even King Alfred himself, the great and good King of the West Saxons. From the beginning, the language was always Englisc.
> Dr. Simeon Potter: *Our Language*

"IT IS THE fate of travelers," an ancestor of mine, returned from an extensive journey abroad, wrote sadly, "to bring back what is old news to those who know, and what is novelty and thus causes incredulity in those who do not." I think I know what he means, and what it feels like. With the present lightning diffusion of information throughout the globe, you don't even have to travel. You can sit watching a TV program bounced off a satellite and be bored or outraged in the comfort of your own home. Or read all about it in the papers.

On June 3, 1977, one could have learned that St. Alban was not English, even though the Dean of St. Alban's was proposing him as England's Patron Saint.

Mr. Andrew Breeze, writing from St. John's College, Oxford, explained in a letter to the Editor of *The Times* that Alban had been born "anything up to 200 years before the English first saw these islands – when 'England' was hardly more than a nest of heathen pirates somewhere near Schleswig-Holstein."

Not only that: St. Alban was indeed a Christian martyr, but he spoke British ("the Celtic language ancestor of Welsh"), not English, and was first mentioned by the Welsh writer Gildas. The Angles and Saxons, in contrast, even tried to destroy Christianity.

Foreigners, especially those who are still asking whether England is in Britain or Britain in England, need strong nerves to face this kind of thing, to use a common English scholarly phrase.

Since there is no English Encyclopedia, and for another reason, I turned to the *Encyclopaedia Britannica* (which is American). Who are the English, I interrogated it, and when does their history start?

The *EB*, confidently enough, starts English History off at the "second half of the fifth century AD" (making England some fifteen hundred years old), which is clear enough, and for which I thank it. It is when it tries to go back further that we begin to glimpse something of the essential nature of the English, something which persists, as I shall show, until the present day.

Mr. Breeze, as I believed all along, was right. The English, then called Angles, came from Schleswig, though, if we want to quibble, it was probably not known as Schleswig-Holstein at the time. The Danes called Schleswig *Hathaby* – which may be one reason why the English like the Danes so much. Other reference books take them farther east than that: indeed, they had migrated to Schleswig from beyond the River Elbe, not too far from Berlin, as it now is. And earlier? But let us stay with the *EB*, for there is more germane information still to glean.

They came with the Saxons, who had been invited by the Briton Vortigern to help with a military problem in his domain, which was later to become England. As great-great-grandsons of Wotan, chief god of the Germanic peoples, the Saxon brothers Hengist and Horsa (some say they were Jutes) had the necessary leadership qualification. They, in turn, hired the Angles for the campaign to sort out the Picts and Scots, who had rampaged southward. They felt unsatisfied with the earlier, Roman, proposal to drive them as far north as possible and pen them behind a wall.

The Saxons soon turned on Vortigern, and found him a pushover. But, quite soon, the Angles were to deal with the Saxons in a more efficient, though bafflingly subtle, way. Although the men of Schleswig were a tiny minority among the mercenaries (and only one component in the Angle-Saxon-Jute, Roman-descended and Celtic community of the land) they prevailed. Nobody knows how; but first they transformed the Anglo-Saxon dialect into Angle-ish, English: then, even more surprisingly, the whole country took their name – England.

Here we find the first traces of that remarkable, baffling tendency which has enabled these people to prevail over countries, continents and cultures. The British are credited with absorbing all later immigrants and conquerors. I am sure that they only did it after the Angles showed them how: and after the Angles had themselves taken over the show from the Britons.

Clues to the reasons for their success are very sparse. How they operated is something which we have to reconstruct from such traces as still remain in English behavior: but more of that later. If you try to approach the riddle from historical sources, you only find conjectures: "the Angles may well have had a cultural homogeneity the Saxons lacked" says one distinguished authority, Barbara M. H. Strang (in *History of English*) – but she leaves it at that.

What the Anglo-Saxons were like is said to be preserved in *Beowulf*, the amazing English poem of the sixth century. People who imagine that this must have been strongly Teutonic stuff might be surprised at the Oriental elements in it.

Here is Ms. Norma Lorre Goodrich, in *The Medieval Myths*:

> The reader will find a strange mixture of paganism, nature worship, the conflict between good and evil so reminiscent of Zoroastrianism, Hebrew traditions. Christian teachings, Oriental dragons, and funeral pyres like those of India... Scholars believe that the Asiatic traits go back to the common Indo-European heritage.

The English tendency to accumulate from anywhere, and then – and only then – to give out their version of ideas and events, which we can still find here today, seems to have been at work in the Dark Ages, and even before...

Hoping to interview some of the surviving Saxons, just to eliminate them from our inquiries as to the origins of the Zoroastrian, Chinese and Indian elements in the English heritage, I contacted the West German Embassy in London. I have it on their authority that the Saxons cannot now be located, as they were dispersed by the Second World War and its aftermath.

The East Germans could not help, either: though the West Germans say that there are Saxons in East Germany. The Democratic Republic's version, however, is that "Feudal survivals and Oriental vestiges have been eliminated by the reality of Socialism."

I could not be quite sure whether the Democratic Republicans were reacting to my query in a spirit of fun: *The Times* has recently recorded that "East Germany is in the middle of a humour crisis," so perhaps I asked at the wrong time. The Deputy Culture Minister said "the lightness of life is not being taken seriously enough" in his country. But, whatever the reason, the sole readily accessible survivors of Angle- and Saxondom are here in England.

I now return to the other point which I promised to clarify: why I turned to the <u>American</u> *Encyclopaedia Britannica*. It actually supports the matter of an Anglicising quality. First, the *Encyclopaedia* cannot be objected to as American if we remember that the Yanks are commonly termed Anglo-Saxons. Further, the word "Yank" – according to etymologists – is rooted in the mispronunciation of the word *English* by the Cherokees. The reason why there is no *English* Encyclopedia, though, rather stunned me. Briefly, it can be stated thus: "English stands for whatever the Angles decide it shall stand for." You can be English even if you are a Saxon or a Scandinavian: or even, look you, a Celt. My authority? No less a one than the *Oxford English Dictionary*, *viz*. under English. When the adj. first occurs in OE, it had already lost its etymological sense "of or belonging to the Angles" as distinguished from Saxons. The earliest recorded sense is:

> Of or belonging to the group of Teutonic peoples collectively known as the Angelcynn... comprising the Angles, Saxons and Jutes who settled in Britain during the 5th Century. With the incorporation of the Celtic and Scandinavian elements of the population into the "English" people, the adj. came in the 11th century to be applied to all natives in "England" *whatever their ancestry* [my italics].

So the English, under the rubric of Anglekin, Angelcynn, emerged in the eleventh century, a full six hundred years after English history begins. Even that date is controversial: the historian Trevelyan starts them off as late as the fourteenth to fifteenth centuries:

> In Chaucer's time [c. 1340–1400] the English people first clearly appear as a racial and cultural unit...

They must be one of the youngest peoples in Europe, by that reckoning. Plenty of Celts who might or might not have wanted to be their kin, were scooped into the collection. So the present-day "English" are not the Angles at all, but the Anglekin, quite a different thing, even if partly a fiction. Why, I wonder, is the country not called Anglekinland? Or Anglelanderland? An American scholar to whom I put this simply said (I think it was in English), "Well, they just endenizened themselves following their relocation": but enough of that.

It is often said, in today's England, that you may become British, but you can't, ever, become English. Indeed, some of the rulers of this country have clearly disliked the very idea. Consider that part of English law officially called *Presentment of Englishry*. Under the Normans, if you killed someone and could prove that the deceased was fair-haired and thus presumed to be (only) English, and not a Norman, the customary penalty for murder could be avoided.

Trust a Frenchman not to want to become naturalized: but today those claiming Norman descent are among the proudest of the English. Although the OED says that the resistance movement against Anglicization continued for a couple of generations, the earliest mention of a literary source for "English" with the present spelling is in the sixteenth century, five hundred years after the Norman conquest. That makes the word "English" as we know it only four centuries old.

For a thousand years or more, England and the English were developing into what we have today, without an over-meticulous chronicling of events. Perhaps as a rejection of Roman pedantry, the English continued to rely, for history, upon myths and legends. They even have a saying, preserved in books of proverbs: "Happy is the country which has no history." That is why we cannot even be sure that there was such a person as Vortigern, the inviter of Hengist and Horsa. Some deny Vortigern's historicity as confidently as others affirm it.

There is, in the English anti-intellectual tradition, a strong indication that the English don't want to be tied down to anything. This influences even their scholars, heirs to the imported, Latin-Continental academic mentality. We need only mention the reputed words of that English man of wisdom, Dr. Jowett of Oxford. One version runs:

> My name is Benjamin Jowett,
> I'm Master of Balliol College:
> Whatever is knowledge I know it
> And what I don't know isn't knowledge.

With surprisingly few exceptions, though, the English academic has avoided the omniscient pose which bedevils learned men elsewhere. It took an Englishman, Dr. Samuel Johnson, to dare to say, accounting for a mistake in the Dictionary which he compiled, "Ignorance, madam, pure ignorance."

Ignorance there may be, but there is plenty of IQ. The woman and man with, respectively, the world's highest and next highest IQs – Ms. Marilyn Savant and Mr. Chris Harding – are both products of Anglo-Saxon culture. And IQ measures not intellect but mental dexterity: which Samuel Johnson certainly had. Although there has been much dispute as to the actual date when the Angles arrived here, the English have overcome this difficulty by an almost superhuman feat of imagination. You can find, in English published sources, that the English were on these islands *even before they arrived*! Perhaps dexterity is too tame a word for it. Just look at what G. K. Chesterton says, in *The Rolling English Road*:

> Before the Romans came to Rye, or out to Severn strode,
> The rolling English drunkard made the rolling English road.

But before the Romans came, there *were* no English, no Angles, in Britain. There wasn't even an England here. See what I mean?

Who was this English drunkard, who got here before he was here? There is only one explanation for it, to my mind at least. Just as "English stands for whatever the Angles decide it shall stand for," so does "England" stand for the tribe itself (or its mentality), rather than for any fixed geographical entity.

Here is some more evidence. We all know that the English are modest, self-effacing and, in the current phrase, low-profile. They accept that people other than the English can have, say, splendid hearts, as one of them (at least) says. How, then, can we account for such lines as

> For England's the one land, I know,
> Where men with splendid hearts may go.

These words from "The Old Vicarage, Grantchester" cannot but import some metaphysical condition subsumed under the code-word of "England." Why, otherwise, "the ONE land"?

The more we read what they write, the more we must suspect that the English have the idea that they were here hundreds of thousands of years ago. Why, I cannot imagine: perhaps they really were. Did you know that children are instructed (in *The Wonder Encyclopaedia*) that when their ancestors arrived, England had jungles, and was populated by Primitive Man?

> The English people have not always been in England. When they came first to Britain, it was very different from what it is today. What is now rich English cornland or green meadow was in those far-off ages pathless swamp or tangled jungle. The pleasant English hills were then shaggy with untrodden forest. And through these forests and jungles roamed Early Man.

How deeply this way of thinking can affect today's English people is seen in, say, Sir Arthur Smith Woodward's book about the "Piltdown Man," the remains displayed in 1912 as having been discovered in Sussex and thought to be half a million years old. The British Museum man's 1948 work on the find (later established as a medieval skull and the jaw of an orang-utan, though that is not relevant to my present theme) was actually entitled *The Earliest Englishman*.

Although clearly not human-orang hybrids (even the Nazi race experts kindly decided that they were Aryans) the English are undoubtedly a tribe, and not a nation as generally understood elsewhere. The difference? Technically speaking, a nation is proud of what it *has*, and the hallmark of the tribe, long accustomed to having very little, is to glory in what it *is*. That's the great difference between the Americans and the English: one has, the other simply is.

And the wandering of the English, even in England, continued long after they hit the Albionic beaches. How many other peoples can say that a major part of them had not settled down six hundred years after conquering a country as nomads?

When the Normans compiled the Domesday Book, the census showed that no less than half the English population had no fixed abode. As Henry Treece, in *The Crusades*, remarks: "We are left with the astounding fact that, in England alone, there must have been a floating population of something like a million souls." The restlessness is amazing, and it produced a great empire. In some parts of it, indeed, English people lived happily where the original inhabitants had been trying for centuries to get out. The British have never ceased to be peripatetic. Cecil Rhodes, the great Empire-builder, in his last will and testament, foresaw not only the reclaiming of the Americans for England, but the final capture of much of the rest of the globe:

> The furtherance of the English [sic] Empire for the bringing of the whole uncivilised world under British rule, for the recovery of the United States, for the making of the Anglo-Saxon race but one empire – what a dream! But yet it is probable.

Probable, he says: not just possible. And, although the country was then (in 1902) called "Britain," and had been for ages, Rhodes is talking about England.

Does any of that sound like any real empire, any real nation, physical or political entity? There is even a likelihood that Englishmen (or -women), far from being rooted in England, do not live here at all. Any who do, always seem to come from somewhere else.

Test it. Go out into the streets of any town or city in the physical England, or into any village or country lane, and ask directions. You know as well as I do that the answer, nine times out of ten, will be "I'm a stranger here, myself." And even if your destination is only "First right, second left: you can't miss it," it's never where they say it is.

And today, with a settled population of sixty million, bereft of the wide-open spaces formerly colored red on the map, with immigration regulations everywhere – where will they go?

Their preparedness to travel, and to live in the most inhospitable environments (the English climate is worse than that of Central Asia), was underlined by Lord Young of Dartington. Aided by Dr. Tony Flowers, he is reported to have attracted five hundred volunteers to live in conditions which "simulate life on the planet Mars," as the *Daily Mail* puts it. This project is not considered particularly odd by the former astronaut and a number of respected academics who are mentioned as backing it. The astounding mobility of the nation is supported by the unprecedented fact – hard to credit, I know – that it has no agreed or defined meaning for the State, either as a British or an English one.

There are laws, legitimately passed by Parliament, which refer to "the State." But the State itself is not defined. Nobody in England denies that there is a State. They just don't know what it is. And that includes their greatest legal brains.

As recently as 1985, an article in *The Times* drew attention to this bewildering state of affairs. It reminded its readers that, in 1962, the Law Lords could not agree whether the State meant the people and the government, or all the people, or only the government itself. There has been no change since then. A jury in 1985 (perhaps because of this uncertainty) acquitted a man accused of communicating information to a Member of Parliament. According to one of the Law Lords, Lord Reid, the State does not mean the government: he thought that the nearest definition was the "organized community." That seems to mean almost everybody. But, in contrast, Lord Devlin insists that the State means only "the organs of government of a national community."

An English dictionary has it that a State Trial is a trial for an offense against the State. Clear enough – if one could find out (or if someone would define) what the State is, in the case of England.

To me, one compelling reason for all this confusion is that the Anglean mentality always keeps its options open. And why? Quite possibly because the Angles, having switched from one state to another, as it were – from Schleswig/Hathaby to Albion, carry their equivalent of a State around with them wherever they wish to go, like their sausages and mash or their weights and measures.

Matthew Arnold, the nineteenth-century English man of letters, unwittingly casts much light on the English mind in this area. Although himself a native of the islands, he spent so much time away from England, living on the Continent, that he became conditioned by the alien concept of the State which is universal there. Returning home, he actually agitated, quite fiercely, for its adoption in England. In so doing, he highlighted – by contrast – the entirely different way of thinking of almost all his fellow-countrypeople.

Instead of admiring the unique mentality and *modus operandi* of the English, Arnold felt that these were flaws which would lead to anarchy. He had become detribalized.

According to him, the English must adopt "the notion, so familiar on the Continent and to antiquity, of *the State* – the nation in its collective and corporate character, entrusted with stringent powers for the general advantage, and controlling individual wills in the name of an interest wider than that of individuals." Few ideas, I would have thought, could seem so foreign from an English perspective. Nearly a century has passed since Arnold's death, and if you look at the history, things were far nearer anarchy then than they are now. And still nobody is any the wiser as to what "the State" means.

Now, if we look at Matthew Arnold's name, finding its etymology from the appropriate reference-books, it translates as "Gift of Yah, Eagle-Strength." In succeeding pages, I give, in brackets, the meaning of various English names. The English themselves always do this when studying other tribes (e.g. Big Chief Rain-in-the-Face), so it evidently gives a clue to the individual personality or nature of the culture. Indeed, from time to time, one may hear it said in England that people come to resemble their names.

Their own certainly bespeak a rugged and adventurous background: Edith (Happy-War); Gerald (Spear-Rule); Roger (Fame-Spear). Even Charles (A Man) has a certain boldness about it, though it is not Anglo-Saxon. It was introduced by the conquerors from France. The inner Anglean gift, whether from Yah or otherwise, is all but eclipsed in Arnold's instinct. And the fine Eagle-Strength, heroically Continental-Teutonic as it is, may somehow have influenced a very unEnglish desire for centralization...

The State, of course, does not correspond in any readily observable way to the English community, past or present. The Inner Anglean is not really talking or thinking about the same country as you and I imagine he is. Run your eyes over the verses published in 1915, by Helen Gray Cone:

> Bind her, grind her, burn her with fire,
> Cast her ashes into the sea –
> She shall escape, she shall aspire
> She shall arise in a sacred scorn,
> Lighting the lives that are yet unborn
> Spirit supernal, splendour eternal, England!

Does that sound like a country to you? It's not as good as, but very close to, parts of *Macbeth*. The witchy parts.

If one thinks about it, there is also something odder than just odd about the way an English politician, when interviewed on television, will speak of "going up and down the country," as if it were vertical – or at least more of a switchback than I have found it to be. Their vision of it is really quite other.

This is also made clear in Wilfred Campbell's "England, England, England, girdled by ocean and skies," when the country is quite substantially bounded by Scotland and Wales (not to mention sandbanks), as well as by water, only a corner of which is, in fact, ocean.

I looked up the figures, just to be on the safe side. The country in this archipelago which comes closest to the "girdled" definition is Ireland, and most of that is a foreign country. Scotland, too, with 365 miles more sea-coast than England, fits Campbell's definition more closely.

The mythical sea "surrounding" England appears again and again in its literature, not least in Shakespeare (*Richard II*) with his "England, bound in with the triumphant sea!"

The description simply doesn't fit. Look at a map and you'll see it bears me out.

Shakespeare promised, "Come the three corners of the world in arms/And we shall shock them. Naught shall make us rue/If England to itself do rest but true." *Three* corners: a triangular world? If the metaphysical theory of England, the Deeper Meaning, did not appeal to me so much, I'd put the English down as just *weak in geography, must try harder*.

Especially when the authoritative *Encyclopaedia* – and the English (1911) and not an American edition at that – cannot decide whether the Welsh coastline is 390 or 515 miles long. It gives different figures in different places.

The allusive nature of English writing, whether by Shakespeare, Ms. Cone or almost anyone else, delights me as much as it seems to enrage Europeans who are still cut off on the mainland. I like it because I think it contains valuable and important teachings, whether or not the English always know it. I am sure, too, that this baffles Europeans and creates the fury which is otherwise hard to account for, especially among the French.

The eminent author Jules Michelet, not exceptionally, found it possible to write, in his *Histoire de France*, that the literature of the island race was the "great vice of the English people." It was "sceptical, Judaic, satanic, anti-Christian."

It is a vast enterprise, you may now begin to see, getting to grips with the English. The impact of their thought, writing and behavior is sometimes almost too much. Faced with such a problem, one might do worse than to follow the advice of Lady Hillingdon, whose *Journal* (though in another context) speaks of lying back, closing the eyes, and thinking of England.

The Other England, we must always remember, runs parallel to the one we see, revealing itself, for the most part, indirectly.

My mind, fuelled by this thought, now tracks back several decades and thousands of miles, to my childhood, when my English nurse, Miss Ursula (means Little-She-Bear) Hampton, taught me a poem. I was to say it at night, before going to bed. The words often kept me awake, puzzling, wondering what on earth they could mean. Finally I decided that there were two possibilities. Either she had lost a child herself, or else the prayer was a blessing that I should invoke for *her* sake:

> I thank the goodness and the grace,
> Which on my birth have smiled,
> And made me, in these Christian days,
> A happy *English* child.

Are those the ingredients of Englishry, I can now ask myself, irrespective of origins, place of birth? Goodness and grace may be all you need, really. Perhaps the goodness and grace are catching, helping to make us foreigners both better and more Anglekin, absorbing the values unconsciously.

Were we – sorry, they – like that in Schleswig-Holstein too: before that great Volkerwanderung took them to Albion? Volkerwanderung? I found the word, invoked to describe the great migration of the English, in a recent English – not a German – book.

Alas, there are only fragments in the histories to give us clues about what the Angles thought. Gildas Sapiens, the British author of *Liber Qaerulus*, may, however, have recorded something important toward understanding the Angle restlessness. According to him, writing in the sixth century, not long after the invaders arrived, they only came here for a limited space of time:

For one of their soothsayers foretold that they should hold the land to which their ships were drawing near for three hundred years.

Unlike most of the other foreigners whom I have met, it is a strange underlying mobility, of both thought and action, which characterizes the English for me. I know that it is customary to assess them as relatively immobile, home-lovers, sluggards even. Not for me. I sense the heritage of restlessness just as strongly as the inertia.

2

Cruel Lords

Unknown
There are no countries in the world less known by the British than these self-same British Islands.

George Borrow: *Lavengro*

"JUST WAIT UNTIL you get to England: that's the place to see." I looked at the fat, middle-aged, sweating man ("of Middle Eastern appearance" in the English phrase) who had sat down beside me in the hotel lounge, after telling the Nubian waiter to bring him a pot of tea.

Khartoum that afternoon was very hot: over 112 degrees in the shade, by the thermometer on the wall. The ceiling fans were feeble, and there was no air-conditioning. The man must have heard my father and me speaking in English, something we often did in the East when we wanted to talk privately. The stranger's English was much worse than ours; but perhaps he had made a fair assumption, that we had not yet been to England. For this was in the days before mass air travel: and we were both wearing the Arabian garb in which we had, only that morning, left Saudi Arabia. The Middle East seemed very small then: only about three people on the

Peninsula, it was said, had been in England: Emir Faisal the foreign minister, Sheikh Hafiz Wahba, the Saudis' London ambassador, and St. John Philby, the explorer, who ran a motor dealership in Jeddah.

"*Bahana bekunem – bego ki narafti*," my father said to me, in Dari-Persian. Afghans often tease people when at a loose end, so I went along with his "Let's have a joke, say you haven't been there."

"What's it like in England, then?" I asked the newcomer, trying to make my voice eager for information and my face light up with anticipation.

He smoothed his short beard with his right hand and screwed up his face, as if seeing the far horizons of a mysterious land.

"England? Well, Manchester is sunny, the warmest place they have. It is a town, very big. But the country is the best. It is all green."

"And what," I asked, wondering about Manchester but wanting to broaden the canvas, "happens in the countryside?"

"You do not know that?" He turned a look of false amazement upon me and sucked at a gold tooth. "The countryside is full of castles. In those strongholds live cruel lords. They wear red coats and ride fierce horses, pursuing small brown animals. If they find no such prey, they turn their whips on the peasants, who pull handfuls of hair, forelocks, from their heads in sullen salutation. This obeisance is rigidly enforced."

"Amazing! How could you have acquired such knowledge, here in the Sudan?"

He wasn't going to be trapped into saying that he had actually been to England. But he wasn't prepared to admit that he hadn't, either.

"Ah, my friend, that is only a little of it. Now, that camera on its strap around your neck. Did you know that it was in England that they discovered how to use it? No. I thought not!" I was shaking my head in disbelief.

"Well, it was found that there are certain minute creatures: *bakterya* is their scientific name. These they capture and imprison in flasks until they have the film ready. Then they enter a room of darkness, to preserve the secret – though I know it – and they throw the *bakterya* upon the film. Instantly the tiny ones chew away each part of the film which contains no picture, and a reverse image is revealed."

"But," I asked, "how do the bacteria know which parts to chew?"

He leaned back, his heavy-lidded eyes closed and his mouth turned up in a triumphant smirk. "They know because the glass at the front of the camera renders, by its nature, other parts of the picture inedible for such as the small insects which I have described!"

"And that is how a picture is made?"

"Not quite. I can see that you have little grasp of modern technology. When the film is ready, it is like glass, only soft, resembling cloth. And shiny. There is a further process. It is called 'the making-it-to-paper.' But that is one of the master secrets. I cannot tell everything of my knowledge to total strangers."

"No, of course not. By the way, which of them – the lords or the peasants – invented the photographic art?"

"Neither. They could not. It was" – he looked around conspiratorially – "it was in England, but it was done by the Turks! People have pretended otherwise, but I know. After all, is not the word '*kodak*' Turkish for 'little one,' and are photographs not merely little ones of the original person or scene? Yes, you will learn a lot, if you can only get to England."

It was then that I thought that some day I would write a book and call it *Darkest England*.

It proved to be more difficult to finish than I had expected. The Romans, so English people are fond of saying, called it a land of magic and mystery; yet at that time there was no such place as England in the British Isles. It was Prythain then, which "may be Celtic, and later meant Wales." The people were decorated in blue, "the men called Brith," from the Welsh word "to paint." And Bret "means a Briton or Welshman." That is according to some authorities. But the redoubtable Dr. E. Brewer is sure that the word Britain is of Middle Eastern origin. "By far the most probable derivation," he says in his *Dictionary*, "is from the Phoenician 'Baratanic' (Country of Tin)."

There is a consensus about the word "England," though: it is named after a village, Anglen, in today's Schleswig, north Germany. That, in turn, may come from the Latin for "the people of the angle," the shape of their territory. Its warriors came here when they joined in with some Saxon freebooters in the fifth century. What we know as England was named (but not united – Mercia held out) by Egbert at Winchester in 829; or it may have been in 925, for the experts are not agreed.

The Middle Eastern discovery of Britain (in the Victorian sense: nineteenth-century explorers were always "discovering" places, such as Timbuktu, which were already known) was in the ninth century. This is recorded by Ibn Rustah (died 910): "In the northern part of the ocean are twelve islands," he says, "called the islands of Bratiniyya."

Why the Saxon Egbert should have christened his kingdom after the minority called Angles is just one of many puzzles. Places like Essex or Sussex, considered to be parts of England, did not belong to the Angles at all. The land strongly held by

Schleswigians embraced mainly Northumbria, Mercia and East Anglia.

The vagueness of the history highlights an important, almost a determining, characteristic of the English today. They are given to shrugging off, or interpreting to vanishing-point, anything they wish. England, for the English, is a state of mind, or one of many states of mind. All this wreaks a strange magic in the mind of the foreigner. As the shelves of many libraries show, it arouses in visitors a powerful urge to study the English and to write books on the phenomena they find. And this in spite of countless warnings by other foreigners that it is hazardous: like the dangers traditionally concealed in a quest for hidden treasure, the Fountain of Youth or the Philosopher's Stone. Patrick Campbell says, in *A Short Trot with a Cultured Mind*:

> It seems to me that you can go sauntering along for a certain period, telling the English some interesting things about themselves, and then all at once it feels as if you had stepped on the prongs of a rake.

I know exactly what he means. You find that you have booby-trapped yourself; and yet when you come to, after that blow on the head, you may well hear yourself saying, like Voltaire, "If I had had to choose my birthplace, I would have chosen England."

The magic, the state of mind in England, and the minefields, are all around us. It is not only foreigners who run into, or come across, them; or even that the influence is confined to the human species. As I started this book, I saw an item on Independent Television News. Thieves broke into a pet store in Oxfordshire and a rabbit, not knowing – or not caring – that it was not a guard-dog, attacked them so fiercely that they fled, empty-handed. No sooner had I absorbed that than

I read how a family had been trapped *in London* by – a herd of wild horses.

I did not, throughout my wanderings, find any cruel lords: and there was little sun in Manchester while I was there. The bacteria which devour the emulsion on photographic film elude me still. But the reality of the land of the one-time Schleswigers proved to be even more astonishing than any of the promised wonders, by the way.

Yes, *by the way*; you hear the phrase on all hands in England. It means *incidentally*, of course. People say this when they do not mean "as a digression" – though they may mean this at times. It has the advantage of prefacing diametrically opposite intentions. "By the way, would you like a cup of coffee?" does indeed mean what it sounds like. But, "by the way, I have a bone to pick with you" is altogether more sinister, and really signifies "there is something important, probably unpleasant, to discuss."

Or, again, it could be a mere jocularity.

3

Damage Control

Somdel I Marvel
Britons and Romans, Saxons and then Danes
So many conquerors have taken it.
I somdel marvel any land is left
              James F. Waight: *Harold*

DARKEST ENGLAND IS very like parts of the East, not only in fauna and flora but in the primate population. "Primate," for the English, has three chief meanings, and it is to two of these that I refer: "principal" and "of the order which includes human beings." The other category, archbishops, has fewer members. Legend, whose custodians are the Press, has it that they are all members of my Club. The legend can only be dissolved by becoming a Member.

The more important mammal primates of England, as I have observed over the years, are those, regardless of location, geographical or social, who have what is known to them as common sense. It is *their* opinion which tends to prevail, especially when allied to aplomb or to one of the many other chief features of the creature.

I recall a discussion between three heated Greeks and a couple of much cooler Englishmen, at which I was present in Petticoat Lane Market, in London. Starting with a difference of opinion about the quality of some trifle of merchandise, it had engendered a broadside of words, directed by the most articulate of the sons of Homer toward an English stallholder.

"You English!" the Greek roared. "I know all about you; I was there, in the Western Desert in the 1940s, when you retreated and left some of us Greeks to take the fire of the Afrika Korps eighty-eights!"

The Cockney didn't have to say (he told me later) that he'd been a Desert Rat himself. I could almost see the jerboa flash of the Seventh Armoured Division on his sleeve as he bawled back:

"Werl, you know wotcha gotta do, dontcher, when them Jerries is about? You just wants ter keep yer 'ead down, that's wot."

Instantly, all was still: Petticoat Lane returned to normal, and people drifted away as the Greek just stood there, his mouth hanging open. I have often thought of this incident, trying to work out if there could possibly have been a better, or more unexpected, way of handling it. There is none.

There is an interesting English phrase "to roll with the punches." But the English know a stage earlier than that. They don't let the punches connect.

Common sense is needed, and found in my own part of the world in such matters as dealing with metaphysical madmen, cranks and impostors. In its traditional form, the term *Sufi* stands for a person of such impeccable virtue and spiritual attainment that none may so style himself (or herself) and still be innocent of vanity.

In other words, if you say you're one, you're not.

But let it not be concealed from you that we, like you, nowadays, are besieged by groups of near-madmen – cultists – who imitate what they imagine to be Sufis, who caper and dress in weird clothes, sometimes taking great liberties with others, and generally behaving in a manner open to justifiable criticism. Instead of seeking power over themselves, they try to acquire control over others.

Real Sufis, contrary to this systematic behavior, often assail such things as fixed thinking-patterns, however laudable these may seem to the converted. The aim is to make room for fresh ideas. Among other things, this flexibility enables people to survive when there is a need to adjust to changed circumstances.

What happens when these putative Sufis invade, or arise in, England? Not far from where I now sit there is what is misnamed a settlement (it is very unsettled) centered on a house in southern England. There you will find strangely clad, gamboling fools, led by a wiseacre in a tarboosh. English to a man – and woman – they have convinced themselves, and even sections of the Press plus some Eastern residents here, that they are Sufis.

When I recently approached their abode, embarrassed that the name of Sufi should be freely used by such as I could see marching and skipping up and down the village street, I noted a local rustic sitting outside the inn, nursing a pint of ale.

I sat down beside him and he said, with the kind of forbearance which bespeaks not only common sense but that propensity for becoming a Sufi which stems from seeing the good and shunning the evil: "Aar, there be the Soofees. Not right in the head at all, but they do have some lovely hives and dainty honey..."

The English people are perfectly all right unless their emotions are so tampered with that they develop fixations. I cannot say that I know how to prevent this: for it can occur, as it were, involuntarily.

Even the most reputable, and the most brilliant, people may become irrationally attached to something: it does not have to be a cult. Look at the example of Sir Robert Watson-Watt. Although he developed radar for the defense of Britain during the Second World War, he was passionately opposed to neutralising the *German* radar defending the Third Reich. But why? Because, according to Professor R. V. Jones in his *Most Secret War*, "it hurt him emotionally to think of radar being neutralized, even German radar."

This statement, not an isolated one, may contain a clue to the problem and its solution.

Watson-Watt did not see the humor of his situation. Lack of humor often goes with absence of common sense. I choose here a more recent example, out of several dozen clipped from the papers.

Professor Abdus Salam is Director of the International Centre of Theoretical Physics and a professor of physics at Imperial College, London. His daughter, explaining one of his theories to a teacher at her English school, was told to abandon it, or she would fail her A-level physics examination. She did fail, and has now taken to the study of – Oriental languages.

A few people in England (probably the darkest parts) seem to believe that dedication, or obsession with trivial rules, is the same as proper diligence or commitment to a cause. They are untypical. This can be seen in such affairs as a recently reported assault in London. Two men chased a mugger (who had attacked an elderly woman) into a train station – where they were turned back at the barrier because they had no tickets. They were not allowed to telephone the police, either. Finally they bought platform tickets and caught the thief.

Common sense can be allied to persistence so as to get things done: indeed, some English people believe that it should be the test for anyone before being encouraged to espouse a cause.

There is a lesson in the case of Harry Wright, a market gardener of Cottingham, near Hull, in northern England. In the 1950s, the Tomato and Cucumber Marketing Board, obsessed by rules, decided to ban the sale of bent cucumbers in Britain. The campaign against this bureaucracy became a national one.

Mr. Wright did not plant bombs, make impassioned, logical speeches, or organize street clashes. Instead, he dressed as Guy Fawkes or as an undertaker to raise questions at meetings of the Board. When he was fined for such unlawful behavior, he refused to pay. Court-appointed bailiffs seized goods from him and sold his equipment. But members of the public bought back his possessions and returned them to him.

I admit that the courts were English. But there are many people in England who insist on calling them "The Caughts"; caught no doubt, by humorless mechanicality.

Getting caught in England, in one sense or another, seems to be all too easy; especially if you are too serious, something which the English really dislike. If I asked you whether you thought Maud Ray was a woman's name or a coded message, what would you answer?

The reason I asked is because I find another episode in English history instructive in showing the mentality of the "caught."

The eminent scientist, Dr. (later Sir) John Cockroft, received a message from his colleague, the equally brilliant physicist Niels Bohr, in December 1940, saying that he and his wife were well, in German-occupied Denmark. Would Cockroft inform Maud Ray?

Cockroft immediately set about "decoding" this message which contained no code at all: Maud Ray was simply the Dane's former governess, who lived in Kent.

Intellectuals, scholars and scientists are often alleged to adhere to the principle known as Occam's Razor. This has been expressed as *Entia non sunt multiplicanda praeter necessitatem* – in the English vernacular, "Don't Make a Meal of It." Choose the simplest explanation for anything. Not so Dr. John Cockroft. He looked at the phrase and rearranged the letters of "please inform Maud Ray, Kent." The message was now much more interesting: he decided that the Dane had really been trying to convey the words "radium taken." That could only mean that the Germans had seized Dr. Bohr's radium.

Three years or so later, when Bohr reached England, he anxiously asked whether his message had reached the worried old lady in Kent.

As one Englishman told me recently, "Common sense can be operated as a sort of damage control method, dontcherknow..."

But we can be sure that Bohr (if not Maud Ray) had a good laugh about all this. I am convinced of it, because of a typical anecdote about the Danish scientist which Cockroft may well not have heard, which gives us a clear advantage over him.

A visitor, noting a horseshoe nailed up outside Bohr's house, asked how a physicist could believe that there was such a thing as magic, and rely on lucky horseshoes. "I understand," replied the scientist, "that they work whether you believe in them or not."

There is an English-type riposte if I ever heard of one: don't let the punch connect. And, if you want a crash course on this, just watch, on your television screen almost any day, one of their politicians wordily answering, with great affability, the question which the interviewer has *not* asked him.

Millions of the watching English are silently absorbing the technique. Each of them will use it, one day.

Judging things too rapidly, by-passing common sense, is nowadays a temptation, when instant reactions are expected from experts. The communications explosion insists on speed; and some people in England do get stampeded by its demands.

I once wrote a book which was published in 274 pages: which would ordinarily be expected to contain some 90,000 words. It was bound in red, with gold lettering – but the total text occupied no more than 1,326 words, occupying fourteen pages.

Some reviewers thought that *The Book of the Book* must be a hoax; others that there was something wrong with the typesetting. Some bookshops sent their orders back, asking for "complete copies."

Only five reviews noted that the story in the book was about quality and not quantity. Critics in two London Sunday papers (being weeklies, their reviewers have time to read books before writing about them) understood what it was about, and praised it.

As the Eastern saying, by the sage Hilali, has it, "One person who understands is worth a hundred who merely obey a custom."

The *Sunday Telegraph*, very English, found it to be:

> An extraordinary psychological test, in that it predicts the complete range of possible responses to itself.

I didn't catch the *Observer* out, either:

> Idries Shah is of course not a joker nor a crank, but a distinguished authority on Sufism, some of whose other books have been hailed as "Books of the Year."

Very kind; and showing that some reviewers *do* read books. But quite a lot of papers sniffed at *The Book of the Book*. A typical remark was "large sales can hardly be expected for *The Book of the Book*..." I'll spare *their* blushes, and not name them. One sat on the fence. That review earned a place in an excellent anthology, *Funny Convulsing and Funny Confusing*, assembled by Denys Parsons, and I am sure that this helped the book's sales. So far, it has gone into five impressions, and a sixth is planned.

Common sense operates as damage control, and requires patience and coolness. This, in turn, needs an impassive outward face. Luigi Barzini, the Italian journalist, spent a long time in England and tried hard to understand its people. In his *The Europeans*, he speaks of the "banal truisms" offered by distinguished men instead of wisdom, and his initial belief that "the English, like most Nordic people, were not very sharp as a whole." One of his great problems was "to separate the dull from the acute."

"In the end," he says, "I concluded that there was no sure way to ascertain if an Englishman was intelligent or stupid."

Mr. Barzini's assumptions may stand in his way. An Englishman can behave as stupidly as anyone if he allows his emotions to rule him, as did Cockroft or Watson-Watt, neither of them stupid men. Hence the damage which common sense prevents. An Englishman will behave as intelligently as anyone else if his feelings are not allowed to gain the upper hand. To assume that there are "intelligent" and "stupid" English people by looking at instances and not at the whole canvas, is, for me, flawed.

But I must admit that I am still puzzling over a notice by an eminent critic, describing, deadpan, the contents of one of my heavier non-fiction books. He delineates the theme and thrust admirably. But the piece is headed "Among the New Novels..."

One and the same action by an Englishman may be misunderstood as evidence of extreme boorishness, of cunning or great subtlety. It can also be used as an instrument of state. Mr. (later Earl) Attlee gave me a remarkable example, characteristically refraining from interpreting it.

A certain scholar had successfully carried out a "tricky advisory job" for the government during Attlee's premiership. Called to 10 Downing Street to receive the Prime Ministerial thanks, he had intimated that he would very much like an Oxford chair.

"I told him I'd do what I could," Attlee said, "and I was able to write him, two weeks later, in the following terms:

"'Oxford chairs, my staff have ascertained, are not up to much these days. I have, therefore, arranged to have a chair sent to you which was made in High Wycombe, which is not far from Oxford and as you will know is the center of the English furniture industry.'"

Deliberately misunderstanding the other person is an English technique of deflation, or humor: or it can be both. One keen observer of the English was the Nepalese Ambassador to the Court of St. James's, General Shanker Shamsher-Jung Bahadur Rana. His titles translate as Prince Brave War-Sword, and he felt that his Gurkha people resembled the English in their eccentricity. "My personal name is Shanker. Two-thirds of my Nepalese titles are in Persian, though we've never had anything to do with Persia..." he said to me one day.

This brought him to the English misunderstandings-with-humor technique. "There is one old and allegedly true story," he said, "about two Englishmen who had just finished, with gusto, a sheep's-head dinner.

"The first Englishman said, 'Long live sheep's head!' This gave the other one his chance to assail his companion's egocentricity, and to call him an animal at the same time.

"The second wagged his finger at him: 'Vanity, sir. Vanity!' he said."

Foreigners, including the Irish, French and Americans, love to make sweeping statements about the English indigenes and the matter of common sense. It rather takes the heat out of things when one sees that they can have diametrically opposed opinions on the matter.

George Bernard Shaw damns the whole lot of them: "No Englishman has any common sense or ever had or ever will have," he says in *John Bull's Other Island*.

Emerson, the American, quoting the Frenchman Montesquieu, weighs in with the exact opposite:

"No people have true common sense but those who are born in England."

But Sir William Gilbert (of Gilbert and Sullivan), a real Englishman even though his middle name was Schwenck, shows us the real link between heatedness and sense, in *Iolanthe*:

> On fire that glows
> With heat intense
> I turn the hose
> Of common sense.
> And out it goes
> At small expense.

Now that's what I call Damage Control.

4

Certainly Not From Trinidad

Follies
England, a happy land we know
Where follies naturally grow.
Churchill: *The Ghost*

APLOMB IS FRENCH for "perpendicularity, as of a lead weight on a line, self-possession"; and *sang-froid*, of course, means "coolness of blood."

It is probable that the English prefer to use these foreign terms for something which is widespread among them because it is bad form to boast of one's own coolness. That is, it sounds better to say, "By jove, that Frenchman certainly had aplomb," to show that one approves of the characteristic, than to claim to possess it oneself. It is left to others to make further inferences.

This is part of the amateur-status preference in England. A compatriot of mine was told, at his first Oxford tutorial, "You are not only here to learn. Try to acquire the appearance of not bothering to work at anything. Let others boast of their studiousness."

It is aplomb which other peoples associate with the English. An American joke may be taken as the standard text:

An Englishman is standing at the long bar of a saloon

in the Wild West. Suddenly a sun-crazed outlaw rushes in, straight through the batwing doors, firing into the air and howling, "Get outta here, you coyotes!"

Everyone dives for the floor or stampedes out of the place. The Englishman, however, is still standing there, as the newcomer skids up to him with staring eyes.

"By jove," says the Englishman, "you were right. There *were* a lot of coyotes in here, weren't there?"

Aplomb may be mistaken for madness or insensitivity but that may be all to the good. One opinion on this was given me by Marshal Sirdar Shah-Wali Khan, our King's uncle and for many years Afghan Ambassador in Paris and London. "An insensitive Englishman is a problem," he said, "but a sensitive one is a disaster!"

A baffled East European once reported to me an experience which, for him, proved British insensitivity: or lack of manners; he was not sure which.

He had been visiting the Foreign Office on some routine matter connected with his embassy, then:

> This Englishman said to me, "One needs something strong," and he put some strong alcohol in a glass, gin it was, very strong drink. Then he added water. Now it was no longer strong. But he wasn't finished, *tovarish*. He put some lime juice into the drink; which, of course, made it acid. And then, into the acid, he put sugar: I suppose to make it sweet. Finally he picked up the glass, and spoke. He said: "Good health!" But, though it was *my* health he was talking about – he drank the stuff *himself*. Had he no manners?

I seem to have been hearing about English manners all my life. Some people claim that they have exquisite manners, others that they have none at all. The nearest that I have been able to get to an answer is that both claims seem to be true. Harold Nicolson puts it like this:

> Admittedly our manners (when we first began to have manners in the fifteenth century) were the product of foreign importations rather than any autocthonous growth.

The encoded message here, to those learned in Englishry, is that good behavior is not native, and therefore can be adopted or abandoned at will.

But was the Slav's assessment right? Did his experience with the Englishman have any connection with sensitivity or manners? I asked a former high official of the Foreign and Colonial Office whether such an anecdote could be true, or even possible.

He shot his starched lace cuffs and gave me a charming smile.

"Yes, indeedy, ol' boy. You see, the fella was obviously showing aplomb. That Russki might have been KGB: trying to find out something. So how to cope? Use up a bit of time, so that your secretary can come in to say you've another appointment, then shake his hand, get him off the premises, that kind of thing. What's the fella's name?"

"Igor Voyenski," I said.

"There you are then! His uncle is First Deputy Clown of the Council of Lunatics over there; something of the sort. I'd watch my step with him."

Insensitivity to Igor's desire for a drink, but, you must agree, great awareness of more important factors.

I acquired my own reputation for aplomb very accidentally. And I have seen English poise which might have been interpreted as something else (nervelessness, for example) in operation so often that I am tempted to trace its origins to similar casual happenings. The difference between English and foreign aplomb may well be that the foreigner is *trying* to practice it, while the Englishman reaches for it automatically.

I probably wouldn't even have noticed my own aplomb if a Finn who was standing by, earnest student of the English as he was, had not identified it and complimented me.

In a stately salon at a London diplomatic occasion, I was watching the usual cosmopolitan scrum trampling the chicken sandwiches into the carpet and bolting the caviar in the usual way, when an Englishman, who had evidently eaten that day and was therefore more detached than the other guests, approached me.

"I say," he said, "are you from Trinidad?"

"No, actually," I responded, "are you?"

He looked at me for a moment: first in bewilderment and then with annoyance. "Trinidad?" he snapped. "I most certainly am NOT!" He lost his head, as the Afghans say, trying to save his ears.

This was when the Finn came up and congratulated me: at least, he did so the moment the Englishman had stalked off. "That was Sir Geoffrey Furlonge, British Minister to Bulgaria," he said, "and you certainly saw *him* off..."

So I got the credit – the Finn spread the word – for being a cool customer, quite without merit. Years later, I still meet people who have heard of my great feat of aplomb.

I am sure that the Finn made the same sort of mistake as Paul Gallico, who once wrote, in the *New York Times*, about the terrible way in which the British were "calculatedly rude." This they may be, from time to time: but I believe that it is rarer than Gallico thought. Mostly, when I've noticed, it has just *looked* like rudeness. In fact, I've almost certainly caught the habit myself.

Gallico's remark is worth noting in full, especially by those who are planning to go to the United States; or by the two and a half million Americans who visit England each year:

> No one can be as calculatedly rude as the British, which amazes Americans, who do not understand studied insult and can only offer abuse as a substitute.

The English, you may have noticed, constantly complain about one another's rudeness: so what are the rest of us carrying on about? Any exceptionable behavior is not targeted at us. It is just a local hazard.[1] Currently a great argument is raging between commuters and Victoria Station ticket-collectors. Each party calls the other rude. If Furlonge, the non-Trinidadian Englishman, had not been so obviously put out by my answer, the Finn might well have attributed his disclaimer to "calculated insult." Try repeating Sir Geoffrey's words in a slow and complacent manner. There you are; it sounds like aplomb, or rudeness (or both) doesn't it?

For me it is the lesson which counts. Just as the apprentice traditionally learns by watching the master artisan, so do the English absorb aplomb from real life. Indeed, the process may not even require special abilities: only the right mindset. Coolness is all.

We used to keep two English donkeys, Boney and Claude, given to wandering unless kept in a paddock surrounded by

---

[1] Quite often, an Englishman will stand up and challenge the entire nation of which he is a citizen, with what would be fighting-talk anywhere else. An English Member of Parliament (quoted in the *Daily Telegraph* of Novermber 29, 1986) calls his own people very dirty, very undisciplined and a nation of moaners.

a wire fence. One day they escaped after watching our cats getting in and out *under* the wire, and then forcing a way out in a similar manner. They just didn't know that donkeys simply do not do things like that. Non-linear thinking helps.

Those who do not learn from aplomb-situations may be regarded as less than English donkeys.

I have, I believe, actually witnessed a first emergence of aplomb-learning, under field conditions, and involving some Englishmen.

I was on a train journey from Italy to France, and the train was crowded. In the middle of the night some tired and unruly Swiss Army men climbed aboard and found that even the corridors were full. In our compartment were three young English backpackers, their impedimenta piled high just where the Swiss soldiers wanted to stand.

Almost nonchalantly, and as the train was passing through a tunnel in the Alps, the Swiss opened a window – and threw all this baggage out.

The Englishmen looked at one another, their faces red. Then one of them, as if remarking on the weather, and staring straight at one of the Swiss, said: "You are no gentleman, sir."

The Swiss took no notice at all, merely settling themselves more comfortably and gnawing at their bread and wurst. That wasn't aplomb: they didn't understand English. But a Frenchman, also in our compartment, who obviously understood the words, cried, "Bravo! What a display of sang-froid!"

One of the young Englishmen said to another, "I must remember that. Might come in useful sometime."

It was this experience, and more specifically the use of the word "gentleman," which caused me to seek out Harold Nicolson, to get a fix on who or what a gentleman might be. Although born in Tehran and having served as a diplomat in the Middle East, nobody could deny that he was very

English. His answer, though confusing to a mere foreigner, was specific, unequivocal:

> The ancient Greek gentleman, the *Kalos Kagathos* of Athens, existed only for eighty years. The Roman equivalent flourished between 98 BC and 46 BC, a period of half a century. The English gentleman lived between 1770 and 1830; that is to say, for sixty years.

I wondered, at the time, whether this was a joke: he was, after all, the author of *The English Sense of Humour*. But Sir Harold argued the case for these datings seriously, and published his contentions, in his *Good Behavior*, in 1955.

Aplomb is often, though not always, related to the actual words used; as I remember from an event of my childhood. Fortunately I can recall it in detail, though at the time I did not know what the phenomenon was called.

It happened in the Afghan mountains. A distinguished Englishman was due to visit us, and considerable preparations had been made to provide a welcome appropriate to his dignity – and also to what we regarded as ours.

Now, our place was well enough fortified, but it was at the top of a winding road, at times infested by outlaws who attacked people as a matter of course. Their motto was "*O darad, man chira nabegiram* – He's got it, why should I not take it?"

On the morning of the visit a fairly wild bandit was in the area, and he spotted the Englishman's Rolls-Royce. With a cry of delight at the prospect of sport and gain, this ruffian fired a warning shot (which shattered a wing-mirror) and began to leap from crag to crag, downhill toward his prey.

The Indian driver of the car jumped out and rolled into the ditch, teeth chattering, as the English celebrity sat becalmed, eyes riveted upon the advancing figure. There seemed no hope for him.

Suddenly, like a scene from a film, another shot rang out, and the bandit fell, drilled clean through the head.

Then, from behind a boulder, also tripping from rock to rock, came a stocky, middle-aged figure, clad in deerstalker hat and Norfolk jacket, a hunting rifle in his hand. It was the formidable Sirdar Faiz-Mohammed Khan, Zikria, our neighbor and a crack shot with a Mannlicher, who had spent a lot of time in England, and spoke the language well.

As he came up to the Englishman, the Sirdar swept off his cap and said, "Good morning, my dear sir. The obstacle to your progress having been removed, you may now proceed."

"But you needn't have killed him," spluttered our guest, which was quite quick thinking, all things considered.

"I had to, on grounds of hospitality," said the Afghan, "the fellow was being almost discourteous."

Between them, the two got the shivering driver back behind the wheel, and the first thing that I knew about it all was the Rolls entering our courtyard to the sound of trumpets, and then the Englishman, white to the gills, muttering "Almost discourteous, *almost* discourteous, almost *discourteous*," like a holy mantram.

My father said, "Terribly sorry about that spot of bother. Lot of it about at this time of year, you know." Having recovered his composure, and relaxing after the feast, our guest asked, "What would His Excellency have done if the ruffian had *actually* been discourteous, instead of 'almost'?"

My father said, "The Sirdar would have crossed that bridge when he came to it."

Now I come to think of it, I can't decide which of them had the greater aplomb. Although the story beats my Trinidadian one, the principle is there: and you can't find many mountain bandits in London.

Here is a report from the august *Daily Telegraph*, perhaps published for instructional purposes, because of its aplomb-content:

> A London employer told a typist that her work was good but her spelling was bad. If in doubt, she should consult the dictionary. "That wouldn't work," she said. "I'm never in any doubt."

You cannot have a real aplomb-situation without something else. This something is defeat for the opponent or an indication that you don't understand that you have been bested. And every demonstration of aplomb must be low-key. If you allow yourself to get excited, or start to argue, or boast, you may win the exchange – but still lose face.

Many people who fancy themselves intellectuals seek to trap one into wrangling: I think because this pre-empts the use of the aplomb weapon.

At one Hampstead party, a voluble English collectivist newspaper writer berated me, as an Afghan, for being a tribal nobody, medievally trying to fight socialism and prevent the gallant Soviet Army and fraternal Russian advisers from sorting out our problems. We were primitive, that was our trouble.

I said, "*Primitive?* But it was a man from *my* part of the world who pioneered algorism, more than a thousand years ago. He was called al-Khwarizimi: the very word 'logarithm,' some say, is your attempt at pronouncing his name! And it took six hundred years before people in England could throw off Roman numerals and use those of our scientists."

Since three or four of the people listening were scientists, I reckoned that this cool-headed, learned rejoinder would align their sympathy with me.

But the political expert was just as quick. "Logarithms!" he said, bitterly. "Without *them* we would have had no nuclear bombs, and fewer crazy scientists, servants of the imperialists…"

Quite neat, I thought; it answered me and outflanked the scientists, in one. Now, at this point, I should have said something which would raise a laugh (like asking why they had scientists in the USSR) or else disconnected from the whole thing. I hesitated, and one of the others intervened. The Russophile writer had, just before, been extolling the virtues of UNESCO, and the scientist held up a hand.

"Just a moment. Did you know that there is one Afghan who has received no less than FIVE international first prizes for his work, in UNESCO's World Book Year?"

The fellow-traveler tried a bit of aplomb. "Yes, I know that, of course, and I'm sure that if he had been here tonight, he would have agreed with every word I have said."

"I'm not too sure about that," said the other man. "He's Idries Shah, the man you're trying to browbeat, who's standing beside you…" Very neat.

My proper course, now, would have been to say absolutely nothing. But there was a picture in my mind of the Russians in Afghanistan, of bombed villages, napalmed children, murder, horror, evil, and I knew that I was going to say something that I should not.

"*Now* will you shut up?" I heard myself inquire. The Soviets were barbarians: I was the civilized one.

Everyone moved away from me. My ally the scientist had won a battle and I had, through not underplaying, lost the war. The English Law of Public Relations says that you can hire someone to boast for you, but You May Not Do It Yourself. I'd lost my cool, just like Sir Geoffrey, the man who was not from Trinidad.

And if *I* did not need to get heated, I have since discovered, neither did he. You see, it really is all right to be from Trinidad. I have this on the authority of Charles Kingsley, who says, in *At Last* (Chapter 3):

> Trinidad is loyal (with occasional grumblings, as is the right of free-born Britons).

Of course, neither Furlonge nor I knew about this at the time of our encounter: but it is registered here, for reference.

Parties offer great opportunities for field-work in the matter of repartee, of which aplomb is the mainspring. Some of my best material comes from the soirées given by that indefatigable explorer and society hostess, Mrs. Francis Fisher. You could always reckon on finding a colorful throng at her place. At one such At Home, I was standing next to a Scottish chief in full regalia and a haughty-looking English officer in tight-fitting mess-kit.

The Englishman looked at the man with kilt and sporran and asked, disdainfully, "How did *you* get in here?"

The Scot rumbled, "I showed my invitation-card at the door." Then, examining the officer's uniform he added, "That's a monkey-jacket, isn't it? No doubt *you* shinned up the drainpipe in it, and that's why you're interested in the matter."

The soldier went blue in the face: no cool, so no aplomb, no repartee.

The Highlander had learned that in England you have to keep one jump ahead. Or perhaps it was Cro-Magnon instinct which came to his aid. My Scottish author friend Lewis Spence was very hot on the theory that the Scots were Cro-Magnon by blood, and superior to the Neanderthal English.

Instinct, which sometimes produces situations that can only be explained in terms of the Marx Brothers, is one of the factors which usually enable the English to keep ahead of the game. All foreigners will know what I mean. Sometimes the Angle gains and holds the initiative while the foreigner is still trying to work out what is going on, and why. We think that cunning is at work, or that a madness has seized the English: or that they are deliberately trying to confuse us, to name but three.

Those of us who have seen as much of it as I have, however, realize that the fault is in us. Two unEnglish weaknesses – premature assumptions and trying too hard to classify things – are getting in the way. Outlandishly, we others demand lucidity and understanding.

I leave you to decide the meaning of a prime example of unflappability for yourself. Unless you care to adopt my own reading: that all will be understood only in the fullness of time.

A powerful English captain of industry was once trying to contact me, urgently, all over the country, his henchpeople leaving messages everywhere they thought I might be. Eventually his private secretary located me and we had a telephone conversation.

"Yes, I am Idries Shah. You say that Sir Rampant Turbid wants to speak to me?"

"That's right, I have been trying everywhere. He *will* be pleased you came through. I'll have to see if he is free. Who shall I say is calling?"

Who is calling? My head swam. *I'm* calling: I'm the man you've been looking for everywhere, and asking for by name, and whom you've just recognized, by his name, when he called you up, for goodness' sake...

Perhaps I'd heard wrong. "What's that?" I asked.

"I said, 'Who shall I say is calling?'"

I took a deep breath. "Madam," I said, with great calm, "you can say that it is The Devil. I'll just spell it: D-E-V-I-L!"

Back came her voice, cheery, confident, self-possessed. "Just a moment, Mr. Devil, and I'll put you through."

I've tried really hard to puzzle it out. Aplomb (or perhaps frequent calls from the nether regions) could account for the lady's lack of surprise. Or maybe Sir Rampant's friends changed their names all the time. Finally, I decided on the Fullness of Time solution.

I have not met this extraordinarily cool lady. Perhaps I should avoid her, because Roget, in his *Thesaurus*, associates "inexcitability" with "frigidity."

5

Angles Down the Road

The Thickest Part
William [The Conqueror] ordered his archers to shoot at the thickest part of the English, so they shot upwards so that the arrows might fall on the Englishmen's heads.
                          Cecil Hunt: *The Best Howlers*

THE OLD ANGLES fitted in so well with the Saxons that even the latter were soon calling themselves Angles. Perhaps because they are so good at Fitting In – when they want to – the English require you to Fit In with them, too. I once fitted in well enough in an English village for the local innkeeper to contrast me favorably with the foreign Welshman whom I had nominated for local Squire.

Leaders are never popular for long among the English, unless they are dead and therefore unable to do much harm to the team. And a team it is, in spite of all the talk about class divisions, ABC socio-economic ratings, and so on. Leaders want *you* to fit into their own vision of reality, so the Angleans don't much like them. It was in England that I heard a leading scholar refer to another academic as "safely dead."

A Harris poll carried out in April and May of 1985 found that a large proportion of the British were worried about "poor political leadership." My guess is that is because they simply don't trust leaders. The word, in English, comes from the idea of showing the way, not from that of domination.

Professor A. J. P. Taylor, speaking in August 1977, could not have been faulted by a fifth-century Angle for his conviction that

> Great men are absolutely splendid in wartime, but they can be dangerous in peacetime, for great men, powerful men, have produced wars, as Napoleon did.

It would not be surprising if the dislike of leadership was shared by the leaders themselves: after all, they are *English* too, as a rule. Leo Rawlings, the artist, in his harrowing book of experiences as a prisoner in the Second World War, notes more than once that the principles of guidance and leadership were weak.

Officer prisoners of war lived a life of ease when the ordinary soldiers were dying like flies from the effects of brutality, starvation and disease. Even men of God whose duty, it might be supposed, was to provide example and guidance, did not all have faith in their shepherd's role. In *And the Dawn Came Up Like Thunder*, Rawlings says:

> Very few Padres I met proved to be staunch believers in their own preaching.

That's how he puts it.

It surprises some people to learn that the English idea of upper, middle and lower classes, which obsesses foreigners and followers of imported philosophies, dates back only to 1772, when the word "class" in this sense is first found. By the time the idea was seized upon by political thinkers, it was still a fairly new term. Far from being ingrained in the English psyche, it was a trendy concept – which may explain its early acceptance by political and economic theoreticians of various kinds.

Fitting In is – and has been for most of English history – much more important. Fitting In is not as difficult as it seems to those who haven't tried it properly.

The best way is to follow the English custom of belonging to a category, as every schoolboy must learn if he is not to be bullied beyond a certain point. He can belong in the ranks of the clowns, the geeks or the rest of the lads, just so long as he fits into the general perception of these groups.

You may be an architect or a priest, run a restaurant, play tennis or pursue any interest from juggling to nuclear physics, and still fit in. An all-rounder, of course, is one of the best English things to be: but it is still a category. And stereotypes are always shifting, here in England. Currently, if you have a regional accent, you can be a comedian, a television announcer or a scientist. Microelectronics is one of the great growth areas of the present fitting-in scene, but it also includes hairdressing and owning racehorses.

In April 1985, the Boy Scouts showed how easily a stereotyped organization can fit in, by shifting into another area. They decided to practice spiritualism, and no doubt will be welcomed with open arms by that community. Most people, when making a dramatic change in their habits, feel it necessary to invoke some plausible connection with their roots to account for it. Not so the Scouts, according to Alan Williams, reporting their decision. He mentions that the founder of the movement, Lord Baden-Powell, once said that spiritualists were "in alliance with the Devil."

An English posture may change, as you see, by 180 degrees. An Afghan, as such, has few stereotypes to accord with. My sister Amina claims she has only one, because of Kipling's words, regularly recited to her by English people:

> When you're wounded and left on Afghanistan's plains
> An' the women come out to cut up what remains
> Jest roll to your rifle an' blow out your brains
> An' go to your Gawd like a soldier.

But, as she says, it only needs someone to write something more arresting and she could become approved of overnight. The trouble is, the Afghans themselves have cultivated a tearaway image for so long that they don't feel the need to do much about it.

We keep it up, even in England. No time ago the medical journal *Current Practice* quoted a Gallup poll among GPs. They were asked if they had been threatened with violence at work. One third of them had: they spoke of alcohol, drugs, razors and psychiatrically disturbed patients. A single respondent, however, was less detailed, laconic:

> Threatened three times in the past seven years, but, being an Afghan, I threatened them back.

The English tribe, like our own, teaches its young what the rules are, and applies shock treatment. Its purpose is to bond the members of the group together. The overt reason for the shock is often secondary, even irrelevant, though strangers to this procedure may misread it. They should remember the English proverb: "An ounce of wit that's bought by care is worth a ton that's lying spare."

My daughter Saira, on her first journey out of this country, found that the official on duty would not stamp her passport, something which surely is the right of every child. "Sorry," he said, "you're British-born. Not allowed a stamp, either in or out." Such rules are only tribal custom writ small. Their purpose is clear.

"If it wasn't for your name, I'd think that you were English," said another member of the Anglekin team or band to my friend Akbar Ali Khan. The man who thought Akbar Ali Khan's name sounded foreign was an Englishman called Rabinowcsky. But names can be important here. An acquaintance of mine, a Beirutian called Isa, wanted to become Mr. (or, better still, Lord) Cholmondeley. But the thing to remember is that English names do not have to be Anglean: they have only to be *established* as English.

A word-count of the *Dictionary of English Christian Names* shows that only one per cent of the names in use today are traceable to Old English. And that is only first-names. The English even have a list of names and how to pronounce them. Look up *Titles and Forms of Address*, and you will learn that the family name Sawbridgeworth is to be pronounced *Sapsed*.

To fit in you must also be prepared, to the horror of many foreign English scholars, to abet the process of giving different, or even conflicting, meanings to words.

If you are French, you will be less than elated to find that *ecrou* has not only been Englished as "screw," but no longer means "nut." Or that a trombone is a musical instrument and not, as in French, a paper-clip. And that *flan* means, in English, custard. If you are a Greek, and are asked for your *diploma*, don't imagine that this still means "something folded, such as a hinge." Or that the *orchestra* is any longer "the place where the dancers perform." If you are a dunce, it may or may not comfort you to discover that this soubriquet traces to a *wise* man named Duns Scotus.

Illiteracy, if not exactly highly thought of, was traditional among English landowners, aristos and kings until comparatively recently, as the record (kept by lowly scriveners) amply confirms. Our Eastern kings were often poets or philosophers, or earned their own livings. Maybe that's why they've mostly been abolished. They swallowed the propaganda about humility, culture and frugality being to their advantage. It's a theory, anyway.

Royalty, among the Brits, can be shifted from one category to another with remarkable facility. According to *The Times* for April 17, 1985, the British Pavilion at the Tsukuba Exhibition in Japan (and organized by the Brits) featured the very English Windsor Royal Family as a "technological achievement."

The word "dunce" may mean a fool misnamed after a scholar: but that is only one dimension of it. The English go further, beyond anything that the most sophisticated Greek philosopher could have conceived. They tell you that it may be to your advantage to be a dunce. There is even a book, published in London, called *Celebrated Dunces*.

It is well established among foreigners that the English are stupid and diabolically clever at the same time. But it took an Englishman, Tom Brown, to produce this well-researched, full-length and illustrated work about famous people who had been adjudged fools. Included in it are men from almost every profession, including science, law, theology, war, administration and medicine. "Dunces," says Mr. Brown, warningly, right at the beginning, "are not always what they seem."

Hunter, Scott, Newton, Sheridan, Wellington: they are all featured, with a wealth of detail about their duncehood. So are Clive, Howard and Goldsmith, and many others.

And in this pantheon the Celebrated Dunces include only one who was not British: Linnaeus, the Swedish botanist. So being a fool is fine. This puts a completely different complexion upon Carlyle's assertion that Britain's several million inhabitants were "mostly fools!" But a mystery surrounds my copy of Brown's book, which I bought secondhand: though from an American who didn't like this word, and advertised his store as "An Emporium of Englyshe Already-Relished Tomes." A bookplate inside shows that this treatise on low-achievers who became famous was presented to an English schoolboy – as a prize for academic excellence!

Being able to feel that one is a dunce, being treated like one, without necessarily being one, seems to be an English characteristic. Jeremy Lewis, writing in the *Daily Telegraph*, notes that English autobiographies represent their authors as "impractical and inept to an almost imbecilic degree." Why? Because, he believes, the English reader sees himself like that, too: he "at once feels the narrator to be a kindred spirit."

What people seem to be is hardly ever what the English think they are: this may be taken as an axiom. I have watched more than one television program in which people were shouting how proud they were to be English, while the English viewers around me looked embarrassed.

The English don't think much of people who parade their patriotism. Their word for this behavior-pattern, *jingoism*, is foreign. It is said to come from the name of Jainko, the Supreme Being of the Basques who were brought here by Edward I to sort out the Welsh.

"Juggernaut" originates with the Sanskrit Jaganatha, Lord of the World. You might consider this to be so close to Jainko as to make little difference. But the English have chosen to use it otherwise than as the name of a deity or to indicate chauvinism. I can just imagine some Englishman saying, "Let me see... 'Juggernaut,' excellent name for one of those large goods vehicles..."

A *legend* means something read, and usually the life of a saint at that. Yet I have a book called *Verbal Folk-Legends of the After-Life of the Pagans*, which just shows what you can do with English if you try hard enough.

Or, among the English, the process can go the other way, with an established usage being changed back into a pristine one. Robert (means Fame-Bright) Graves once begged me not to use the word "system" in relation to ideas. It was derived from the Greek for a box made of pieces, he explained, and it was surely inappropriate for thought to be imprisoned.

More than one English dictionary, including the venerable and sometimes venerated *OED*, can rub your nose in it, if you try to get to grips with meaning or derivations.

Take the word *typhoon*. I felt as if someone had been lying in wait for me when I looked up the word and saw what the book said about its origins. The combined efforts of the English lexicographers had seemingly determined that it could be from the Persian *tufan*; or from the Greek *typhon*; yet again, if you prefer it, the origin might even be sought in the Chinese *Tai Fung*. No wonder Scotus was called a dunce, I thought. I am sure he wouldn't have admired such pragmatism.

When I spoke of such mysteries of the *OED* to a grammarian, he was quite equal to the challenge. "You should remember," he said, "that the first English dictionary only appeared in the seventeenth century. And, furthermore, the *OED* is authoritative but not paramount."

Of course, it was my fault for having misinterpreted the role of the scholar. There really was no excuse for this. I already had in my notebook an affirmation by no less an authority than Miss Patricia Barnes, Deputy Keeper of the

Public Record Office in London: "One thing I know about scholars is that they will oppose anything."

I can now visualize the stalemate between the *Dictionary*'s scholars, after long days and nights of opposing one another about the etymology of "typhoon." They obviously decided that it was a dead-heat, and the miscellaneity of the authoritative derivation was born. But there are a lot of people who respect dictionaries. One lady journalist who interviewed me made quite a point in her article of the fact that, though already the author of twenty books in English, I did not own one. So I feel that some examination of dictionaries is useful in studying the English.

To resume: a minister is an important person nowadays, but the word used to mean "an inferior person," as dictionaries insist. This equivocal nature of the language may go back a long time. Look at the word *Minch-House*, which is traced to the Anglo-Saxon for "either a nunnery or an ale-house."

"Valentine" is another complex one. In England today, a man may ask a woman to "be his Valentine": many ladies await February 14, St. Valentine's Day, with eager expectancy. They hope to be a Valentine. But Valentine is from *galantin*, "a (masculine) lover." That is, unless you accept the alternative origin. This is "the Lupercalian festival, when youths whipped young girls." In early times, many Valentine messages were almost insulting, and not associated with love at all.

The lesson seems to be that the English won't let anything remain static for long.

St. Valentine's miracles, by the way, have been traced to two Persians, Marius and Martha; so perhaps the English have a right to celebrate February 14. Their language is linked with Iran.

Dr. Schele de Vere, an American (though there has been no shortage of British scholars who think the same) writes, in his *Studies in English*:

> The youngest of all European idioms, our great and noble language, has yet spread farthest over the globe, and now rules the world without a rival... English is a child of the great Aryan family, so called from its ancientist homestead in Asia, now known as Iran.

I have always thought how Iranian in conception is the English statement, seen so often in print, that English has one of the largest vocabularies of all (nearly half a million words) "though the average educated person uses only one per cent of these."

The secret language extends beyond words, to habits and customs, which are constantly changed. If you can't keep up, you won't fit in. I was surprised (I should not have been, of course, and few things have that effect on me now) to find that the English used to dislike gold wedding rings. They were a sign that the wearer was a Continental Catholic. It was a pagan custom, adopted by the Church in the ninth century. So you knew where you were: a married woman *without* a plain gold band on her third finger, left hand, was English, and a Protestant. Then, probably just as foreigners were getting used to this, the English took to wedding rings. You know the result.

It used to be considered vulgar to wear both wedding and engagement rings, status indicators, together. Some still think that it is: "You can't be both married *and* engaged at the same time, can you?," one haughty beauty told me. But the matter of kissing on meeting is even more striking.

English and other books are full of accounts of how this was once a very English habit, and how it astonished Continentals to see all that kissing on both cheeks going on over here. They didn't like it, either. It was regarded as an odd and awful *Persian* custom as far back as Herodotus.

Try it today and you will be thought French or Italian. You wouldn't fit in at all.

The English were once renowned garlic-eaters, too.

Some think that fitting in is made more difficult because of hostility toward outsiders. But it may be due to misunderstandings, even mishearings.

One day I found myself standing beside a distinguished-looking Englishman, near Trafalgar Square. He was escorting a party of Islamic dignitaries, and we were all waiting, trapped on a traffic island, as a procession passed. They bore a banner identifying them as war veterans, and members of an ethnic minority. The tall patrician pursed his lips. "Look at that," he said to the nearest Moslem devotee, "not a Christian among them…"

The complexity arises when we discover that he did not say that at all. I had not heard the actual words, only the phrase repeated inaccurately to me by another Englishman who was also on the island. He then took issue with the noble Lord. This was a most improper thing to say, the more especially about ex-soldiers – and a lot more besides.

The offender stayed calm, and disposed of the entire complaint in a single sentence. "Get your ears washed out, man: thought they were nuclear disarmers, frequent in these part, always carry banners with questions on 'em; what I actually said was 'NOT A *QUESTION* AMONG 'EM.'"

You not only don't fit in if you don't understand: you can run away with a lot of false ideas, collecting what seems to be information, but is no such thing. Our proverb, "Haste is from the Devil," might well be an English motto: don't rush in. I have done it, though; and often enough.

As I stood there, right in the middle of London, I remembered the day I had driven into the country, as far as East Anglia. After a long and dusty journey, I stopped the car in a village street, where a very Nordic-looking old cowman was waiting for a bus. I tackled him.

"I'd like to find traces of the Saxons," I said. "And the Angles, if possible, though that's more difficult."

The old countryman removed a pipe from his mouth. "Don't know about *more* difficult. There's plenty down the village. Follow your nose."

Amazing! "How many?" I asked.

"Oh, there must be hundreds. A new lot just came in, with the buckets and things."

Hundreds of Angles! I might have to amend my theory about their melting into the Saxon community. With buckets, too: so they still maintained some sort of cohesion and activity.

"Iron, they are," continued the gaffer, "and you put nails and screws through 'em. Down the ironmongers. Mind, they call 'em angle-irons down there. It bee three moyles."

My face must have dropped, for the kindly old man continued, "You'll find the Sexton, though, much nearer'n thaat. The church bee only half a moyle down the road."

Yes, it is complex all right. If I had impetuously stopped the conversation at an early stage, I might have driven off thinking that the man was talking about *my* Angles, and that they were alive and well and ranging the country with buckets. I might have put that misleading information into a book, even this book. Then I would never have fitted in.

And it was a book that featured in my next adventure in darkest England.

6

Pliny Rules in Badgersden

Not Yet
For we are the people of England,
that have not spoken yet.
           G. K. Chesterton: *The Secret People*

THE MISUNDERSTANDING OVER the parade had been sorted out, but the Arabs, the English Lord and I were still talking, standing now at the top of Whitehall.

One of the visitors turned his large eyes toward me and said in Arabic, "Thou art from Egypt?"

"Nay, this suppliant is from the eastern territories which Your Presence's people call those of the Ajam, the dumb, those who do not speak the Arabic tongue," I told him in the same language. He nodded, and peered closer at me, as if trying to understand dumb-talk.

"Unfortunately, I am one of those whose stumbling phrases, disconnected and unuttered for many a year, may displease Your Presence by their inelegance. May your life be extended." I touched my head, eyes and heart, in a suitably ceremonial way.

"Thou talkest like a book," he muttered.

I searched my repertoire and resumed, "Noble Sir: the sacred Arabian tongue has been, for us rough mountaineers, largely a language of the books for even unto a thousand years. This humble indigent begs permission to state that we recklessly fought your gallant armies for a hundred years, and were eventually conquered. After that, however, our own atrocious idiom prevailed once more. The negligible person now being permitted the audacity of addressing Your Long-Living Sheikhliness is one from among those known as the Afghans. The name has been said to derive from the Arabic word signifying 'The Turbulent.'"

"Enough of this. You mean that you speak Farsi?" the words from the center of the beard were now in Dari, the tongue of my ancestral glens. The Sheikh had, he told me, been Minister-Counselor for three years in his country's embassy accredited to the Afghan Court: and that is how I got to know Sheikh Anwar Al Agali, of the Gulf.

Early the next day, having learned that I was working on a book about the strange land of Inglaterra, the Sheikh sent a car for me and dispensed cardamom-flavored tea in his suite at the Dorchester. "I am bidden to a feast, being held this day on a large grassy space in a settlement in the Emirate to the southeast of London, known as The Emirate of Kint," he told me, gravely.

"The light of your countenance will make the grass grow even greener," I assured him.

"The visit has been proposed by the Council of the British and, moreover, agreed to by the Overseas Bureau of Whitehall; and it is of some importance that I should attend. Why? Because not only is the Emirate of Kint in the hand of a scion of the ruling family of this land, The Douk af Kint, but it is the dwelling-place of important people from the East." He ticked them off on his fingers. "Sheikh Tajir of the

United Arab Emirates owns land there, so does the Imam of the Yemen, and Kintian castles are maintained by the sheikhs of two or three important tribes."

The British Council and the Foreign Office had, I thought, been well briefed.

"I too, have pitched a humble tent in Kent," I said, "though, as at present, I often visit London."

"So the Dumb have also found the place, bravo!" He slapped me on the back. "You must accompany me, and I can make a pious visit to your palace there. I also need information and experience. Did the learned Al Ghazzali not say, 'Happy is he who is warned by the experience of others'?"

"Look here, Sheikh," I said, reverting to my rough Afghan style, "I'm getting a bit tired of this business about 'The Dumb.' I know you Arabs always call us that among yourselves, but we don't really go for it, you know. It's one thing for *us* to use the word, from modesty, but…"

He had not been in Afghanistan for nothing. "My dear friend," he cried, switching to the refined speech of the Kabul Court, "I beg forgiveness a thousand times, miscreant that I am. I was behaving toward you as I would be a brother Arab, treating you like one of our very own. But I see my fault, and offer you in apology the lines from the great Hafiz, Nightingale of Shiraz:

> "A Shah no other than thyself, aspiring Hafiz craves:
> Oh! Were he in thy doorstep's dust, one of thy common slaves!"

I winced, for I had been among the English for quite a long time, and these words, though usual enough in the East, now sounded excessive. He went on, "You are my guide, my pilot through these unknown waters, as Rumi would have put it. You are my Noah in this ark. Did the great Saadi not sing, in his incomparable *Rose Garden*:

> "What have we to fear from the waves,
> If Noah is our Captain?"

"That's enough," I stammered.

"Not quite. We must remember that you are a man of intellect and learning..."

Luckily the right quotation swam into my mind, for in the East you must match a compliment with another, or with a poetic disclaimer. Intellect and learning...

"Did the sublime Jami not allude," I asked, "to these very things in his words

> "Leave boasting of intellect or learning: For intellect,
> here, is a shackle and learning, foolishness?"

The Sheikh leaned forward. "Are they as stupid as that, then, these Franks? No, I think that there is a subtler meaning behind your speech. All the more reason for you to accompany me. We leave in half an hour for the feast. In the meantime, have some more tea and tell me why the English upper lip is rumored to become so easily paralzsed. Omit no detail, however trivial it may seem to you. It may contain a clue."

"They haven't had a Stiff Upper Lip for very long, you know," I told him proudly. "The *Oxford Dictionary of Proverbs* gives the first instance of the use of the term as J. Neal's *Brother Jonathan*, in 1825..."

The Gulfian crinkled his nose. "Rather give me an example of it. I am not concerned with its history."

"As an example of stiff upper lip," I began, "there was once an Englishman who was on a ship..."

"And what was the purpose of his journey?" I looked at him and saw from his serious mien that he would brook no evasion. Our conversation had slipped into the Eastern form, in which fact and fantasy mix so readily.

"Commercial affairs," I said. Sheikh Anwar stroked his beard.

"It is true that the English are great traders. You may proceed."

"This trading Englishman was on the upper deck early one morning when a storm blew up."

"A storm. Was it serious?"

"I shall come to that in a moment," I added. "May your life be extended!" as it might well have to be if this tale were ever to be finished, I thought. He signaled me to continue.

"A foreigner was also there..." I resumed. The Sheikh raised his finger, and I added hurriedly, "He was a Patagonian, born in Bosnia, of Ethiopian extraction, who spoke English." The Sheikh beamed; he was obviously fond of information: and the more the better.

"Wishing to start a conversation with the Englishman," I continued, "the foreigner said to him 'Have you had your breakfast yet?' And the Englishman replied, 'Rather the reverse, actually.'"

Sheikh Anwar narrowed his eyes and then nodded three times, in measured reflection.

"It is my opinion," he pronounced, with slow deliberation, "that this Englishman had vomited. That would account for his reply, and also for his upper lip being affected, if that is, as I take it to be, your point."

Almost at once the Sheikh rose, and I felt like Scheherazade of the *Thousand and One Nights*, after a particularly difficult stint with the Caliph: dazed but relieved. Sheikh Anwar might, after all, have asked me questions about the story, wanted matters of detail, which I might not have been able to supply. Like exactly what the Englishman had for breakfast, for instance, or the precise moment when the storm blew up.

Explaining English and the English to foreigners is very tiring.

I cannot say that I was looking forward to the prospect of a day at an English country fête under these conditions, no matter how essential the Foreign Office and the British Council thought it might be for the Sheikh's edification. In the train from Charing Cross I came across a perfect description of some English fêtes in a piece by Peter Ackroyd, of *The Times*. Admittedly it was in the course of a television review, and not intendedly relevant to the present subject. But it accorded with some of my experiences on village greens. He wrote of the "peculiarly English combination of genuine horror and spirited comedy."

Luckily, for once, the Sheikh broke into my thoughts by asking about what our attitude should be toward the natives.

"Since this is an English occasion, with its own characteristic rules and manners," I explained, "we must comport ourselves in a manner such as would be assumed by an Anglo-Saxon when faced by foreign native peoples. They have experience and have blazed the trail."

"And that is?" the Sheikh asked.

"That," I said, "is amply yet succinctly laid down in the instructions to travelers penned by a Mr. Fogg. Although he wrote in 1875, I do not think that his wisdom has been superseded."

"Wisdom," intoned the Sheikh, "if it is truly such, can never be superseded. Have you this sagacious tome upon your person?"

"In my briefcase, at all events," I said. I took it out, opened it, and read:

> One should drop that haughty air of disdain and superiority, and so far as is consistent with propriety and comfort, mix with the people in a dress that will not attract special attention of everyone he meets.

"Humility is my normal attitude," the Sheikh assured me. "And, as for the dress, what could be more normal than a *thaub*, *agal* and *kaffiya* such as I am now wearing?"

"What indeed, O Sheikh? But we should always remember that English villagers traditionally regard their compatriots from other parts of the country as foreigners. You and I may, therefore, be considered equally strange."

"Now," he said, taking Fogg's book in his hands and looking at its pseudo-Oriental cover design with due respect and admiration, "tell me the title of this writing. The man sounds almost civilized."

I said, "It's *Travels and Adventures in Egypt, Arabia and Persia*, by W. P. Fogg. Coincidentally, Mr. Fogg published his *Round the World Letters* when Jules Verne was writing *Around the World in Eighty Days* with a Mr. P. Fogg as its hero. This observation of mine," I continued without a notable effect upon my companion, "may be, for all I know, a minor literary discovery."

I was surprised to learn that this was not the Sheikh's first foray into the English countryside. "You thought that I was a tyro in things English," he smirked, "but as I have said, I have some knowledge of the rural life here, and I may even be able to advise you about our conduct at the impending feast. I have merely been testing your knowledge, in my queries about behavior. It is a way of passing the time.

"Our guide," he continued, "whom you saw when we met yesterday in London, was an English Lord. I met him through a friend, a large landowner at a place some hundred kilometers from the capital. This man conveyed me to his castle for a day in the middle of the last week. He had asked me if I liked hunting, and I told him that I had some experience of it. 'Come and join our hunt, then,' he said, 'for the day. Midweek is best, since we don't have those office workers who turn out on Saturdays.'

"I of course accepted the invitation, but I was interested to know what kind of hunt one could carry out on a single day. I was also intrigued to learn that the Lord could not preserve his privacy from mere office-workers. And we were expected to arrive at the castle at ten in the morning – which seemed very late. As you know, at home we usually start hunting at, or before, dawn.

"Outside the castle, by about half-past ten, there had collected a large and miscellaneous swarm of people, men and women, without weapons, variously mounted on good and bad horses and accompanied by dogs and dog-masters. Few of these people had the look of experienced hunters, in eye, in age, or in suppleness of body. Some were actually on foot.

"I inquired as to what quarry they proposed to seek. Wild boar, I reckoned, would scare many of them to death, wolves could outdistance them, and decent-sized bears would undoubtedly knock others off their insubstantial mounts. I realized, of course, that there were no lions, such as I had tackled in Africa, and probably few if any snow-leopards, which I had tracked in the High Pamirs of your own part of the world.

"Now, as you know, our sages, like theirs, have advised that one should on no account embarrass the natives, or allow a host to lose face. I was providentially prevented from unwittingly doing either. Luckily I had not mentioned any real game: because, when I asked the purpose of the expedition, I was told, 'As usual, we shall pursue foxes, which will be chased and then assailed by these hounds!'

"Naturally, I would have been utterly disgraced at home if it ever leaked out that I had taken part in such an activity. On the other hand, as a guest among these well-meaning people, I could not disclose my feelings. On no account should I, I realized, let them feel that I had the slightest sense of condescension. They obviously regarded fox-chasing as a form of hunting. I racked my brains for a means to escape from this situation.

"The sages have said, 'It is an honor to be humiliated, if thereby you save the repute of another.' I was, therefore, about to lie, and to say that I did not know how to ride, when an inspired alternative – to plead fatigue and illness – came into my mind. This I accordingly did, and passed the day touring the estate. Everyone's face was saved."

He leaned back in his seat with a look of benign satisfaction, and I was spared further reminiscences as the train drew in to our station.

A taxi took us from the station to the village which I shall call Badgersden, five miles away.

It was a Saturday, and the charity fête on the village green was in full swing, under the benign tutelage of the local Vicar, and, more directly, organized by the numerous lady activists of his flock.

The fête was the usual kind of thing: tents and lemonade, and hoopla and bottle-stalls, adjurations to guess this cake's weight. We dismounted amid the festivities, and the Sheikh, after inquiring kindly as to the religious persuasion of the Vicar, assured him that he, too, was "an admirer of the Prophet Jesus, who was an excellent man." The clergyman took this in his stride, perhaps having heard equally egregious things said by English theologians. He took us on a tour of the stalls.

At one there was an enormous pile of, well, very old shoes. "These," Sheikh Anwar said, "are for throwing at recalcitrant servants no doubt?"

"No doubt," I concurred, and steered him to the nearby tent, where he scowled at a lady, dressed as a Gypsy, who was telling fortunes. "We put this kind of thing down very severely in our country," he told the lanky, rumpled Schoolmaster who had come running up, "because it excites erroneous beliefs among the people. Can you control your bedouins, great man of wisdom, when they become inflamed by the false assertions of fraudulent prophetesses?"

"Tell the Sheek," said the Schoolmaster, "that English law forbids predicting the future. Vagrancy Act, and all that."

"And soothsaying is contrary to Scripture," snapped the Vicar. The look he gave the teacher showed that the two were at odds.

"You wouldn't know much about this," neighed the clergyman, "but I suppose it wouldn't do any harm to mention that the church here is Perpendicular."

"What's the Nazarene Mulla on about?" asked the Sheikh. I told him.

"Perpendicular? At right angles to the horizon? I'm glad to hear it. Did he suppose I believed it to be horizontal, or perhaps underground?" The Sheikh had an idea. "Or is it some kind of jest?"

"It's a style of architecture," I said.

"Architecture? Observe that he says nothing of the faith of the people, mentioning only the external aspect of their devotional building," said the Gulfian.

"The Sheikh is most interested in what you have said," I translated for the Vicar, invoking permissible English equivocation. The Englishman assumed his most ecumenical smile and, encouraged, started to talk about choirs, vestries and even gargoyles. "Tell him," he simpered, "that *nobody* has ever 'walked up the aisle' to be married."

This was a new one on me. "*Nobody?*" I asked. "Haven't you got a license to marry them, or what?" For a moment I wondered if he'd been unfrocked or something.

The Vicar was delighted. "I thought I'd catch you out," he giggled, "you see, 'the aisle' is, properly speaking, one of the two side passageways. It means 'wing.' The bride and groom proceed up the center of the church, neither left nor right. They are separated from the aisles by pews on either side. I am sure the Sheek will be amused: tell him, would you?"

I interpreted as best I could.

The day continued thus until the Sheikh sat down on the grass, and the rest of us grouped ourselves around him. "They may spread the feast here," he announced.

"Oh dear," said the Vicar, "fête, feast: I see. Yes, well it's not exactly fleshpots in Badgersden, you know. But we might just manage some tea and sandwiches."

I said to the Sheikh, "These good people would be honored if you would condescend, exceptionally and as a sign of your courtesy, to partake of their frugal native diet."

"That is, indeed and verily, a charming thought," he said, "providing of course that it is not associated with prohibited aliments. This is sheep country is it not?"

I was able to assure him that the food would be permissible. While waiting for it, I kept the conversation going with some useful information on names recently gleaned from the pages of Dr. Brewer (who may have had a vested interest in the subject). In England, he avers, what may look like humble or even objectionable surnames are often, in reality, of great distinction.

Pigg means "slasher," a warrior, and Bacon is a fighter. Hogg is Anglo-Saxon for either a scholar or a "high" (Germanic,

"*Hoch*") person. Brewer traces his own surname not to beer, but to the French *bruyère*, the broom-plant. This enables him, in an inspired throwaway line, to associate it with the surname of the Plantagenet royal family.

Discovering that the Vicar's name was Gaiter, I was able to tell him that it came from Saxon for an arrow-man. The Schoolmaster wondered aloud whether a man of the cloth should have a name connected with violence: so I did an Angle on him, and shifted my ground in the interests of harmony. I immediately admitted that another authority, Dr. Simeon Potter, avers that the meaning of Gaiter is "watchman."

The teacher's own surname was Smith, which Brewer explains is not from the simple plebeian blacksmith of ordinary attribution, but may be traced to something far more interestingly red-blooded. It signals descent from a mighty warrior: a Smiter. Even Miller (the name of the lady who was handing round sandwiches) really means Mauler or Fighter. "I conclude that they are all the descendants of men from warrior clans," the Sheikh announced, when I had explained all this to him.

This excursion into the world of linguistics gave the Schoolmaster-Smiter the idea of trying out his rudimentary army Hindustani on the Sheikh, though his enterprise was not adequately rewarded. Sheikh Anwar merely remarked that the teacher seemed to have a throat infection. A decoction of *anis*, aniseed, or *qarawiyya*, caraway seed, might help, he thought.

This seemed to give the Vicar an idea, both geographically and linguistically. "*Semper aliquid novum ex Africa*," he declaimed in a loud voice. "Always something new from Africa, eh, what?" His moon-face panned across the crowd, which had closed in around us and now rustled interestedly. No doubt they were deeply impressed.

"*Africa semper aliquid affert*," I responded automatically. "Or *Ex Africa semper aliquid novi.*" That was the way I'd heard it, anyway.

The Sheikh was smiling benignly, unaware that a trial of strength was about to start. The Vicar looked at me suspiciously. So did the natives. Surely I, a stranger, wasn't correcting the Vicar, even if it was in a foreign lingo?

To fill the vacuum, I said: "Pliny, you know, *Historia Naturalis*." A hundred eyes moved from my face to the clergyman's, seeking any sign of weakness. But the Vicar wasn't English for nothing.

His face lit up as if my words gave him the clue to my strange behavior. "Oh, *Pliny!*" He gave a light laugh. It had just the right pitch and insouciance.

Even the Sheikh caught the confident tone and looked carefully at me. "Bleenie," he affirmed gravely.

The crowd relaxed: Oh. Pliny – that explained everything. I knew what was going on, of course; but I could not help my brows knitting in what must inevitably have looked like the perplexity of the man without an answer. I already knew from living in the Emirate of Kint, that these people were experts in body-language. And it was, after all, an Englishman who had pioneered the study of one-upmanship.

Still, there *was* the honor of the side to defend. I decided to do an Englishman on him, as we say in my family. That is to say, make an equivocal but pertinent sally. The informal English war-cry, *Illegitimi Non Carborundum* (Don't let the bastards grind you down) – recently quoted by Professor H. H. Huxley in *The Times* – ran through my head. I would try a counter-attack:

"Pliny also said, '*Nemo mortalium omnibus horis sapit*' – No man is wise at all times..."

But people accustomed to command, especially in England, can say anything and get away with it. "Don't let it bother you at all, my dear man," the Vicar said graciously. "*Nil desperandum*, as it were." He spoke so decisively, and so loudly that even the dimmest yokel present must have recognized his authority and seeming victory.

I had a fleeting vision of how the inspired, so English, Lord Tennyson, when his hair caught fire, once forestalled derision by saying merely that such a conflagration was not accidental, but repeatedly necessary in his particular case.

"Pliny," the Schoolmaster was saying, "was, of course, merely quoting from the Greek. *Unde etiam vulgare Graecuae dictum*, you know."

The Vicar, evidently from long practice, had his measure. He nodded sagely.

"Yes... the Greeks *always* had a word for it, didn't they?"

But the man of learning was zooming back into the attack, from another direction:

"Vicar, with regard to that lecture you gave last night, about the local manor being so important, I hope you'll amend your text before you use it again."

The parson gave him a baleful look. "If you mean that the term 'Manor House' did not come into use until 1576..."

The Schoolmaster rubbed his hands, "No, not that, though people do, erroneously, think that manor houses as such date back farther than the late sixteenth century. I have been looking at Peel's *Englishman's Home*, and I have discovered some disturbing things, which show that all this 'To the Manor Born' business you were reveling in is, well, a load of nonsense. You watch too much television."

"The Manor," hooted the Vicar, "represents the distillate of the ancient values of our people."

The Schoolmaster snorted triumphantly and pulled an old envelope from his pocket.

"In that case," he roared, obviously addressing the village multitude, "you may care to hear a really authoritative extract, again from Peel." He peered at the paper. "Nineteen seventy-two edition, page ten." Then he read:

"'The earliest manor house was a hall or communal living quarter, topped by a single storey, which contained sleeping accommodations for the lord's family... The retainers slept in the hall, on straw or pallets. Very likely, the house was made of timber.'"

"And the animals slept in the house, too. I knew *that*, you silly!" fluted the man of God.

"'Baronial' is upstart, 'Manor House' is arriviste, preoccupation with them is downright common!" spat the teacher.

"Then you'd better admit that you're common yourself, you're obsessed by the subject!" snapped the priest.

Things continued like this for another half hour; petering out in some exchange which I missed, but which enabled each to decide that he had won.

I now had, for my book, an example of something which Dame Edith (Rich War) Sitwell had once defined. It was nothing less than proof of "that peculiar and satisfactory knowledge of infallibility that is the hallmark of the British nation." Each one in this case, the Vicar and the teacher alike, was able, by virtue of this convention, to preserve his own conviction unthreatened.

It was also a perfect illustration of Novalis's dictum, "Not only England, but every Englishman, is an island."

"'England is safe, if true within itself': Shakespeare," I muttered, but the Sheikh wanted more.

"Exactly what," he asked, "has passed between the three of you in your learned discussion?"

He was not satisfied when I offered him a précis: "Points about classical texts and the humble origins of allegedly noble edifices." But he was so astonished at my subsequent literal translation of some of the exchanges that he made light of the fact that there had been no whole roast sheep at the English feast.

I, for my part, left the fête certain that both the Vicar and the Schoolmaster were admirers of Churchill. As he wrote in *My Early Life*, Sir Winston was impressed by the "enormous and unquestionably helpful part that humbug plays in the social life of a great people dwelling in a state of democratic freedom."

The Sheikh, at that point, offered me a *dinar* for my thoughts. The helpfulness of humbug seemed too intricate a subject to explain, so I merely said, "Winston Churchill."

"Ah, Shurshill! I recently met a Frenchman who heard him speak at a dinner in Paris after the liberation of France," the Sheikh said. "His words caused the wildest possible applause, the man told me. So I memorized them. Shurshill always insisted on speaking French in France, you know."

Here was a piece of living history: and I realized that I must acquire and preserve it. "What did he say to them?" I asked.

"His exact words," said the Sheikh, "were '*Il faut, toujours, faire la bonne.*' He believed in good things."

After struggling with languages all day, I felt grateful for Winston's literal and thought-provoking translation of a simple English phrase.

Yet, strangely, when I quoted it in France, I was to find that the reaction was not consistent. Some people looked surprised: others clapped me delightedly on the back. That was before an Englishman asked me, in puzzlement, "Why should Churchill 'always want to make the maid'?"

7

The Cipher

Take Your Pick
The face is the index of the heart
English Proverb

The face is no index of the heart
English Proverb
Wilson: *The Oxford Dictionary of English Proverbs*

I TOOK THE Sheikh back to my place, not far from Badgersden, and we talked of hawks and camels. At least, I did, explaining that the word "mews" was originally French, and from the Latin.

"It comes from the King's Mews, near Charing Cross," I said, "the buildings reserved for moulting hawks. 'To mew' means 'to molt.' Later, such places became stables. Nowadays people live in them, and pay a lot for the privilege."

"How very distressing," was his reaction to that.

With camels it was, at first, even worse. "In this country they say that a camel is a horse designed by a committee," I told him brightly. The Sheikh cast his eyes upward, as if seeking heavenly succor.

"Committee, committee?" he snarled. "I've had enough of them! When I arrived in London, I was met by a committee. Then I sat and talked to people in a committee. It is typical of them to insult camels. If you ask me, a committee is a horse designed by a camel." If you think that this has suffered in translation, all I can say is that this was exactly what he said.

"Anyway," he continued, "why do they keep them in zoos over here? Just look around you: this is quite good camel country. A little damp, perhaps, but you could graze, say, a hundred on your own land, around the house. You could race them – a top-class racing camel is worth a million *dirhams*, £200,000, in Dubai – or start a caravan trail to the north, carrying produce. You did say that there is an abundance of economic activity in the south, didn't you?"

"Silicon chips," I said.

"That would do. There is sure to be a demand for them in the hotter, more arid, areas of the north, where the oil wells are. There are oil wells in the north, are there not? Ours are in the north."

I had to admit it. "But very far north: the platforms are…"

He clasped his hands together and interrupted me. "That shows you how easily problems can be solved, given a little thought."

As the night wore on, and the Sheikh had kindly discussed in greater detail what he called my preoccupations with hawks and camels, it became clear that there was something of greater moment on his mind. As is our way in the East, he threw out hints and spoke of "seriousness and urgency" while I waited for him to come to the point.

"There is a matter of some importance to discuss," he said at length, leaning back in his chair.

"At the Emir's orders," I answered, automatically.

"I have had it in my mind since we first spoke, when I heard you talking like a book. I see that you have many books in your library, and find that you have even written fifty books yourself."

"Only thirty or so, O Sheikh."

"Thirty or forty, then. We have few at home, you know. Nowadays the young people are reading the adventures of Qumandan Jimiz Bund, a dangerous British Agent and English spy. His number is *sifr, sifr, saba*." He traced the Arabian numerals 007 in the air with his finger, and continued: "and he is in the service of the English Queen."

"Yes, *Diamonds are Forever*, and so on," I said, to show that I was following him.

"Diamonds mean Always," he corrected me. "A clever concept. Coupling their hardness with their durability. Now, there is a connection. I am being increasingly concerned, for reasons of State, with the renewed interest of the prosilient English spies in the affairs of the Arab World."

"I don't think that I can help there," I said, hurriedly because it had always been my policy to keep out of politics, espionage and international matters where I might get hurt.

The Sheikh raised his hand. "But you *can*, my friend. And nobody need know, for it will be private advice, spoken, while the need for confidentiality subsists, only between these walls. Besides, I am your guest" – here he barked the hallowed Arabic word establishing it – "*Dakhilak*! You can now refuse me nothing."

So I had to agree, though you may think it foolish of me. I lacked the English capacity to get out of tight corners, especially where matters invoking a host's role is concerned. I might fancy myself an Anglekin of sorts, but in the Sheikh's eyes I was not a host who could get away with a mustard and cress sandwich. That "*Dakhilak!*" had bound me, by immemorial chivalric tradition, to aid and defend him, even at the cost of my life.

I braced myself, recalling our ancient wisdom: "Once the caravan has had one setback, a thousand demons fall on it."

"Honorable Sir," he said, using the flowery phrase which he could now afford, since I was so entirely in his clutches, "you will keep this secret for as long as its sinister meaning remains in your mind."

From the folds of his robes he took a tiny object wrapped in a handkerchief, and handed it to me. A book: or rather, a fattish booklet, it carried the label of a famous London bookshop, and it was priced at fifty-six pence.

"That," said the Sheikh, "is a secret codebook of the kind which is doubtless to be employed in *jasusiyyat*, espionage, by certain agents."

"It does not look like such to me, O one whose life should be prolonged," I told him.

"That is precisely the point. Secret things are always disguised." The Sheikh was querulous. "They have even gone so far as to put it on public sale, to lull possible suspicions, such is their confidence in the supreme artistry of its camouflage. I have, however, understood some of its purpose."

That sounded interesting; and, beguiled by the words and the implacable certitude of the speaker, I looked at the object with mounting excitement.

SAY IT IN ARABIC, shouted the cover. Inside were the words "Everything useful, modern, no dead wood."

"How did you discover its secrets?" I asked the Sheikh, whose English, I knew, was less than perfect.

He let his eyelids drop for a moment, while he fingered his rosary.

"That is an intelligent question, which shows you are beginning to understand. One must be ever-vigilant. Now we are alone here. Why? Because I have left Dawood behind in London. And who is Dawood? He is my Lebanese interpreter.

Through him I learned the meaning of the book, while he was reading from it to me."

"So *he* broke the code, and not you?" I was trying to understand. After all, I had been called intelligent.

"Not so. He is a Christian Arab, a Nazarene. There are millions of them, you know. He did not notice the secret meanings for that very reason. He does not share our high morality. He merely read it out, but I, who am Anwar al Agali, I understood."

He took the book from me and opened it, then pointed to a sentence. "This was the one which put me on the right track."

I looked. And then I really did understand the reason for his suspicions. The phrase offered to the innocent traveler was the very last one which any sensible person would try out, anywhere from Morocco to the Arabian Sea. Yet there it was, fighting talk if I had ever seen it: "How is your wife?"

But that did not make it a secret code-book, or even a manual for an *agent provocateur*. I hurried to my bookshelves and took out a volume. Books the Sheikh respected, and books he should have.

"O Great Sheikh, Commander of Wisdom," I cried, "allow me to explain that the customs of the Franks are different from those of other lands. They say and do all kinds of things which are regarded as – inappropriate – elsewhere."

He looked unconvinced, but did not interrupt, merely folding his hands on his lap and smiling. I showed him the title of the book which I had grabbed from the shelves: *Travels in Arabia*, by Lawrence d'Arvieux. Then I opened it at a passage relating a conversation with an Eastern prince:

"'The Emir and his whole Court,'" I read out, translating the while into Dari, "'heard with some pleasure the little detail I gave them, but when I told them of the handsome liberty the men have with the women,' that is, in Europe,"

I stressed, "'I observed that the Prince blushed and that all his Court were out of countenance. Our custom especially of saluting the ladies seemed insupportable to them; nothing shocked them so much as that; they could not comprehend how a man of honor could suffer his wife or his daughter to be kissed before his face by way of civility – it is with them to injure the honor of the whole family.'

"The ways of the Franks are often opposite to those of the People of the Firm Faith," I ended.

I looked at him, expectantly: and when he answered I realized how close, in some important respects, are the minds of the English and the Afghans. The Sheikh was speaking in our common language, and he now used the phrase *Har balai ki bashad* (roughly meaning "that rot apart"), which is a close enough approximation to the essence of Englishry, *Be That As It May*. As with them, so with us. No backtracking can follow this positive slamming of the door: even if you have proved your case.

Unlike the English, I sometimes know when I am beaten, so I inclined my head with such grace as I could muster, and invited Sheikh Anwar to continue.

"I have not yet decided exactly what the policy behind this document actually is," he went on, "but further examples will show you, quite unequivocally, that it is not what it purports to be."

Following the pencil-marks in the margin, and reading out the passages, I heard his interpretation.

"'Give my regards to your (boy, girl) friend' we can treat with the astonishment which it deserves," he told me, passing quickly to "I love you." "Now perhaps you see what I mean? Even d'Arvieux, your traveler in Arabia, did not say such things, though I admit he came close to it, presumably also for some espionage purpose."

"But..."

"There can be no but where there is clearly no but," he rebutted. "Now how about this one, for a code-phrase: 'I speak only English.' If he speaks only English, why is he saying it in Arabic?"

He shot me a triumphant glance.

"Further, 'How much do I owe you?' is not rendered by those words at all, in the Arabic version given here. It clearly says, against that, 'How much do you want or need?' And there is a strong suspicion attached to the purported use of the telephone. The alleged traveler is supposed to be trying to make a call to a long distance. This is dust in the eyes: for the parallel passage plainly translates the word as 'abroad.' It does not refer to a trunk call. The agent is trying to make a foreign contact."

"James Bond was never like this," I breathed.

"Exactly. Now you are beginning to see the intention of the thing, and I for one don't like it at all." In my fevered state I almost imagined that a British intelligence chief from a John Buchan novel was speaking. The Sheikh's voice had that ring of quiet authority which I had read about in English books, and yet had so seldom heard. Perhaps this was, indeed, the real thing. And the Sheikh, by some alchemy of the English air, had become the all-wise spycatcher.

I discovered the next suspicious phrase all by myself. It was the traveler, again, this time speaking to someone at the reception counter of a hotel.

The sinister words could surely have been intended only for a terrorist: "I would like to get the money from the safe." Speaking to a confederate, no doubt.

"You have missed an important point inherent in that passage, which I have studied with care," the Sheikh informed me when I essayed to share my discovery with him. "They give both the masculine and feminine version of the words, which means that there are female terrorists involved as well as men. You are right in thinking that they are planning to get money which is not their own. The correct phrase, addressed to the receptionist, would of course have been, 'I would like to have *my* money/travelers checks from the safe, please.'

"There is no limit to the depth of their mendacity."

"And," the calm voice went on, "there are Latins involved as well: Spanish or Portuguese, or the like."

"How so?" I cried, unable to bear the suspense and frantically flicking the pages of the tiny book.

"It is simple. Look at this page: the alleged traveler is asking about the Mambo, Rumba, Samba and Tango. Now, I ask you, since it says at the beginning, 'everything useful, modern, no dead wood,' how can this be reconciled with the fact that everyone goes disco-dancing nowadays?"

But I was now hot on the trail, too. "O Sheikh," I stammered, "just look at this. Here is a list of words positively labeled USEFUL ARTICLES. They include," I jabbered, "'A CAMEL, A SILVER COMPACT, A DOG...'"

"And HORSE and VASE," he interrupted, obviously having the abominable text by heart.

"Everything useful – no dead wood, ha!"

It was not until much later that further, more personal, connotations came to me. The Sheikh had taken his leave, promising to keep me informed if any agents of the publishers of the travel guide were ever found in his country, and I had gone to bed. I woke very early in the morning in a muck-sweat.

I had just remembered something that had happened many years before.

My father was working, before breakfast, in his study. On that day he had asked our English maid to bring him his "tea and boiled egg concurrently."

Jenny had returned with tea, an egg – and currants.

There had almost certainly been an enciphered meaning in that act of the female spy. Who knows what damage she wrought before being dismissed for saying "go" (which means "excrement" in our language) while handing a coin to an innocent wayfarer soliciting alms. But we had no book or sheikh, or even any suspicion, to alert us in those clays.

And we had not digested Churchill's warning, given in 1936: "England is a curious country and few foreigners can understand her mind... she is very clever." The meaning is clear, even if the grammar is not.

A more recent book than the one which the Sheikh discovered has, for me, put a completely different complexion on the matter. Charles Berlitz, in *Native Tongues*, published in 1984, has given the show away – insofar as people ever do reveal such things.

There has never been a language, he says, which has been influenced by so many others as English. In fact, it consists of part of "most of the world's languages," containing words from places as far apart as Japan and Armenia. This leads him to feel that anyone can adopt it without qualm, quite apart from it being the most widely used of international tongues. He even foresees the possibility in the next century of "a worldwide tongue based on English."

Are you surprised that I see the Anglean hand in this? First the Saxon takeover, then the Celts and the rest, then international airlines, communications – finally, the world...

The travelers' phrase-book shown me by the Sheikh may indeed be some small part of that program. It should be added that the publication was not British, but American. Yet it was on sale in England and, as we shall see later, there is no lack of British and American authorities who swear that the North Americans are in fact English.

Of course, two centuries of pursuing their own objectives must have caused some at least of the Anglean tendencies to become blunted on the other side of the Atlantic. The Yanks do not exactly come over as cunning schemers with a wealth of ingenious political activities in the international field. I was reflecting on this when I came across a book – Edmond Taylor's *Awakening from History* – which provided two very important pieces of information, vital to my researches on the English character and how it is employed.

Taylor, an American journalist, lived for many years in Europe before the Second World War, representing, among others, the *Chicago Tribune* and CBS. When the United States came into the war, he found himself working with the British PWE, the Political Warfare Executive. This was a highly secret organization, located in the country, in "romantic isolation." Its activities were "more imaginative and frequently more ruthless than any Nazi psychological warfare I had studied." The people of this secret service included Richard Crossman, Ritchie Calder and Sefton Delmer, all figures very well known to the public. And also, "eminent, and eminently respectable, bowler- or brass-hatted servants of His Majesty who sat on this committee" – among whom Taylor "recognized several of them from various international conferences I had covered before the war."

They were, in a word, not just the rag, tag and bobtail whom one might have expected to have been thrown up by the maelstrom of war. Their importance and wide experience, now totally placed at the service of Machiavellian schemes as if this were the most natural thing in the world, made Taylor think hard. "From what secret peacetime drawers had the British taken out all these recipes for exploiting human weakness, all these mental philtres, all these scoundrel skills, accumulated through centuries of power struggle in every quarter of the globe, which they were now so generously making available to an upstart ally and potential successor?"

He came to the conclusion that "there had always existed the indispensable foundations for rapid expansion: a pool of trained personnel, a current technology of clandestine operations, and the necessary structures of administrative control." He never discovered, Taylor says, the answer to the problem of how power attitudes and certain power skills are transmitted among the Brits. So maybe the Sheikh was not as paranoid as he seemed to me, and the American originators of the phrase-book had proved worthy recipients of the ancient English lore which – for my money – could only have been brought from far-off Asia, such is its sophistication and intricacy.

There is another point which I unearthed for myself, and which would certainly have appealed to the Sheikh. It may be summarized in the words "The English do not need phrase-books for Eastern languages at all."

If you find this rather difficult to credit, see a telling passage in Dr. D. J. Renier's *The English: Are They Human?* He is battled by what he calls a contradiction in the English character. They are, he says, "incapable of learning foreign languages" – but also wizards at it:

> How is it that [they] are among the best Oriental linguists in the world? How can some public schoolboys who scarcely know their own language suddenly become acquainted with four Oriental languages if they are transported beyond the Suez Canal... Surely, Eastern languages are much more difficult than French or German?

Up to a point, Dr. Renier. The very Oriental cast of mind in the English may well make these languages easy for them. That, and the sure signs that they are prepared to consider almost anywhere in the world to be England, probably mean that they have made a calculation. The calculation that, although people like Dr. Renier will learn English and save these public schoolboys a lot of trouble, some Orientals are less obliging – and, besides, Eastern languages are not really all that difficult if you set your mind to it, don't you know.

I wonder whether it would have reassured the Sheikh if he had been told that the East, which has been insinuating itself into England from the earliest times, is stepping up its role in Albion, and over a wider area than that of the English spies in the East?

I see the following news stories in today's papers:

UK TYCOON'S YACHT SOLD TO SULTAN

EGYPTIAN MILLIONAIRE MAKES SHRINE OF EX-KING EDWARD'S HOUSE

ENGLAND NOW HAS 680 MOSQUES

COMPULSORY PUNJABI LESSONS FOR ALL WOLVERHAMPTON SCHOOLS' PUPILS...

8

Gy-i Fee-a

Hisses and Buzzes
The phonetic structure of English – the assemblage of sounds that constitute it – is marked by a multitude of hisses and buzzes.
C. T. Onions, in *The Character of England*

PROPER ENGLISH, STANDARD English, Southern English, BBC, Oxford, all those other kinds of English are, today, largely fantasies maintained by the popular Press, by foreigners, or by some of the upwardly mobile. You often can't tell a person's class, certainly not his or her income-group, by listening to pronunciation.

Lord O'Neill of the Maine went on record (in *The Times*) in 1978 as insisting that American English is English English, and that "The Establishment" in Britain today does not speak with an "English" accent at all.

There is an interesting curiosity, though. This is the matter of the dropped "g," the added "r" and the pronunciation of words like "house" or "mouse."

Like other matters English, it is a paradox, and may be stated thus:

At the very top and very bottom of English society, many words are pronounced similarly. Both the Cockney and the aristocrat (though you can be both in England) will say "goin,' seein,' thinkin'," and so on – the dropped "g." Again, people from both ends of the social scale will each tend to add an "r" to words ending in -a: *viz.* "Indiar, Chinar, I sore it." And the rustic from Oxford or Bucks will say, instead of "house, mouse," *hayss* and *mayss*, enunciations which are to be heard from the lips of the Highest in the Land, and are regularly mocked by television comedians. Likewise four-letter words, increasingly avoided mainly by the genteel.

This is all very confusing to those who hail from beyond these shores (and some from within them) who are trying to upgrade their pronunciation. No sooner do they learn not to drop their "g"s, to avoid being thought Cockneys, than they have to remember to drop them again as their upward-mobility demands that they should not be mistaken for members of the middle-class.

Things became so confused by 1985 that Major General Pelham Witherspoon had to write *The Drink Spotty Book* (Bantam Press). It instructed the Middle Classes on many vital pronunciations that both the duke and the garbageman already used, and had for ages. Examples are *wiskin-sader* for "whisky and soda," *crydidrome* for "crowded room," and *arnair* for "oh no."

But there are limits, or, at least, caveats. My father, when he was a student in England, came across the invisible barrier which does, or did, separate the quality from the rest.

He was looking for an address near The Strand, and stopped a costermonger to ask for a landmark. "You can't miss it, cock," the man told him. Apparently it was just near the Gaiety Theatre.

So, continuing along the street but still not quite certain where the theater was, my father next approached a distinguished-looking gentleman and, after referring to his phonetic transcription of the Cockney's words, asked for directions.

The Englishman looked down his nose at him, and then replied, "If that is your idea of a joke, I must tell you that it is in very poor taste," and pushed past.

What my father had said, naturally taken as an impertinent sally, was, "Excuse me, cock. I wonder whether you would be so very kind as to inform me as the location of the *Gy-i Fee-a*!"

So, remember, "Indiar Hayss" is perfect for India House but, unless you are a Cockney, *never* "Gy-i Fee-a" for Gaiety Theatre.

English people, however, know the rules and the usages as intricately as any protocol official at the Bourbon Courts of France, Spain or Naples. But never try to get an English person to explain meanings. One of the best conversation-stoppers you can use at a social gathering is: "What is the difference, in English, between 'the middle of the road' and 'the center of the road'"?" Everyone in his right mind knows it already. Few can explain it.

It's like belonging to a secret society, once you have got the hang of it, even if there is no actual initiation: you get there by osmosis. Beryl Graves, the wife of Robert, unwittingly had a Spanish professor of English almost hysterical when she asked me at a picnic, "Are these *these* apples?" And he started to moan when I actually seemed to understand her, and answered, "Yes, I think so."

"One can't *say* that in English!" he shouted. But you can. We were sitting under an apple tree, Beryl had an apple in her hand, and she was referring, of course, to the apples on that particular tree.

Perhaps it is that English is not only spoken, it is lived, or acted. Without the context, the picnic and the props, the tree and the apples, Mrs. Graves's sentence would have been meaningless: like one of those languages which are partly spoken and partly whistled.

Another Spaniard, misled by a further feature of English – its local or minority usages – said to me, "I met a policeman today and got talking to him. He pretended to be clairvoyant, but he was a fraud."

"How so?" I asked (instead of the customary English "Oh, really?") because it did sound rather intriguing.

"Well, he said 'You favor the Italians, I'm thinking.' He was claiming, you see, that he could tell by telepathy that I supported Italy in the current international football championships."

He could not understand it when I tried to explain that "to favor" in England can mean "to look like." Could it have been just such a misunderstanding which caused the Romans to conclude that Britain was a land of magicians and soothsayers? There are other examples of this kind of thing, of course, apart from those one finds in the United Kingdom. Enough, I think, to form a theory that occultism and the supernatural may to a great extent depend upon linguistic misunderstanding. For instance, a Swiss-German writing to me asked what seemed at first to be a highly metaphysical question:

"How can J become a work-permit?"

It was only after consulting a German scholar that I determined that "become" was a German attempt at an English version of his own word "to get," and that "J" was the letter which German typewriters use for the English capital "I." The whole matter may, one hazards the guess, lie at the root of the English distrust of foreigners. By and large, the English do not like things which smack of esotericism. One only has to imagine an Englishman receiving a letter from "J" and having no German scholar handy, or less curiosity than I had (curiosity is bad manners in England), for him to conclude that it was just the ravings of another of those weird people from abroad.

After all, a recent English king, George V, is on record as saying that he had "been abroad and it was horrid." But some curiosity is permitted, especially among the less educated. An English workman once said to me, "You've been out foreign, then? What's it like?"

I took refuge in the traditional English cover-all phrase, "Oh, it's not too bad."

"Thass all right, then," he said.

The English distrust of foreigners coupled with their sense of humor can provide openings if you know how to work it. The young man whom we came to know as "J," and who wanted to get a work-permit had answered my advertisement in *The Times* for an "Au Pair." His references were excellent, and so I wrote the Home Office, seeking the necessary permission. The reply said, "'Au Pairs' cannot be other than female. In these circumstances the Home Secretary cannot see his way to granting the permit for which you have applied."

I decided to try Oriental cunning. I had obtained a permit for an Iranian couple to work as domestics, on the ground that I needed people who spoke Persian for my staff. They had then decided that they didn't want to come to England after all, so I was left with a permit for two Persians and none for the Au Pair. So I wrote back to the Home Secretary's minion:

Would the Minister feel inclined to allow me to import an Au Pair boy if I swapped him for two Persians?

The answer came almost by return of mail: yes. And, for quite a time we were able to entertain our English guests with "This is J, our Au Pair boy. He became a work-permit when we swapped him with the Home Secretary for two Iranians, you know..."

They like that kind of thing: that's what makes them so good at solving crossword puzzles.

The code-phrases in England are numerous and effective. One soon learns a goodly number, though not without some pain and perturbation. "Do you really think so" decodes as "I think you're lying, or stupid, or both." "I can't say," or, simply "Dunno" means "I'm not co-operating." "Be that as it may" is probably the best. It means "What you say is true [etc] but I don't give a damn." Then there is "What do you mean by not/gone/sorry/[etc]?" This is multi-purpose. It gives one time to think; it can stop almost anyone in his tracks, because it implies that there is something absurd about what he's just said.

But other people's throwaway lines do not always transfer directly into English. I picked up one, in Ireland, which I thought rather charming and a sort of general pleasantry: "Just to show there's no ill-feeling." Believe it or not, several times when I have used it in England, I have either been met with blank stares or with the reply: "What do you mean, ill-feeling?" I'm still working on the significance of this.

Another Irishism, or at any rate a phrase I learned in Dublin, is not recommended either. This is: "The reward sweetens the labor." The first (and last) time I used it in England the rejoinder was: "Not for me it don't, mate."

So, as I advise all Afghans who seek my counsel, go carefully in the matter of code-words and imported phrases. Mind you, even a lifetime of experience cannot guarantee success. I once heard a Frenchman, who had lived in England for forty years and was bilingual, claim to an Englishman that the word "cul-de-sac" was not good French. The right word to use was *impasse*.

"I prefer cul-de-sac," the Englishman told him.

"But cul-de-sac can mean 'behind the belly,'" insisted the Parisian.

"Sounds like an impasse to me," said the Englishman.

Then, good easy man, when you think that your knowledge of real English full surely is a-ripening – go deeper into the colloquial speech, because some people think that this is where it is all at: or a lot of it. There's a lot of it about:

> [In] the English "them blokes ain't got no go" not even a single word satisfies the standard exacted by pure English... not merely uncultured but illiterate: yet the speech is straight from the shoulder, the meaning unmistakable.

This is Eric Partridge's dictum in *Usage and Abusage*. I once sought a view from Professor Gilbert Murray, one of the most melodious speakers of the language that I have ever heard. As a polished academic he was worth listening to. Briefly, his theory was that the whole difficulty lay in the hostility of the masses toward scholars. "If they didn't dislike the academics, they would try to enunciate more clearly and musically."

But why should there be this hostility? I asked. I was indeed curious, for I had found it even among scholars themselves.

"It's quite simple. Freud taught the English something that they had always suspected anyway: that people who try to do something are often over-compensating. Scholars, then, are seen as people who are not too intelligent but want to appear so. Public speakers, you may have noticed, often have some sort of impediment in their speech."

So, I asked, scholars were not really such at all?

"They may overcome the drawback of finding it difficult to learn, as do many other partially disabled people. But they always represent learning as difficult – because *they* find it so."

And the hostility of the well-spoken man toward the Cockney pronunciation of Gaiety Theatre?

"Hostility toward what he thought was mockery, not toward Cockney. But you should study your English people carefully: he was perhaps not English at all, but Australian or something. How was he to know that a practical joker had not enlisted your father's help in rubbing in that the man was not *quite* English?"

Gilbert (Bright Hostage) Murray, of course, was himself an Australian.

He is dead now, so I could not go back to him with some recent evidence which seemed to question his assertion that scholars are not over-intelligent, as I had understood him to say. I knew that the British strength is in compromise, and would have liked to know how he reconciled his views with those of a more current authority.

Richard Parlour, writing in the *New Scientist* (and billed there as a cosmologist) says that the country needs less academic research, and "not an academic recruitment drive but a campaign of wholesale sackings." Because the scholars can't do their jobs? No, because universities are "simply too congenial."

The theory continues that the cleverest dons should be returned from their colleges to the community as a whole. This would infuse new life into it; otherwise it would remain intellectually bankrupt.

When I submitted the argument to a professorial friend, he spotted the weakness at once. "Both Murray and Parlour are right," he told me. "Murray did not say that scholars were fools, only that they had trouble studying. Perhaps it is even true that the extra effort needed by the less able enables them to try harder, like the hire-car agency which is Number Two and advertises itself as such. Perhaps we're not balls of intellectual fire, but we may deliver the goods just the same."

Since Parlour says that British universities are both overstaffed and "effortlessly the best in the world," I asked the Professor if this meant that here quantity made up for quality. "Almost true. We need very few dons compared to what we have. The word 'effortlessness,' here, distinctly means that they have got the method and the content right. It does not necessarily imply that they are naturally brilliant."

This all took me back to the difficulty of understanding exactly what people meant when they said something in English. As Churchill once declared, in the House of Commons, "The English never draw a line without blurring it." Even here, we cannot guess whether the plural he uses is a mistake for the singular, or whether he is only talking about a number of English, all drawing a line, together. There is a precedent for this, in the case of the (English) Wise Men of Gotham, who tended toward Anglo-Saxon type communal activities. Like fencing a thicket to imprison birds.

But cosmologist Richard Parlour seems definite enough when he levels his gun at others in the country which he seeks to help: all the best brains are at the universities, and this "explains why we are afflicted with banana-skin politicians, tunnel-visioned bureaucrats, industrialists who are so inept that when they actually make a profit it is front-page banner headline news." For him, at least, academics are clever.

He goes on to say that all this "could be rectified virtually overnight." Just return most of the cleverest dons to the community.

One of the great reflectors of the English character is Samuel Butler, and I turned to his *Notebooks*[2] to check how much reliance I should place upon things read in the Press. "The most important service rendered by the Press and the magazines," he states, "is that of educating people to approach printed matter with distrust."

---

[2] Edited by Keynes and Hill, London 1951.

Fine: but how can Parlour's advice be taken if it is distrusted? Perhaps an extract, from P. E. Smith, of the North-East London Polytechnic, writing to the editor of the *New Scientist* on another subject the following week, may clarify matters. "Unfortunately," he says, "students believe what they read in your magazine, so please get it right next time."

Whatever the scholars or the Press may think or write, I have no doubt that it is the Anglean group-mind which ultimately directs what shall and what shall not be English. No scholar or journalist would have dared, for instance, to transform the meaning of the word "gossip" as the native culture has done. Originally it stood for "godparent." And, although you may co-opt foreign words into the language, you must always wiggle them about a bit before accepting them as naturalized. Take *Na-ranj*, Persian for the fruit called "No sorrow." In English this is too simple; so it is not "a norange," but "an orange."

An English grammarian, I notice, laments the fact that this word, with inaccurate spelling, was imported from the French. "In Spanish it is *naranja*, which is very close to the Persian original. If we had adopted the word direct," he says, "no doubt we would have been more careful than the French." No doubt; and in that case, is it merely to keep us on our toes that the English have taken their own word "ewt," and instead of referring to it as "an ewt," elide the indefinite article, to produce the creature thenceforward known as "a newt"?

One is almost tempted to christen the whole process Linguistic Chauvinism, because words are frequently changed in meaning to such an extent that foreigners cannot be expected to keep up with the changes.

Reading old books only baffles you, thus slamming the door upon the secret writings of antiquity. "Naught" used to mean wickedness: now it means "nothing." "Silly" means both harmless and senseless. "Nice," according to my dictionary, can stand for accurate, hazardous, delightful – and no less than fourteen other things. *Harlot* was originally French for "a base fellow." And "let" formerly signified "to prevent," not, as now, "to permit." So "let me if you can" has entirely reversed its meaning.

Mind you, newer books are not always as clear as they might be for tyros. The 1966 edition of *The Oxford Dictionary of English Etymology*, which I consulted to see what it said about the word "Postmaster," defines it thus:

> Scholar of Merton College, Oxford. Of unknown origin... one who receives a prescribed portion has been suggested.

Who knows what motivates these people? They have turned *syrup* (Arabic for "something to drink") into a sort of treacle, which you can't drink. Treacle, on the other hand, was originally an ointment against the effects of snake-venom. Perhaps there is a clue in the *Dictionary*'s Introduction, by the great Dr. C. T. Onions. He speaks of words being "admitted to citizenship from other languages." An interesting phrase, this may mean that the word has to undergo some kind of test of function or desirability: perhaps both.

My own belief is that form and substance are involved. The English are innovators and traditionalists at one and the same time. Other people change either the form or the substance of a thing. The English will change either, or both.

Something other is distinctly in charge, and for some – perhaps fell – purpose of its own. Before adopting English as the future world language, let us foreigners make sure that we know what we could be letting ourselves in for.

Foreign native English speakers, those whose mother-tongue it is, now outnumber UK-born Anglophones five to one. But the latter still have the ball at their feet. It will stay there for a long time.

Two or three days ago a Malaysian lawyer whom I know rang me up. A charming and cultivated man, he had been destabilized by a recent experience.

"I am in terrible trouble," this gentle and innocent (English) graduate gasped. "I asked the porter at this apartment block to find me a plumber. When I got back after a day at the office, and asked him about it, I could not understand a word he said."

"What were his exact words?" I asked.

"*Lit. et verb.*," he stammered, "the man said, 'Oh, he's come and been and gone.'"

Psychoanalysis, he thought, might help. "There's nothing we can do about *him*," I said, "because he's just part of a whole program. This difficulty is with *you*. In cases like this, only a very long period of rest can hold out any hope of recovery."

Military strategists recommend that one should mentally put oneself in the other fellow's shoes, to penetrate his thinking; so let us ask ourselves, "What would I do if I were English, to ensure supremacy?"

The first requisite would be to make sure that one is not fully understood. I have this on the authority of Sydney Smith, no less. He quotes the words of an English missionary in India:

> Wherever we have gone we have uniformly found that so long as people did not understand the purport of our message they appeared to listen; but the moment they understood something of it, they either became indifferent to it or began to ridicule.

In the face of such experience, who would wish to be understood: could even afford it? Nobody wants his efforts to be counter-productive.

But why did India, almost a continent, yield so readily to British rule, especially if the people understood anything that the English were saying? It took me some time to find, from English sources, the real explanation. Finally I tracked it down. Algernon Charles Swinburne, the poet, explains:

> India knelt at her [England's] feet and felt her sway
> more fruitful of life than spring.

What's the betting that that sway had something to do with the English language?

The interplay of words, actions and objects which makes up English speech marks out both the tribe and the tribe-within-a-tribe, the clan, in this country. Its operation is so intricate, so changing, that much observation, patience and study are needed to acquire competence.

Living near a country town not far from London, I walked into a harness store and asked the girl behind the counter for some saddle soap. Simple enough, you might think: but nothing is simple in England, and only patience will help with the complication of it all.

Her eyes took on that detached look which, here, presages something – or can simply mean disinterest.

"Certainly, sir. Which is it you have – bar or can?"

It seemed simple enough. Do you want, she was saying, the hard kind in a cake, or the soft, which you sponge on and therefore has to be in a can?

I rather liked the phrase "Which is it you have?" It implied that you were a regular customer. Or, at least, a regular user of saddle soap. An acceptable person, that is. Or so I thought; quite wrongly, of course.

"Bar," I said.

"Of course," said the salesgirl. "Trouble is, there are so many of those people in the new commuter estate – Mullion

Court they call it – that we've had to get the canned stuff in for them. Weekend riders, and foreigners, mostly."

So the question, her first words, had been a hidden test. I looked at her again. Her rural accent did not bespeak a classical, even a prep school, education. She wore neither twinset nor pearls, and seemed like a girl who would think that "champers" meant horses who chewed energetically. In a word, she was very much a product of the toiling rural masses: not County or Sloane. But she knew the right stuff to put on your saddle. And that it might be non-English not to know it.

Yet the test had been carried out so casually that a Mullion Courter would surely never have guessed. But did such a person not have a fifty-fifty chance of being right, given only the two options, cake or can? Probably not, I reflected, as I drove homeward. First, it is the done thing at Mullion to use cans. Second, it is not really English to take the soft option, to use cream instead of bar soap.

I can report, too, that events such as this have a positive functional advantage – if you emerge with a pass mark. Now I'm always served before the gaggle of executives' daughters with Diana hairdos, Mullioners all who used to make it difficult to attract attention in the place.

And the local horsey people must have heard, too. They now greet me with a wave or shout, instead of a frozen smile, as I crawl, in first gear, past their interminable strings of hacks, along the leafy English country lanes.

I have passed; have Given Off The Right Signals, don't you see. This phrase, revealingly, is employed to refer to the correct assembly of verbal clicks and buzzes, movements and *actions* which are essential to a right employment of the English language among the twenty per cent who form the Anglean segment of native-born English speakers.

9

The Dear Martian

Englishman's Bible
Collins's old Peerage-Book... is properly all we
English have for a Biographical Dictionary;
nay... for a National Bible.
 Thomas Carlyle: *Latter-Day Pamphlets*

ANY STUDY OF the English system of aristocracy and titles, it seems to me, must eventually have recourse to Outer Space analogies, for the scope and nebulous nature of the whole thing seems to belong nowhere else.

Great Britain and Northern Ireland is a monarchy, which means that one would expect it to have a hierarchy of nobility: and it does. Yet, in one study carried out in England in 1927, and a second in 1983, nobody, repeat nobody, in samples of 600 and 1,500, could correctly name the order of ranking of the dukes, earls, marquises, and so on who comprise the nobility.

Ranks and titles have existed among the English, remember, only since they came here. Then, after a few hundred years, the Normans got rid of most of the English titles, substituting French ones. These two factors are at the root of the uneasiness which one finds among the English about the matter.

A story which they tell, combining discomfort and pretension, is based on the fact that the feminine of marquis is marchioness: a woman recognizes a certain Lady Someone at a party and gushes: "Marchioness, how nice to see you. And how *is* the dear *Martian?*"

I like the connection with the inhabitants of Mars, not only because it was an Englishman, H. G. Wells, who invented them, but also because, as you will see later, there is a strange affinity between the English and extraterrestrialism. Perhaps that concept is the real point of the joke.

But let us backtrack to marquises.

A marquis was originally a Prefect of the Marches, and his title comes from Late Latin. He is known as Lord, evidently a generic term for a headman: (in Old English) "Bread-Keeper." The Lord kept the bread and gave it out to the men who fought for him, the Gesiths. Somewhat confusingly, to me at any rate, these fellows were "probably all of them Earls" (Eorls), although, as we shall see in a moment, they could be a pretty hard-up bunch, very different from later bearers of coats of arms and ermine, for centuries associated with big houses and affluence.

The marquis's wife was, of course, a Lady, which translates from the Germanic for "Bread-Kneader." The traditional English Lady Bountiful, dispensing food to the poor, is thus only following the logic of the title. The genteel Lady Bountiful, one of the type more familiar to us, would have been surprised to learn how harrowing the lives of her titular ancestors were. The Lady had to do much more than give out the product of her kneading and baking, of which her husband was the Keeper. She made and looked after the clothes of the gallant Gesiths: who could not have been much fun, as they did not like to work, and slept on the odoriferous equivalent of today's drawing-room floor, in the "hall."

One English lady was so disturbed by this revelation when I told her, that (unlike the marquis, her husband, who liked the idea) she refused to believe it. For others like her, I document the situation here. It is from Samuel R. Gardiner's *A Student's History of England*, painstakingly, if not eloquently, written by a man with no less than two law doctorates who is described as a Late Fellow of Merton College, Oxford:

> A body of Gesiths once approached their lord with a petition that he should take a wife, because as long as he remained unmarried there was no one to make new clothes for them or to mend their old ones.

No wonder their proud name of Gesiths was "gradually abandoned for that of Thegns, or servants." I dare say the gentle Bread-Kneader had some say in that.

But this species of lord, surely, cannot be the kind which rides about in red coats being unkind to serfs, as alluded to by my Khartoum informant? They sound almost like the Knights of Old, who weren't always as dashing and chivalrous as they might have been. Indeed, we find that they did get a bit above themselves, since the etymology of *knight* is given by many authorities as "servant." Perhaps they were promoted when the Gesiths sank to servanthood. And at some point the Knechts, the servant-lads, managed to get hold of servants of their own. These are the people still called squires: what my local innkeeper kindly thought I could be styled.

So the squire was not of illustrious origins. Indeed, the fellow seems to have been a bit of an upstart. It is stated in more than one English book that he was originally engaged to attend the knight, carrying the shield. His duties included heaving the knight on to his horse and picking up and re-attaching pieces of metal which fell off during this operation or in battle. Some sources say that he was a sort of apprentice knight: which is quite possible, since in early times knighthood was not as rare as it is today. Not only were reluctant people forced to be knighted (to make them liable for knightly taxes) but they were even hunted over hedges and ditches, to have the honor thrust upon them. Moreover, one knight could "make" any number of others at will, just as you can make more yogurt from heated milk once you have got a starting batch with enough active *bacillus bulgaricus* in it.

Quite soon, as the records show, the squires became men of a certain amount of property. How they did it is, alas, not well understood. There must have been some secret, which enabled them to leap from knave or varlet to owning land: something which not all knights could themselves achieve. Perhaps they did it by saving the money they would otherwise have had to pay in taxes on becoming knights.

I like to think of the original squire as the equivalent of the former major who is traditionally to be found in his favorite seat at village hostelries, throwing his weight about a bit and owning a little property in the neighborhood.

Of course, nowadays in England, every man is called Esquire, abbreviated to Esq., on letters. The fact that these missives so often come from tax men and the like, employing peremptory commands, tempts me to speculate that such officials are traditionalists, thinking of us as the old scrap-iron pickers-up rather than as respected landed gentry. I recently received one such communication, styling me Esquire. It begins:

>Dear Sir,
>You are required to...

Imperious, yes: but the bureaucrat is also according me an honor which I probably do not merit. An English book on precedence clearly states: "Without being a Barrister-at-Law or possessing the MA degree of Oxford or Cambridge University, few are entitled to be styled Esquire..."

Perhaps the ranks of the trainee knights were formerly filled mainly from among advocates and Oxbridge men.

And even if I *am* an esquire, the servant of a servant, what is the status of the civil servant who writes to me? Looking at the letter again, I see that I have myself acquired a lackey. He signs himself "Your Obedient Servant."

In case you feel that this is no longer a live issue, I refer you to *The Times* of November 27, 1984. Here, on page 15, Mr. Richard Seddon gives a list of those legally entitled to be called Esquire, according to the authoritative official, Richmond Herald.

Skipping up to dukes (another Latin title) we find that there is some reason for their snootiness: on the Continent they were originally independent sovereigns, something like the Duce Mussolini of Italy or, more felicitously perhaps, the Doge of Venice, both styles also being derived from the Latin *Dux*, a leader. No wonder some of the twenty-six dukes of the United Kingdom are said to look down their noses at monarchs. The latter's reply (as I have it from one of them) is "Dukes are an innovation in England, post-Norman."

They are aware, these dukes, and sometimes even remind us, that "king" means "a man of good birth," at the best, and "belonging to a tribe, or 'kin'" at the worst, depending upon your source. But, surely, we might say, a king (or queen) is a Majesty, and dukes are not. Ah, no. This has been true in England only since Henry VII, who was first called Majesty by the French King Francis in 1520 "and liked it so much that he took it home with him." Deeper delving reveals that crafty Francis had himself translated, and then appropriated, the title from the Arabic *jalalat*.

Much of the time, then, Henry was a plain Highness (German, *Hoch*), and so was Queen Elizabeth I. The republican Cromwell was styled Highness too, even though he was only a Protector. Highness is therefore not an exclusively royal title.

Nowadays, people assume that Highness is attached only to a prince: and that the son of a king is a prince. But it was nearly a thousand years before the sons of kings were princes in England. Before 1301 they were merely "Lord." That is logical enough, since "prince" means the supreme ruler, and such a title cannot be shared. Strictly speaking, therefore, there is only one prince in a country, and that is the head of state. The present inflation of princes started, in England, with the adoption by Edward I of a foreign – Welsh – title, *Tywysog*, for his son.

And queen? "Queen" is derived, so say the references, from the Greek *Gyne*, meaning "woman," which is logical enough.

The English keep shifting their opinions on royalty; sometimes showing love and respect, sometimes quite other sentiments, toward their monarchy. Their feelings are occasionally tepid. In 1937, a writer in the *Sunday Times*, though effusively loyal, allowed his concentration to slip:

> When our sovereign was born he was given, among other qualities, the rare boon of youth.

The media and the satirical programs on television, too, are not comfortable with the regal habit of saying "one" or "one's" instead of "I" or "me": though this is probably only a hangover from the nursery. My nanny, too, reproved me for using the first person singular. After all, one should not assert oneself, should one?

This attitude seems to be based on a very rare instance: the English reacting to criticism from outside. In the early nineteenth century Don Manuel Espirella wrote a book, *Letters from England*, which was a runaway best-seller. In it he said:

> A remarkable peculiarity is, that they always write the personal pronoun with a capital letter. May we not consider this Great I as an unintended proof how much an Englishman thinks of his own consequence?

The English have always been avid readers of books about them written by foreigners, even though these are sometimes very hostile. Robert Southey showed that the English can beat any foreigner at his own game – he wrote *Letters from England* under the pseudonym of Don Manuel Espirella. So it wasn't an outsider at all, criticising that personal pronoun.

The ubiquitous "one" has given rise to at least one joke. One of the English Royals had died, and was hovering beside the golden gates, calling out, "Has one arrived yet?"

Back came St. Peter's voice: "One? There's *millions* of them here, stupid!"

But at least the media joke sends the Royals to heaven...

There was, for me, an unexpected twist to this story. I had assumed that it was intended only to emphasize the outlandish use of "one." But the English are more sophisticated than that. When I said this at a social gathering, some English friends were kind enough to expand the context for me. The millions did not only refer to numbers. It meant people with royal blood!

And St. Peter's "millions"? Yes, indeed. English genealogists have calculated that *most of the population* is of royal descent. Their opinion was cited by Dr. John Tanner, CBE, DLitt, FSA, in the 1984 printing of the (English) Reader's Digest publication *Who's Famous in Your Family?* "In a room containing 100 Englishmen, over 80 will be descended from Edward III." Eight out of ten... Add the people carrying the blood of all the other monarchs, and your chance of being the scion of a king or queen, these worthies seem to say, approaches certainty.

English kings have graduated from being "the man," to royal status, and have been martyred, sanctified, and reviled in the process and afterward. Every time there is an accession to the throne, or even a royal birth, the newspapers carefully inform their readers as to the exact proportion of English blood in the newcomer. We are assured that they are getting more English all the time. A recent book combats the "German" sneer by citing the royal descent from the ninth-century King Egbert, who was a Saxon. Yet the ambivalent attitude lingers. The English writer does not omit the fact that the Queen is also descended from a London plumber named George Smith. And the bated-breath attitude toward royalty is noted by Donald Home (in *God is an Englishman*) to be rather new. The "Oriental," magical aura attached to British monarchs dates only, he says, from the late nineteenth century.

With Queen Victoria, both the English and the German, the popularity and the reverse, came together. We have all heard of the great crowds which turned out to cheer her, and the heights to which patriotism rose during her reign.

But she also held a record for the number of attempts which her subjects made on her life. They tried to kill her seven times in public: an average of one attempt to murder her was made every nine years, although at one point in her long reign two whole decades passed without an attack. People tried to shoot her six times; but the only soldier to have a go used a club, and he was the one who came the closest to success. A former Hussars officer, he was more accustomed to non-explosive, if sharper, weapons.

My theory is that it is hostility even unto the second or third generation which gave rise to the unlikely allegation about Victoria's grandson: Prince Albert Victor, Duke of Clarence. Hypnotized by Sir William Gull, Physician to the Queen, he is said to have confessed to being the multiple killer nicknamed Jack the Ripper.

Although the Victorian period is generally thought unique, it was a perfect sounding-board for many aspects of English behavior. An English courtier once espied a Continental nobleman leaving a royal levee in floods of tears, and moved forward to console him. "The Queen spoke so kindly to me," sobbed the European. "Don't take on so, dear chap," said the Englishman, "I'm sure she didn't mean it!"

The popularity of the monarchy is now on the upgrade here, in spite of the dethronements which continue abroad. Time may well prove that King Farouk was right about one thing. He told Lord Boyd-Orr that, within a few years, the only kings in the world would be the four in a pack of cards – and the British monarch.

Nowadays, of course, the English do not use physical means to control their royalty; but they keep them under close scrutiny nonetheless. A royal wish is, nowadays, very far from a command. An appeal to the Prime Minister for the Queen Mother to be allowed to visit Iran by Concorde in 1975 was turned down on safety grounds. The Queen Mum had to wait ten years to go on a supersonic flight. Recording this, "Albany" of the *Sunday Telegraph* says, "Lord King of Wartnady, Chairman of British Airways, is arranging a birthday treat for the Queen Mother." Giving a queen a treat, even at Mach 2, doesn't sound like obedience so much as a concession.

The monarchy is kept in its place by a sort of threat-and-promise system, operated mostly by the Press and public opinion. *The Mail on Sunday*, which is always appropriately dutiful toward the Throne, does not suppress the allegation that the legitimacy of the present incumbent is contested. Under the headline of HAIL KING KEN! the paper, on September 1, 1985, spoke of "The man who could be the real King of England"; Ken Lightfoot, descended from a bootmaker in London's dockland. If the documents adduced to support this claim – of a marriage between George III and Hannah Lightfoot – are genuine, it asserts, even Queen Victoria had no right to the throne. The legitimacy of the House of Windsor is challenged.

In the *Sunday Times* (no especially republican paper) of August 11, 1985, Julie Burchill was able to write:

> The institution of monarchy, which we consider our grandest, most epic, most civilized asset... is an institution we share only with countries where Missionary Mignon only recently came off the menu and countries where the biggest event is coming fourth in the Eurovision Song Contest... the somewhat dull, ponderous Windsors themselves seem almost embarrassingly decent and sweet, the state their subjects get themselves into over them is truly repulsive. They bring out all that is worst in the British – snobbishness, sentimentality, deference and superstition. Grovel, you peasants.

The 1984 edition of Graham Jones's admirable *Forked Tongues*, nailing untruths by public figures, devotes more than five pages to criticized utterances made by or for the Royals.

Foreseeably, an English king has dealt with this problem. George VI said, "We're not a family, we're a business." In business, as everyone who's ever bought or sold things knows, the truth has to be flexible.

Being English, the people of the House of Windsor are very flexible, and can make a joke out of almost anything. That's why Ms. Tina Brown's description of the Heir to the Throne as a "hen-pecked wimp" is unlikely to cause other than gales of laughter at Buckingham Palace. Even the words "Teutonic boorishness" applied by the former Editor of the society journal *The Tatler* to Prince Philip will have no lasting effect. Perhaps that's why she used them.

Continuing with our survey, research reveals that *baron* is also from (Late) Latin, and signifies the same as king, inasmuch as it also stands for "A Man." "Charles," according to some, means "A Man" as well. So when the present heir to the Throne succeeds, he will be King Charles III, or Man Man III: that does seem to me to have a certain style. Of course, he's also Philip Arthur George, so we can't be sure.

Fictional English aristocrats are not the only ones to show unexpected talents. Lord Nelson of Trafalgar is a Detective Sergeant in the Hertfordshire (the name of this English county is pronounced "Haafudsha") Police Force. Lord Teviot is a baron, and listed in *Who's Who* as man enough to be a "Bus Conductor and Driver." His title is the lowest rank in the nobility: and its lowness may be the reason why there are so many low-down barons in the old story-books. Yet even barons (established 1338) can claim to antedate majesties in England: the latter only appeared 182 years later.

Just how out of touch with things members of the general public in England are is shown by their unshakable belief (in spite of the efforts of knocking gossip columnists) that aristos here are rich and inherit priceless castles and art collections.

Taking some in alphabetical order, we find representatives of each class – below duke – as taking part in productive labor without much regard to poshness. The Earl of Breadalbane (and Holland) is said to be "so poor that he holds his trousers up with string"; and there is a viscount who has been a waiter. The Earl of Dumfries has been a laborer, and a Premier Baron (of Ireland) was once a bingo-caller. The Countess of Mar describes herself as a "Telecommunications Sales Representative," and the Marquis of Tweeddale, formerly a bricklayer, is listed as a "farmer and lobster fisherman." The Earl and Viscount of Ypres, whose baptismal name is John Richard Charles Lambart French, is a hall porter. No doubt the English though, have a saying like this one of ours: "The man of dignity makes honorable the tattered cloak."

"I'm a republican monarchist, actually," one English peer of the realm, formerly a labor union leader, told me when I asked how he reconciled his rank with his ideology; so that explained that. Since an English dictionary definition gives the meaning of *peer* as "an equal, a fellow," as well as "a nobleman," perhaps my question was redundant.[3]

He gave me tea in the Upper Chamber, and spoke lovingly of this most English of institutions and some of its less ordinary denizens.

In truly English fashion, some peers come from a foreign country: the Republic of Ireland. Some live abroad. Not all were born to the purple, reared in the workers'

---

[3] Or perhaps, given that this is England, not. A jury in a case reported in the London daily *Independent* as recently as November 6, 1986, asked the judge whether they "could be informed what a peer is?"

struggle or trace their ancestry to the god Wotan. A peer can be anything and anywhere, or originate anywhere. The founder of the Churchill family was a village blacksmith. Baron Calverley was, until his succession in 1971, plain Police Constable Rodney Muff. In the same year Viscount Soulbury was living in seclusion as a holy man in Sri Lanka. Lord Gardner of Uttoxeter in the County of Stafford dwelt in a village in Uttar Pradesh, North India. Others live in France, Africa, America and the Far East. Lord Sinha is of Hindu extraction. Lord Headley figured in the London newspapers as "the English Moslem Peer," a worshiper at the Woking Mosque.

The noble Lords count among their number people who are authorities in all fields, from nuclear physics and law, education and administration to – yes – Flying Saucers. Things in England have a compelling circularity: I knew we would get back to the Martians.

A Russian I know puts down all the confusion about aristocracy to the fact that the English were never fully tamed and indoctrinated by their rulers. "They never used the knout, you know," he told me. I forbore from alluding to what the Russian peasants had done to their own aristocracy, and sought a comment from my standard English sounding-board, Mrs. Ethel Linda (Noble Snake) Coggins.

She listened to my notes on rulers and ruled in England, and sniffed. "I dunno about Martians, but them nobs is a very mixed lot," she confided.

I asked her whether she meant this in terms of blood or performance.

"Nar," she said, "wo' I means is, they mixes things up wo' don't mix at all. They're forever tryin' to make out that it's them as is the syme as the coun'ry. It's all wrong. Look at that there 'Land'v 'ope an' Glory.' Useter expeck us ter sing it, they did. But ya know wot we sing?

> "'Land'v 'ope an' Glory
> Muvver cort a flea
> Pu' i' in the teapot
> Myke a cupper tea'"

She went on: "The Queen's luv'ly, though, ain't she? I blyme it on them toffs and the peepuw she's serrounded by. She orter 'ave a reverlushon, that's wot. Make a clean sweeper the lotturum. Give all the minks and hermines and gins and tonics to the workers. Then they'd get the country outer trouble, see?"

I asked whether there would be enough mink, ermine, gin and tonic to galvanize the entire labor force.

"Course there would! It's all proper gander, sayin' there ain't. Foolin' us, and the Queen, too, Gobbless 'er, I shouldn't wonder. Mind you, she's got 'er 'ead screwed on. Seed in the paper she's put 'er foot down. Not goin' ter fly about in them old hairyplanes wot they've bin fobbin' 'er off wiv. Gonna 'ave some nice new ones. Worn out they woz. It's a cryin' shame."

That concluded the *vox pop* session, as Mrs. Coggins had a previous engagement, to watch a television social drama about English aristocrats oppressing the poor and makin' pore gewls go wrong.

My original interest in the aristocracy of England came about through a coincidence. One of the members of the boundary commission after the last Anglo–Afghan war was a marquis. This, he had explained to his Afghan opposite number, Colonel Iskandar, originally meant Prefect of the Marches, the Boundaries of the Realm. And here he was, looking after the farthest reaches of his country's dominions, just as one of his forebears had done.

Iskandar was in his eighties when he reminisced, at a feast, about his English colleague. We had just eaten one of those enormous pilaus, with roast chickens buried in spiced rice (which we crave in exile as much as any English expatriate does his bangers and mash) and the old man was denying someone's claims that the English are "ill-intentioned."

"Why," he asked, "should anyone be ill-intentioned when natural confusion can gain all the necessary advantages?"

We all looked at him, puzzled.

"It's all to do with the English and their way of doing things," he said.

"Our two delegations were charged with the task of delimiting the frontier between Afghanistan and British-administered territory. I soon noticed that the maps handed out by the Marquis were printed in Delhi, and drawn at the British cartographic office there. They showed British Indian territory as extending, in places, as far as thirty miles into Afghanistan!

"I said to the Marquis, 'Excellency, if your maps are right, then *I* was actually born a British Subject, and I don't think our King would like that at all, with all due respect.'

"He laughed, and said, 'Just a little slip by those armchair-wallahs, Colonel. I hope you realize that an Englishman wouldn't use sharp practice. We muddle through.'

"And the maps were reprinted, without frontiers marked, for us to fill in jointly."

"How interesting," I said, "that the English sent a hereditary guardian of the frontiers to deal with us. It shows an amazingly well-organized people."

"Better than that," said the Colonel, "it shows a proper sense of the fitness of things."

And though he said this phrase in Afghan-Dari, I'm pretty sure he originally heard it, all those years ago, from the English Warden of the Marches.

10

Wise Men Never Tell

> *Revelation*
> God is decreeing to begin some new and great period in His Church... what does He then but reveal Himself to His servants, and as His manner is, first to His Englishmen?
> <div align="right">John Milton: <i>Areopagitica</i></div>

THE ENGLISH, FACED with something foreign, may adopt in whole or part: but they generally effect at least some adaptation associated with the national genius for compromise. I recently saw a large Indian spittoon in a house in Surrey. Used for its intended purpose? Of course not. It was brought out for mixing punch in. Adaptation may go as far as reversal of concept, name or function.

Take clothes. Borrow the outdoor garb of a Persian (and the name, *pyjama*) but wear this garment *indoors* instead. The English are not people to show special favor. Having looted the pajamas, they turned their attention to the tasseled fez, coat and slippers of the Turkish religio-judicial authority, the *mufti*, and put that on as well. Subsequently, the Army, Navy and Air Force captured the word and used it for "anything that wasn't uniform."

Yet the original, Victorian English mufti outfit, to be seen in antique prints, was amazingly standardized. This non-uniform was far more uniform than anything you would find among any group of real muftis. Some of the old Turkish clerics wore turbans, for example, or boots rather than slippers, some sported cloaks instead of the mufti coat which has become the Anglo-Saxon's dressing-gown.

Adaptation and reversal go hand in hand.

Finally, Christian priests adopted the word. I never hear an English padre speak of being "in mufti" – dressed, that is, as an Islamic theologian – without wondering at his ecumenism.

So being "in mufti" today doesn't signify "dressed as a Turk," but "dressed like an ordinary Englishman": though the phrase is an imitation of the French *en mufti* (dressed *as a mufti*), I wonder what it'll signify next time they change the meaning?

I went so far as to quiz Sheikh Abdel-Latif Khater, the Grand Mufti of Egypt, asking his opinion on this interesting question. Being a man of the law, in which all practitioners, worldwide, are brothers, he at once said, "If you would do me the courtesy to indicate the relevance of your submission to my function as the highest legal authority in the Arab Republic of Egypt, I would be glad to offer a ruling on the question."

It is not considered correct, nowadays, to say dessert if you mean pudding. Americans may say it; but it is a French word and the two great Anglo-Saxon peoples, whatever their differences, have effected the necessary reversal: changing its meaning. They may not concur in its definition, but agree that a dessert is something brought to the table. In French, on the contrary (after all, it is a French word), it analyzes as "something *taken from* the table."

And a country dance is also from the French. In England it means "something from the countryside." Yet it came here from France as a *contre-danse*, an alternating dance – which came, contrarily, from the towns.

There is no statutory law about all this, as I have to inform alarmed foreign friends, more accustomed to regulation by legislation than the English are. If you perform a country dance in a town, call a pudding a dessert or even wear pajamas – or mufti – in the street, you will not find yourself helping the police with their inquiries.

But you should be careful of this last phrase, since it does involve the English reversal of meaning. An old lady of my acquaintance was unaware of its hidden significance. She had tried to telephone her favorite nephew, Edgar (Happy Spear), only to be told that he was "helping the police with their inquiries."

"You can't imagine how delighted I am," she told me, "that Edgar has found a respectable interest at last. Why, it's almost as if he was in the legal profession! They must think a lot of him down at the police station."

Thinking a lot of him, I mused; but in what sense? I had the uncomfortable feeling that it would be the police who were helping *him*: to remember some probably inconvenient things.

Certain English stores specialize in reversal. In other countries you may stride into any store with the confident assumption that you have a right to be there, that people want to sell you things, even that you will be attended to promptly. English people know, however, that you may well not be noticed at all unless you slink in, clear your throat nervously and say – if anyone looks in your general direction – "Excuse me, I wonder whether you could let me see…"

Just arrived in New York from London, I saw something that attracted me in a storefront window. I went in and was immediately pounced on by a man in a white singlet. "Good morning," I said, "I notice that you have a radio in your window. Might I possibly see it?"

When he had stopped laughing, the man said, "Why shouldn't you? Got no money?"

I got to see the radio: but only after the salesman had called a colleague, with "Get a load of this guy; he's 'wondering if he can see' something..."

Not long afterward, I saw a man in a white coat standing in the doorway of a drugstore. Approaching him, I asked what is, Englishwise, a perfectly good question: "Are you open?"

His answer was "No, I'm crazy. I come here every day, put on this coat, and stand in the doorway just for the hell of it."

As with other vital elements in the British character, their linguistic craftsmanship must have been going on a long time. The excellent Dr. Brewer, an admirable if often unwitting guide to recondite aspects of English, has reminded me of this.

He notes that if you say that you are going downstairs, you are in fact using the Saxon word ("down") for going *upstairs*. Descending, he instructs, should properly be described as "I am going a-down." Who could have inverted the meaning? One is tempted to see in this the weapon by which the Angles confused the Saxons and took over the show themselves.

And Dr. Brewer, in addition to being unconscious of the bizarre nature of this inversion-of-meaning question, failed to notice that it is *a process* among his compatriots. Once I grasped this, it took no time at all to find examples everywhere.

If I said to you, "I met a nice person today," would you conclude that I meant "over-particular"? Milton might; but even he might not have understood Shakespeare, for whom "nice" is "strange or foolish." So Helping the Police may, one day, mean just that – or something completely different from anything we can imagine now.

Edgar, as I discovered when I went to bail him out, was charged (among other things) with transmitting by radio without a license. The police affably explained the English attitude toward such things. "You can *buy* any kind of transmitting equipment in this country," said the station sergeant, "but you better hadn't use it, that's all."

You can own all kinds of things, make them, buy, sell or exchange them, borrow them or lease them, he informed me, "But you mustn't actually *use* them." These things include telephone redialers and devices to detect speed-trap radar on roads. You could, he said, open all kinds of stores on a Sunday, but not *sell* anything in them. You might possess all kinds of dangerous weapons, but must not take them out of the house.

I said, "Why should one be allowed to have something if you are forbidden to use it?" The policeman looked at me wearily: I believe that they are trained to do that. "This is England, sir. We don't want to infringe the liberty of the subject."

"The subject's liberty to sit in his house with a dangerous weapon, looking at a mute radio transmitter, knowing that if he went out he might find a store open, but that he couldn't buy some of its stock?" I asked.

But he wasn't English for nothing, and declined to be provoked. "That's about the size of it, sir," he said. "After all, until recently it was unlawful to try to kill yourself, you know." In a more conciliatory tone, he added, "Of course, we've liberalized that…"

"Well, then," I asked, "how about explosives? I bet I'm not allowed to have any of those, even if I don't intend to use them. Then there's poison darts. What's the exact position on them? English books are full of accounts of people bringing in 'native darts whose points are coated with deadly poisons unknown to science.' Where does the liberty of the subject begin and end?"

It is rumored that spooks of the British or United States intelligence services, or both, monitor international telephone calls with computers programmed to record any conversation as soon as a trigger word – such as "explosives" – is used. Something similar may exist in the English police brain.

The sergeant leaned forward. "*What* did you say your name and address were, sir?" he asked.

Being English, his attitude had little of the Dark Menace which the English find in that of Continental policemen. But I wouldn't have called it Light Menace, either.

I told him I was Baldwin (Bold Friend) Adrian (of Adria, in Italy) – with an equally imaginative address – made an excuse, and left.

Adoption, the great English habit (which included adopting much of Albion from its inhabitants), has decorative, educational and utilitarian advantages. You can collect an announcement carved on stone for Thothmes III, and bring it to London, change its name to Cleopatra's Needle (it had nothing to do with her) and put it up near Embankment Station. You can then keep it there just to look at, and torture unfortunate schoolboys with questions as to its location under the heading of General Knowledge. Or list it in guidebooks, stimulating bewildered tourists to ask what on earth this quite unneedlelike object has to do with England's capital city.

You can adopt (nobody knows from where) the word "dhow," and decide to use it to mean an Arabian sailing ship. This enables people like the late (and justly famous) Colonel H. R. P. Dickson to spend years in the Gulf doggedly asking puzzled seagoing Arabs where he might actually find a dhow.

They referred him to baghalas, kutiyyas or dangriyyas, spoke of sambuks, shuais or batils, offered him huris, huwairiyyas and balams, described mashuwas and bakaras – they are great boat-builders – but nary a dhow. The Colonel noted all these craft in his diaries: but only one Arab, it turned out, seemed to have even heard of a dhow. Dickson duly records this in his huge and valuable book, *The Arab of the Desert*, published in 1949:

"I have asked many Arabs what a 'Dhow' is, but none of them have heard of it at all," he writes, rather inaccurately, for he goes on to tell of the one who had.

The Sheikh of Kuwait, known as a man of great courtesy, told Dickson that he had found the word used once, in a book. But it has been suggested that this avowal is a classic example of bedouin politeness, so nobody can be sure. And no description, let alone location, of a dhow is forthcoming.

If anyone could have found a dhow, we may be sure, it would have been Colonel Dickson. He was not only indefatigable – an essential English trait – but his wet-nurse was a woman of the noble Aniza tribe, supplied by Sheikh Mijwal of the Mazrab Clan. This desert chieftain himself married Lady Digby (formerly Lady Ellenborough) who, with English thoroughness, thereupon adopted the desert life. With such connections, if there had been hide or hair of a dhow to be found, the Colonel would have been apprised of it. Characteristically, although adopted by the Aniza, Dickson insisted upon adopting them, en masse.

Adoption and adaptation go hand in hand in the case of good old Farmer Giles. The name conjures up a vision of a besmocked or begaitered, clay-pipe-smoking, middle-aged or older, rubicund figure, leaning smilingly over a gate, wishing the townee good-day. But the name Giles is French – and from a Greek word for a young goat. *Farmer* is from the Latin for "fixed price." A fixed-price goatling, a Greco-French Kid for a Farthing, has become, through English linguistic magic, an old codger in a battered hat. (A codger, in turn, is said to be from Persian *khoja*, defined as "a contentious and importuning old cleric of a type found in Bombay.")

The English will even adopt something from themselves, and then adapt it into something else. I have in mind the origins of the Old School Tie. This was invented in 1880. It originated when students took the ribbons off their hats and knotted them around their necks. Why they should have had ribbons on their hats, and why they suddenly felt the need to place them around their necks, we are not told. But the matter is at least dated, by Gordon Grimley, in his *The Origins of Everything*, published in 1973.

Did you imagine that the English idea of fair play and sportsmanship originated among the English? Well, it did not – and they don't mind putting you, very firmly, right on that one themselves. Sir Harold Nicolson declares, after investigation, that sportsmanship came to the English from the Dutchman Erasmus, and was not to be found in any other books of the period than his *De Civilitate*, a textbook on behavior used in England in the sixteenth and seventeenth centuries.

Turn Cinderella's originally fur slippers into glass ones (*vair* into *verre*) and you have material for quiz-games; rather like the Americans, your cousins, did when they called some of their Germans, in Pennsylvania, "Dutch." It must have been a special delight in England during World War II, for people to give false directions to inquirers, "just to fool the enemy" as the phrase then had it. And, more than forty years later, this saying still crops up in conversation.

I confessed my bewilderment at the seeming inequity of English to an international jurist: Sir Muhammad Zafrulla Khan, who had been President of both the International

Court of Justice at The Hague and of the General Assembly of the United Nations in New York. How, I asked, could they dress as muftis without being muftis? In the East, people studied for years to reach that dignity.

"The English," he ruled, "have poor memories, or are absent-minded. They take, say, the mufti's rigout, remember that it is 'mufti,' but forget to go in for the necessary law courses and examinations to become Islamic muftis themselves." It seemed an intriguing idea, but I demanded more evidence.

Zafrulla referred me to this, from *Wit, Wisdom and Foibles of the Great*:

> Lord Palmerston once said that the Schleswig-Holstein question was so difficult that only three men had ever understood it. The first was Prince Albert, and he was dead; the second was a Danish statesman, and he had gone mad; and the third was Palmerston himself, and he had forgotten it.

In spite of the book's title, it is not divided into sections by subject: so we cannot be sure whether this extract is offered for its Wit, Wisdom or Foible content. This uncertainty is, however, not unusual in England.

The reader will observe that the matter referred to was that of Schleswig-Holstein, penultimate rootland of the English. I hoped that Zafrulla would be familiar with this nuance, but he showed no sign of that and, ignoring my excitedly pointing it out, he offered an historical citation to clinch his argument:

"Forgetfulness, among them, may start very young. Richard Cobden, an English politician of the last century, relates that his small children used to ask, 'Mawm, who is that gentleman who comes here sometimes?'"

Uniquely, English absent-mindedness can be linked, at one and the same time, with alertness. If you think this improbable, just look at the definitions of the word *oversight* in English dictionaries. It can stand *either* for "verifying, noting, superintending," or for "a failure to notice, not verifying."

Hence a factory foreman might say his job included the oversight of the oversights of others. This noting-and-not-noting syndrome can even come in waves and suffuse a single encounter.

This example comes from Richard Tangye's *Reminiscences of Travel*:

> At Ismailia we stopped some time, and a lad wanted to clean my boots... I told him to black the bare feet of a brown boy who was standing by. This he proceeded to do... The shoeblack then brought an ebony Nubian, whose skin was already a shining black. He asked me if he might do his feet, but I made him understand that it was quite unnecessary.

At that point, it seems, another kind of oversight took over, for Mr. Tangye continues, "A grave-looking Turk observing the proceedings gave a look which seemed to say, 'Mad English again.'"

Something like amnesia may be involved in the English attitude toward religion, which displays the genius for adaptation in full flower, so Judge Zafrulla Khan may well be right.

On the other hand, I had been running into him for decades without knowing whether he really believed everything he said; so you will have to make up your own mind on his dictum.

I shall note, later, the disappointment of a foreign man of the cloth who came here as a missionary and saw little or no evidence of religion, whether *en mufti* or otherwise: but for the moment I am after other meat.

According to various British authorities, Christianity has been actively promoted in these islands for over seventeen hundred years: others would make it nearly two thousand. Some clerics, on the other hand, claim that "it has never really been tried at all." They should know, I suppose.

A British Israelite recently told me that Albion is really Palestine, and all the events in the Gospels actually took place here: but he is, admittedly, far to the right in the community. And it was an Englishman, one Richard Brothers, who declared himself Prince of the Hebrews and also, for good measure, Ruler of the World, as recently as 1792.

Perhaps, in a sense, both of them are right: Professor Gordon Childe cites the evidence of their peculiar pottery to prove that the aboriginal inhabitants of these islands came from – Palestine. This evidence, as he insisted to me, is "absolutely conclusive."

My first contact with the essentially English attitude toward religion was years ago when a local clergyman started to visit me regularly and complained (that is the only word for it) that all his fellow students, or the cream of them, at Oxford, had become bishops. He alone lacked preferment. This refrain was maintained from one visit to the next, and his episcophilism extended, week by week, to all sorts of recondite details of the origin, function and nature of bishops.

I was only able to get rid of him by pointing out, with a technique I have learned in England, the inconsistency of his position. "If," I said, "as you have explained so thoroughly, a bishop was the name given to a high civil servant in the *pagan* Roman empire, perhaps you should now apply to the Civil Service Commissioners in London or the Pagan authorities in

Rome, or their legal successors. Further, if as you say, bishop only means 'overseer' in Greek, you could go to Athens and work on a building-site. They might well promote you to overseer, bishop, rank. I understand, too, that Greeks value men of learning, philosophers and so on."

You may think that I was taking advantage of a sophistry: but there is ample precedent for secular authority promoting otherwise unqualified people whom they feel should be bishops.

The English King George III made the Duke of York, then seven months old, Bishop of Osnaburg. One pious writer was therefore able to dedicate a book to him as "The Right Reverend Father in God," when he had attained the age of three years. He must have done a prodigious amount of spiritual work in the twenty-nine months which had elapsed since his enthronement.

I wonder whether the King (or the Bishop) duly celebrated the feast which falls today, November 27: that of Saint Jehosaphat. Although this Christian saint's dates are not known, the full account of his life has been found contained in – the life of Buddha, who was born six hundred years before Christ. Buddhism, of course, is not alien to the English mind. Public opinion polls have shown that many people here believe in reincarnation. The same people don't go along with Hinduism: exactly Buddha's sentiments. I have noted elsewhere that a number of professed English Christians have stated in opinion polls that they prefer Buddhism to *their own faith*. And idols and suchlike, though said to be disliked by both Buddha and Christians, are often treated, in England – as among Buddhists – with respect: fetching high prices at auctions.

Sir Hugh Rankin (Harrow and the Royal Dragoon Guards) is not only a former Senior Vice-President of the Western

Islamic Association, but describes himself as a practising Non-Theistic Theravada Buddhist.

There may even be a less well-known, underground Buddhist influence at work in this Christian land. Among my reasons for saying this is the attitude revealed by a conversation I once had with Mrs. Coggins.

I had shown her a photograph of the giant standing-Buddha statues in the Afghan valley of Bamiyan, world-famous and admittedly very imposing. "I bet *their* priests was livin' in palaces when ours was sittin' around in caves, them monks," she said, with approval. Actually, whatever those Coggins priests were doing (living east of the River Elbe in Germany, or farther eastward still, according to the best authorities), the Bamiyan monks *were* dwelling in caves. There are thousands of such cells there, still showing signs of occupancy.

She didn't stop at that. Looking at a photograph of the Dalai Lama in an illustrated paper one day, Mrs. Coggins (wife of Mr. Albert – Germanic: "Nobly Bright" – Coggins) said, in a dreamy voice, "I wouldn't mind being one of *his* wives…"

And she is quite hostile to some clerics, too, while staunchly describing herself as Church of England. She was really annoyed by the following news item:

> Rev. Ben Crockett, of All Saints, Mickleover, Derby. He's refused to marry Helen Warner to Robert Madeley on Saturday afternoon because he wants to go to a football match.

She wholeheartedly approved of Ms. Warner's observation, which was reported as:

> They say God's House is always open – but in this case, it seems, only if Derby are playing away.

As I was working on this book at the time Mrs. Coggins was bemoaning, with sisterly commiseration, the plight of Helen Warner (what about her fiancé?), I tried to console her by mentioning the derivation of *Hip-hip-Hurrah!* I had just looked it up.

"It's not English at all," I explained. "It is a German exclamation, though it comes from the Hungarian. It means 'Jerusalem is lost to the Infidel – *Hierosolyma est perdita...*'"

"Ass royt," she said, "you just write and tell the old Vicar that. That'll learn 'im."

But might the Reverend Crockett's attitude not simply be due to the English habit of adaptation? After all, it might have been possible to get married on Saturdays in his church in the past, but football has its place as well.

Under Ripon Cathedral is a Saxon crypt, thought to be the earliest place of continuous Christian worship in the kingdom. It has a hole in the wall through which accused persons were made to crawl. "If they succeeded, they were blameless, if they could not they were unquestionably guilty." And unmarried damsels crawling through the aperture would be sure to be married within a year.

"Be that as it may," says Harry How, the reporter who describes it, using my favorite English phrase, people still believed in it. Though my knowledge of Anglican theology is limited, I suspect that this is an adaptation, by the new church, of the old Anglo-Saxon beliefs.

I do not suggest that this is typical, any more than Mr. and Mrs. Coggins provide the only possible English opinions; but the religious picture is both eclectic and careful. Note how elegantly the Church named its most solemn annual event, Easter, after the heathen goddess of the spring equinox: and how the English Parliament was able to abolish even Christmas, as it did in 1647.

There is much evidence for an independent attitude toward religion. *Hocus-pocus* is said to come from *Hoc est Corpus*... this is the Body. "Tedium" describes the effect of exposure to extended spiritual activity. The use of orange blossom, adopted from Saracen brides in the Middle East and now common in England, was permitted by the church as "an emblem of fecundity, not of pagan faith." Again the adaptation.

A Bishop of Ripon (very much older than his colleague of Osnaburg, and therefore a reliable source) told an interviewer a story which well illustrates the capacity of the clergy for adaptation, even in prayer.

The headmaster of his school was holding prayers for some of the boys when the bishop-to-be saw a nervous boy, afraid that he had been absent from some obligatory service, creep into the room. The Bishop continued, "Dr. Turner looked up, and said, in the same tone as he was reading, 'Go out – go out! Somebody put that idiot out!' Then he went on with his reading exactly in the same voice."

To join people just because they are at prayer may be as unnecessary, if you see things in the right way, as to want to be married on a Saturday afternoon.

William Henry (which means "Will-Helmet House-Rule") Maule, Justice of the Common Pleas of London, is an example of the kind of Englishman who likes to keep his options open, in religion as in anything else. He will operate the religion; but he will not necessarily commit himself to it. Thus the record:

A small girl was being examined to discover whether she could be allowed to take the oath.

"Do you know what an oath is, my child?" asked the judge.

She said that it meant that she must tell the truth.

"And if you do always tell the truth where will you go when you die?"

"Up to Heaven."

"And what will become of you if you tell lies?"

"I shall go down to the naughty place, sir."

"Are you sure?"

"Yes, quite sure."

"Let her be sworn," said Maule, "it is quite clear that she knows a great deal more than I do."

The trials of a bishop in England may have been underestimated by my friend the complaining vicar. I do not know anything of the vocational hazards of Osnaburg: but nearer home Lord Thurlow, Lord Chancellor of England – for one – had a short way with prelates.

He was staying at a country house where a bishop, a fellow guest, voiced his hope that the Baron would come to the local church to hear him that Sunday.

"No," answered the noble Lord, "I am obliged to listen to your damned nonsense in the House of Lords, but there I can answer you. I am damned if I am going to hear you when I cannot reply."

In religion or any other area, the English are determined to adapt the input. Whether it is done for their own convenience (as with pajamas), or for a higher purpose, they decide case by case.

As with so many other things English, religious foreigners seem to misunderstand English attitudes to an extreme degree. Father Batista Angeloni, for instance: the Jesuit whose observations were published in England in 1755.

"You would be amazed," he writes to Rome, "to see how degenerate this nation is become." Speaking of the assemblies of English men of wisdom which he has attended, he goes on to describe his feelings when science reared its ugly head.

> At the meetings of these philosophers, gazing with raptures at a cockle-shell of a new kind,

admiring the aptitude with which each animal is fitted to his definition in nature, wondering at the hummingbird and his nest, built with so much art, and instinct; I have beheld them with the utmost contempt, conscious that their intellects were not strong enough to see the fitness of religion to human kind.

The Reverend Father's greatest mistake (if we except his decision to come to England in the first place) seems to be that he has the category-mania of so many of his Continental fellow-observers. He looks at the Quakers, at the men, the women, the politics, the musicians, the married, the single, the Presbyterians, and so on, always in isolation.

In England, that approach simply does not work. To understand the problem, let alone any of the answers, you have to let your mind run free, range over the whole of the horizon, seek and find hints and glimpses here, there and everywhere. In a word, you have to be either English or from the East.

Adopting this method, we can note further intriguing facts about the state of religious feeling, and even about the basis from which the English proceed in their spiritual life.

The Press makes a great deal of noise every time a man of the cloth does something like running off with his organist, as is not very infrequent. Or when a bishop proclaims that he does not agree with what other churchmen think is Christianity. But, as in other spheres, the English are at work formulating their own system, without too much regard for what the supposed authorities say or think.

In *Eavesdroppings*, a splendid collection of bizarre overheard remarks edited by Nigel Rees, a lady from East Barnet records this piece of lay theology:

I don't actually believe in the Resurrection, but I do think that there's something going on up there.

And they are up to something down here, too: the religious leaders, I mean; probably waiting until they know the sense of the group-mind. I see in my paper that a thousand churches have been closed in the last fifteen years: that points to an awareness of consumer reaction. Another journal quotes the fascinating wording of an advertisement for a church vacancy. Have you ever read anything more English than a request for applicants to work in the church, which adds that a "knowledge of the Christian religion would be helpful"?

A contributor to *The Times* notes that "it is impossible to buy a copy of the New Testament in English" – you can only get various versions. They contradict each other from time to time: sometimes giving totally opposite meanings. Such variations actually change theology.

Perhaps all this means that something very undercover is about to be brought to the surface? Some time ago there was a clue, a discussion between Lord Shaftesbury, then Lord Chancellor of England, and a Major Wildman. "Notwithstanding those infinite divisions caused by the interests of the priests and the ignorance of the people," they concluded, "all wise men are of the same religion."

Was the secret about to be revealed? A lady who was present "demanded with some concern what that religion was." Alas for our hopes, Lord Shaftesbury immediately answered, "Madam, wise men never tell."

Other than this we have only hints. But Bernard Shaw may have known something which he wrapped up in these words from *Saint Joan*:

> How can what an Englishman believes be heresy? It is a contradiction in terms.

Adaptation is what they're up to.

P. D. James, the famous novelist, who should know if anyone does, told an assembly at one of London's premier learned societies in 1985 that the best detective stories had "much in common with the Church of England." She added, "and I make the comparison without irreverence."

Of course, it is very rare for anyone to come right out with it, and say that, whatever the historical facts, the English feel more at home with whatever they can decide is to be their own religion, and never mind about foreigners. Rare, I say, but not unknown. The Right Reverend A. T. P. Williams really gave it away, in his essay in the anthology *The Character of England*:

> It is a fascinating but generally a futile pursuit to attempt to trace the origins of the threads which form the confused tapestry of English religion... It was natural that there should be English customs, followed by England alone.

He could have been even more specific, though. Archbishop (of Canterbury) Matthew Parker was. "When Almighty God is so much English as he is," was the way he put it.

In the fourth and early fifth centuries, when the Angles hove on to the British horizon, a monk of these islands, named Pelagius, formulated his own version of Christianity. His followers were important enough for St. Augustine to condemn them fiercely, and to be condemned by Pope Zosimus in 418. This Pelagian heresy, reckoned both to have been a seriously powerful one and to have been wiped out, has, for me, uncanny echoes in the mentality of the English ever since.

The Pelagians, as Dr. Brewer summarizes it, "denied the doctrine of original sin or the taint of Adam, and maintained that we have power of ourselves to receive or reject the Gospel."

The Englishman's sureness of himself, his feeling that he is essentially right – or good – and his need for his own form of religion may be the bequest of that old monk...

11

Tribal Rituals

Dinner With the English
If an earthquake were to engulf England tomorrow, the English would manage to meet and dine somewhere among the rubbish, just to celebrate the event.

Douglas Jerrold

KURDISTAN, IN THE instantly recognizable prose of an English feature article with customary grammatical hiccup, is "a country of doughty fighters poised like a dagger aimed at the vitals of the Middle East." The author soldiers doggedly on: "There are Kurds in Iraq, in Turkey, in Syria and in Iran. A people without an independent national state, they are yet a distinct and worthy stock."

Firoz Kirkuki was a Kurd, and to his worthy doughtiness was added the fact that he owned several oil-wells, though not in Kurdistan; those belong to the various governments of the countries in which Kurds form minorities.

He was in London for the first time, on business, and I had called on him because we had distant family links. The Kurds are not unlike the Afghans: we can even communicate after a fashion, each speaking in his own language.

"You will help me with the English," said Sheikh Firoz. Here we go again, I thought. One of the duties of every Easterner in this country is to be an unpaid escort, translator, adviser and everything else to his fellows when, however rashly, they decide to come here. This useful convention overrides all other commitments.

Kirkuki took my hand, crushed it in his paw, and then enveloped me in a *baghl-kashi*, that Eastern bear-hug which can have serious results. My reading-glasses, in my breast pocket, crumpled.

"More than that, I shall be entirely at your service," I answered mechanically, wondering what Mr. Cohn, my English optician, would say. Over the years I have almost run out of excuses: he can hardly believe that any normal person can break as many pairs of spectacles as I do.

"Very well. Sit down and we shall talk."

His first question was about an unusually puzzling Englishman, a fellow-tycoon in the oil business, whose motivation needed some interpreting.

"Though a colleague, he speaks enviously of another man whom I intend to meet, because of a business in which the latter is engaged, which he himself would much like to enter," Kirkuki told me.

"It sounds rather involved," I said, "and, perhaps, beyond my skills, for I am not in business. Can you be more explicit?"

"I can," said the Sheikh, "and the facts are these: I had told my English friend that I was going to see this other man, an American, to discuss organizational matters. But the Englishman has, I fear, other things on his mind which may influence his judgment. He replied, and I give you his exact words, 'that feller couldn't run a whelk-stall.'"

Kirkuki frowned, "I conclude from this that he is anxious to attempt the retail, open-air sale of whelks – a type of snail – and that this was preying on his mind."

"*Istilah* – a metaphor!" I cried, delighted to be able to get that out of the way so easily.

"He does not mean whelks at all?"

"No, he means that the man is incompetent, whelk-stalls being considered uncomplicated to run."

"Ah," said the Sheikh, "I have heard of this allusive English speech. There was an Assyrian who went to London and he told me about it. Indeed, he gave me important information about it, supported by a telling anecdote.

"It appears that they use a figure of speech here for certain necessary bodily functions. When you are admitted to a house someone says, 'Would you like to wash your hands?' The Assyrian was forewarned, so no confusion ensued."

"Did he wash his hands at home?" I inquired.

"Nearly right. When he arrived, the lady of the house said that he could wash his hands in a small room opening off the front hall. The Assyrian replied with an equally discreet use of the euphemism. He said, 'No, thank you. I washed them on the lamp-post before ringing the doorbell.'"

I just managed to explain (I think) why I was laughing when Sheikh Firoz announced that he had a special interest in English hospitality. "You see," he confided, "I have to dine at the house of Sir Bart, my oil colleague, tomorrow night. Let us review the possible pitfalls, for I would not wish to be guilty of a *faux pas*."

I began to brief him. "The English," I said, "use some words which may seem like cipher to you. They are, in fact, foreign words (for some reason they love Eastern titles) and most often employed when someone or something makes them feel uncomfortable."

"Such as?" He took out a notepad. "Such," I said, "as *Tycoon*, Japanese, or *Nabob*, from India: actually *Nawab*, for 'a rich man' like you. Such as *Kamikaze*, Japanese, for 'suicidal'; such as *cash*, for 'money'; that one is Chinese, of course."

"Of course," said the Sheikh. "And further?"

"Further," I continued, "there are *Guru*, Sanskrit for a teacher or expert. Race, from the Arabic *Raas*, Rank, Persian *Rang*, for 'status,' and *Mandarin*, which is Chinese, for Senior Civil Servant. Then there are the Greek *Xenophobia*, which stands for 'dislike of foreigners,' *Grandee*, Spanish, which can mean 'aristocrat,' and *Mogul*: Mongolian, for 'big shot.'"

At this point, as is the way of the rich, the Sheikh became bored. "Tell me how to get them to turn off the television set," he said.

"Under what circumstances?"

"I am going to dine with these infidels," he reminded me, "and whenever I have dinner in my hotel room and switch on the television set, I see that they are showing a program about some disease or surgical operation."

"Yes, I'd noticed that," I replied, "this is indeed peculiar to English TV; but in houses such as the one which you are visiting, it is not the convention to watch television during meals, so that's all right."

"Very good. Now, what about men and women sitting side by side at meals?"

"Yes, they usually sit, alternately, one man and one woman..."

"Husband and wife together, of course?"

"No, that is not allowed, I mean customary..."

"Amazing! All the evening?"

"No, the women leave first."

"To prepare for belly-dancing?"

"No, to allow the men to talk together."

"Ah. Is that all they do?"

"They also smoke, if they wish, often cigars, and pass a cut-glass wine flask around the table in a certain direction: always clockwise."

"I shall be obliged to partake of alcohol?"

"No, you can just pass the decanter on. It contains something called port."

"They cannot afford a bottle of wine each, or have no servants to pour?" He had written, in Kurdish, "Wine-flask = DIKANTAR."

"It is a custom, nothing more."

"Good." He made another note. "And what is this rumor about nonsense phrases?"

"Which one, exactly?"

"I have been told by a professor at Cairo University that although you may say 'Heigh Ho!,' which means nothing, you may *not* say 'Yah, Boo!,' which also means nothing. These words are not in the dictionary, at least not in that form."

"If I were you, I'd avoid all meaningless phrases," I suggested. "The one can mean 'I'm tired,' and the other something like 'I don't like you.' But that is quite advanced stuff. In English, especially the colloquial, there is little or no relationship between the words and their meanings."

"It is the same in Korean, I believe," said Kirkuki. "Now tell me why Mr. Michael Chalhoub of Cairo is known in England as Omar Sharif."

"I don't think that the subject is likely to come up, Eminence. There are other things that we have to cover, and the time, considering the complexity of the question, is short."

He quickly recognized this Eastern way of saying "I don't know."

"You are right. Then let us speak of the rituals of the occasion."

"That's just what I was going to do. First, remember that people here eat with their shoes on."

"Amazing! No delicacy at all."

"And they may well sit, after dinner, with the sole of the foot pointed at you."

"And this means no disrespect? Tell me more." He leaned forward attentively.

"Yogurt is sometimes flavored and eaten with sugar or fruits..."

"*Sweet yogurt?*" He burst out laughing. "You'll be telling me that they put on special clothes for eating in, next."

"They do – sometimes. Less than they used to, though," I added, lamely. I decided not to refer to penguin suits or black and white ties.

"Can it be true that they consume soggy baklawa? And that they even thread sliced *peppers* on the skewers of their shish-kabob? It has been hinted that they prepare kabobs without fresh coriander leaves, but perhaps this is a calumny spread by detractors."

I smiled equivocally. "It is, indeed, alleged that this has been known to happen, O Sheikh."

"It is said," intoned my friend, "that they actually use last year's rice."

"Even the year before's."

"Even from the crop of the year before? Incredible."

"And they handle food with their left hands, without intending any insult."

He skidded the heel of his (right) hand off his forehead at the thought.

"Enough! Tell me what they discuss after eating." He finished a cup of coffee in the regulation three gulps as I continued:

"First, remember that, unlike us, they do not start cooking the moment you arrive. The food is ready. This means that they dispense with the two or three hours' wait for the food customary with us: you do not have to fortify yourself with a meal before going out to dinner."

The Sheikh was pleased. "That is an interesting innovation, and one which I may well adopt myself. And they eat in silence, just as we do?"

"On the contrary, all are expected to *talk* during the meal. And you do not leave as soon as you have finished."

"Talk? They certainly turn things upside down, don't they? They don't sing or recite poetry, by any chance, while they're eating? But I am prepared to make sacrifices, even to behave badly, in order to please my host. Now, as to topics?"

"Topics," I said, "are wide-ranging. Much will depend upon the nature and background of the company. Various kinds of people have their own preoccupations."

"They behave like tribes, in a word?"

"In a word. Now, you should be safe with little anecdotes and unusual information. Nothing controversial."

"I can ask about English manners and customs?"

I said, "I'd be careful about that. I know a Chinese diplomat who thought that he was making small-talk at a dinner here, and committed a real blunder. His name was then marked on the hostess's list as 'NOT to be invited again!'"

"Indeed?" said the Sheikh. "Whatever can he have done?"

"He said," I told him, "'Tell me, madam, is it true that your honorable people bathe in your own dirt, and do not shower it off after soaking?'"

"Naturally," laughed the Sheikh, "they do no such thing. The very idea is preposterous!"

"Just the same," I warned, "be careful. But the English love general knowledge. They like to learn odd facts: whole television series are built upon this peculiarity. That and the ability to remember facts. People are actually acclaimed for having retentive memories. They call them masterminds. I'll let you have material from my list of gambits. They are known, naturally, as conversation-starters. The Chinese diplomat's remark, equally obviously, is one of the class called conversation-stoppers."

I then recited:

"*Sovereign* is misspelled; it should be 'souverain'; black lead is not lead, it is carbon and iron; there is no such thing as 'rice' paper; catgut comes from sheep, and the word 'pen' originally meant feather."

The Sheikh clapped his hands with delight, wiped his eyes and cried, "Of course, they do it on purpose!" Encouraged, I continued:

"'Chamois' leather is really sheepskin, and is not from the goatlike antelope of that name; 'Camel hair' brushes are in fact made from squirrel fur, and a 'ream' of paper is called that from the Arabic word *rizmah*, 'a bundle.'"

He was still gazing, entranced, at me, as I went on:

"And here is a very good one, for few of them know it. There are those who boast, in a restrained sort of way, that their land is listed in the Domesday Book. This is a catalog prepared for the Normans, and today signifies antiquity..."

"Ah," interrupted the Sheikh, "to this ostentation I am immediately to answer, 'But *my* property is far older than that': am I right?"

"May your life be infinitely extended," I said, "but that would be considered in poor taste. No: here we use subtlety. Hold up your hand as if respectfully asking for permission to interrupt. Then, but not too loudly or firmly – mildly in fact – you say, 'I presume that, in speaking of the Domesday Book, you are using the vulgar nickname of *The Book of Winchester*?'"

He was so pleased that I threw in another ploy which I had given to an American, who later told me that it had changed his social life. He had been sorely tried for years, by being told that his national sport, baseball, was only a derivative of the English children's game called rounders.

"A powerful ploy, Sheikh," I said, "can be used if anyone has been condescending upon you: especially if he talks endlessly about cricket. Remember that its rules are called Laws. They require that the bat be held with one end on the ground, and only moved to receive the ball, which must never be bowled under-arm. There may be no hole in the turf, and mixed teams of men and women are impermissible."

He looked at me with puzzlement. "I know all that, as it happens. I have memorized the Laws of Cricket, in case I am invited to attend a match."

Time to put on some spin. "Now hear this," I said, "as with baseball and rounders, the present 'Laws' of cricket are not really old at all. And they are quite different from those of the traditional game which gave the thing its birth. If, therefore, people weary you with talk of cricket (particularly if they claim that it is an old and hallowed pastime), you interrupt, politely but languidly. You say, 'Oh, you mean that game originally called Hondyn? In its earlier forms, of course, the bat was held up in the air, the bowler tried to throw the ball – under-arm – into a pit: and women played in the same teams as men!' Guaranteed to have an effect."

"Bat in the air? Under-arm into a pit? Mixed teams?" Kirkuki sounded as amazed and affronted as any Englishman could be. "And what, pray, is your authority for such extraordinary statements?"

I scowled and skittled him. "My dear Sheikh: I am as sure as anyone can be, and I have it on the best authority. From the very lips of the great historian Sir Arthur Bryant. He gave me references to published sources, which are available if you wish to have them. *And* he was the illustrious author of *The Story of England*, and a pillar of the MCC."

The Sheikh's manner changed in an instant. Appealing to published authority is respected in Kurdistan. "You are indeed a man of great learning," he said, "but now tell me something connected with yet deeper scholarly wisdom, that I may astonish the Ingliz even more."

Reaching, as it were, into my researches, I came up with another tidbit.

"English dictionaries," I recited, "cannot decide whether 'custard' is Welsh for sour milk or English for a pie with a crust. It is defined either way, according to which authority you consult. Even odder, when you first see custard you will instantly perceive that it bears little resemblance to either milk or pie."

"Excellent, O man of wisdom!" he cried, slapping me on the back. "They serve much custard on such occasions as the one to which I am bidden?"

"Er, well," I said, "you can nearly always contrive to bring custard into a conversation in England." I had just read the latest statistics from Taylor Nelson's Family Food Panel. "In the last six months," I added, "the British have consumed 331 million servings of custard: nearly two million dollops a day. It has also been announced, in another report, that the menacingly named 'spotted dick' is their favorite pudding to keep in the freezer. But remember, on no account are you to refer to it as 'frozen dick.'"

"Good." He was scribbling furiously. "Now give me just one more fact, some intricate one, to use if the jollifications extend to a late hour, and I run short of inspiration." I could only think of one: though it seemed a bit more complicated than the other examples.

"There is a saying here," I told him, "that something unpleasant and bad for you, the epitome of bitterness, is 'like wormwood.'"

"The Wood of the Worm. Yes. I can see that. It sounds quite horrible."

"Ah, but if we consult the reference books, we find that the English have entirely confused the meaning. The herb was, in Anglo-Saxon, originally so called from the combination of the words *wer*, meaning 'man,' and *mod*, which signified 'inspiring.' It was, in fact, a tonic."

"So the real derivation of the name of this substance is the exact opposite of what they think it is?" Kirkuki, though no philologist, seemed to have got the drift quickly enough.

"Incredible though it may seem, that is quite true, O Sheikh."

"Now," he said, "tell me if there are any little misconceptions about the East which I might usefully clear up for our English friends."

"*Any* misconceptions?" I echoed. "Where shall we begin?"

"So long as you *do* begin, I shall not complain," the Sheikh said, kindly: reminding me that I was getting too excited for his usually placid Kurdish temperament.

I got a grip on myself. "Very well: what is 'a sheikh'?"

"A sheikh is a grave old man."

"Wrong," I told him, "it means, in England, a young and romantic one, much given to carrying off young women, usually on pure-bred snow-white steeds. Or on milk-white racing camels. It also usually means a kind of nobleman. Always wearing bedouin garb, too."

He wrote this down, muttering, "Interesting…"

I continued, "What is a fez?"

"*Not* 'a Fez,' O Shah, but 'The Fez.' That is the name of a great imperial city in Morocco. I have been there. 'Fez,' properly 'Al Fas,' also means 'hatchet.'"

"Wrong again! In England it is what they call a 'tarbush,' the sort of rimless cap the Turks used to wear."

He picked up his pen, saying, "They don't seem to know much, but they know a lot about it."

While he was scribbling, I gave him still more of it: after all, I had been on the receiving end of English expertise on the East for some time now, and felt I had some ground to make up. "Moreover, they call a *hijab* a 'yashmak,' and a s*aif* a 'scimitar.' They think that we all eat sheep's eyes and camel-hump. You'll be lucky if they don't serve what they call curry at the dinner. They think we all revel in peppery food." When he had digested this, he put aside his notebook and said, gravely, in a very sheikhlike manner: "Do they not know that Sultan Salahuddin Ayyubi was a Kurd?"

"They call him 'Saladin,'" I informed him, "and you shouldn't really confuse them with that. They are convinced that he was an Arab."

He was so incensed at this that I shifted focus slightly by adding, "They use, goodness knows why, all kinds of *Turkish* words to describe both you and us, and even the Arabs. Like *muezzin* or *vizier*, even 'café' – or 'coffee' – for *Qahwah*."

The Kurd's mouth had dropped open as he tried to assimilate these new wonders of the West. Then, collecting himself, he asked, "But surely they have books, written by their wise ones, which speak of us, who we are, and our great men, towns and cities, lands and crops, flocks and literature, artifacts and warrior code?"

"Up to a point, Sheikh Kirkuki," I said, and went to the bookshelf. As always, the *Oxford English Dictionary* was my first choice. But there was no listing for "Kurd" in the main body of the work. Afraid to face the man from Kirkuk, I scrabbled desperately in the Supplement. Thank goodness, there it was:

KURD: One of a pastoral and predatory race of Aryan stock, which gives its name to Kurdistan in Asia.

Fortunately Kirkuki was not annoyed by the use of the word "predatory." "Yes, it is true. I have heard that there are bandits among the Kurds. I suppose that the English have no robbers, so they would naturally write about ours."

The *Chambers Dictionary*, however, brought out a more aggressive streak in my friend, when I read out its definition:

Kurd, one of the peoples of Kurdistan. Iranian in speech, often blond, Xenophon's *Kardouchoi*.

The Kurd fixed me with his deep blue eyes. "There is only one people of Kurdistan. So, what is this 'Iranian' business?"

"O Sheikh! 'Iranian' is a word used by the Franks to refer to a group of languages. They actually call both your language and mine 'Iranian.'" I hoped that the very eccentricity of the thing would mollify him.

"O Aga Idries Shah! Inform them of the facts, for that is the duty of a scholar. If they do not know what is an Iranian and what is not, that is no good reason to call all sorts of other peoples by the name. It makes the English look ignorant, too."

I told him that I'd give the matter some thought; but he was really not listening, for he went on, fiercely:

"And who is this Zanfoun, pray? I have never heard of him, and I know everyone of note who has been in Kurdistan! And how did *we* become 'Zanfoun's Kardoukwi'?"

"Sheikh, Xenophon is the name of a Greek, and the apostrophe denotes not ownership but that he has dealt with the matter of the Kurds in a book."

"If he can't pronounce 'Kurd,' I doubt if he has ever been to Kurdistan," shouted the Sheikh, adding, "I doubt if the owl would dare to try, in any case. Kardoukwi, indeed! He obviously means 'Kirkuki.'"

I calmed him by placing my hand on my heart and asking, "While we are on the subject, respected Sheikh and brother Kirkuki, are there any puzzling points about English life that I might clarify for you?"

"Yes, that is good. Why talk about Greeks when we're in England, eh?" He was in a better mood now.

Sheikh Firoz linked his fingers, bowed his head for a moment in thought, and then said, "I have myself made a study of the English, from films and television. Some things are, however, still obscure."

"Say on, O Sheikh."

"Well: unusual things have happened in some houses here. The programs show that the cooking staff entertain policemen in the below-ground kitchens; the butler is a murderer whom nobody suspects until some unlikely outsider unmasks him; women jump from giant cakes on tables; and the Queen's fat and bearded son smokes large cigars continuously..."

I had to stop him at that point, and explain. It disappointed him somewhat to learn that in England, home of tradition, some things do indeed change or are altered – and even reverse themselves capriciously. Or that fact can be mixed with fiction. He thought that that only happened in the East.

A model of propriety, the Kurd was slightly uneasy about the presence of women at the forthcoming dinner, and asked me how he could assess them, since he was not used to mixed company. By now I was weary, and simply handed him a photocopy of a page in the *Oxford Dictionary of Proverbs*, listing types of women, which he gravely read out:

Fair and foolish, litl and loud
Long and lusty, black and proud.

Fat & merry, Red and bad,
High cullor choler showes;
And shee's unholsome that lyk sorrell growes.
Nought ar the peeuish, proud, malitious.
But worst of all the Red shrill, jealous.

He asked me about several other things, but I had to leave him, to attend to problems of my own. I left him still wondering why maids no longer cry themselves to sleep in attics. He could not imagine, either, where all the men with club feet who formerly lurked outside London houses had now gone, since peasouper fogs had been miraculously banished.

The following morning I opened my *Daily Telegraph* to find a reminder, in an article by Christopher Booker, that English history as taught to children is not to be trusted. King Alfred (Elf-Counsel) is not on reliable record as having burned any cakes; King Arthur ("the name perhaps means Bear or Stone," my dictionary says) probably never existed; Harold (Army-Rule) did not get an arrow in his eye at the Battle of Hastings; Richard (Rule-Hard) III did not really have the poor little princes murdered in the Tower of London – and much else.

I scribbled an update for the Sheikh and tried to telephone him, but he was already out. His program, left with the hotel telephonist, included seeing a Swedish film, hearing a lecture on Nineveh, and viewing Dutch paintings in Bond Street: all of them attractions listed by that day's *Times*. Nothing like London to give you an insight into what interests the English. I switched on the radio to immerse myself in Englishry. The programs were about India, Nicaragua, the United States, Russian deserters in Afghanistan, a Dublin bomb suspect, Doctor Savimbi...

I learned later that the dinner had gone well. The only thing which had puzzled the Kurd for a moment was his hostess's invitation to "belch if you feel like it, Sheek."

"I soon realized," he told me, "that eructation must be an English sign of satisfaction with a meal. So I managed a small burp, in spite of having taken sodium bicarbonate beforehand to neutralize the effects of the impending culinary horrors. And the lady, noting my effort, smiled with pleasure. So I think I may say that I acquitted myself adequately."

"You did well," I said.

"Yes, I believe so. By the way, for your notes, I have to report that the English eat animal-fodder: maize, which they call sweet corn. As you might have guessed, this vegetable is neither sweet nor corn. It may, however, have been served in pretended humility: they are indeed a complicated people. Have you heard of the little Samaritan community, in the Levant, who eat a moldy crust after a meal, to show that they have not forgotten that there are others less fortunate than themselves? This is, of course, unconscious hypocrisy, but it may originally have been genuine concern."

I made a note. "And after dinner, how did it go?" I asked.

"After dinner, all went well. One of the lady guests was wearing an engraved base-metal plaque on a gold chain around her neck. This was a 'precious talisman for safety' given her by a Real Sheek at the Pyramids. She asked me to translate the Arabic words on it."

"And did you manage to read it?"

"Oh, yes. It said:

"Please do not talk to the driver of this motor-coach. Lack of concentration can cause accidents."

I said, "Surely you didn't *tell* her that?"

The Sheikh stroked his beard. "I managed all right. I acted in accordance with the wise injunction, 'When the lion buys a fiddle, it is time to learn to dance.' I translated only the second sentence on the pendant – and she was delighted."

"Well done, Sheikh Firoz!" I said.

Then I remembered the matter of the man whom his friend wanted to cut out of their business relationship. "Tell me," I said, "what Sir Bart had to say about the man who couldn't run a whelk-stall."

"That was a very important matter," the Sheikh told me. "I had been tempted to work with this man, and if Sir Bart had not helped me by delineating his terrible and dangerous characteristics, I might well have come to grief."

I asked, "What were these characteristics? Is the man a crook?"

"I do not think so," said the Sheikh, "but that is not at issue: the affair goes deeper. We have here a matter of great subtlety, which only an Englishman can fathom to its extreme depths. Sir Bart took me into his confidence, explaining in fascinating detail exactly how this man was disqualified as a possible business associate. I made a covert note at the time. We must memorize certain important facts."

I craned my neck to read the words in the tiny notebook which the Sheikh now pulled from the inner pocket of his robe and held tightly in his hand. He had written, in minuscule handwriting:

"Utterly unreliable, proved by the fact that he drinks Perrier water, drives a Porsche or a Mercedes, eats in restaurants – and has *business cards*."

"Did Sir Bart go into any details as to the meaning of these arcane habits?" I asked, in wonderment.

"Yes, indeed. You see, Perrier is drunk as an affectation: to make people think that you are upper class. Porsches and Mercedes cars *used* to be status symbols. And the really top people never go to restaurants."

"And business cards?"

"Business cards carry your name, that of your firm, and your address. People who really *are* somebody are already known, so they don't have to give their name. Yamani, Rowland or Krupps do not have to run around with cards. Similarly with their firm: everybody knows, or should know, what that is. As for the address, this is the private concern of the man and his intimate friends. As Sir Bart said, can you imagine the Queen of England handing you a business card? With 'Buckingham Palace, SW1' on it? Oh, yes, then there is the matter of the candlelight."

"What about it?"

"What, you ask, about it? I thought that you had spent time with the great ones, the tribal chiefs and the amirs and vizirs, of this nation? Evidently you know, at best, only the merchant class. Sir Bart strongly emphasized that nobody who is anybody would dine by candlelight."

I looked at Firoz with admiration. I had learned much from – or through – him. As our proverb has it, "Whoever tries to learn on his own has a fool for a teacher." Sheikh Firoz's Englishry really was progressing. He must have been a great hit at the dinner-party.

Now that he had, effectively, graduated, he had little further use of my expert guidance; apart from one small point, on which I was happy to put him right. He had been rather baffled by the difference, if any, between "English" and "British." "What, for instance, is a Briton?" he wanted to know. I explained, with the aid of the *Oxford English Dictionary*. "It says here," I told him, "that a Briton is (1) a native of Britain, of the southern part of the island."

"But what about the north?" asked Kirkuki.

I scanned the entry. "Under (1)b, it says 'A native of Great Britain.' So that includes the Scots and Welsh."

"Ah, so you have to be born in Britain, in the British Isles to be British?"

"Up to a point, Sheikh. It also says that it could be a native of the British Empire."

"Only the British dependent territories?"

"Yes, er, no, hold on." I had just found that it could mean "of or belonging to Brittany, Breton."

The Sheikh got a bit testy at that, implying that I was not quite right in the head. A dictionary could not be so imprecise: it must be me doing it to him. He would not believe that a Breton, from France, could be British.

"I was, as it happens, born in Cyprus, fifty years ago," said the Kurd, looking at me narrowly. "Does that make me a Briton?"

"I speak as I find," I said, "and I beg of you not to think any the worse of me when I insist that, according to this book, you are a Briton, or were one at one time, if you were born in the Empire."

"And that means?"

"That means if you were born forty-odd years ago in India, Pakistan, Sri Lanka, Malaysia, large parts of Africa, some places in Oceania, in certain South American territories, in Cyprus or Hong Kong. Or Brittany, though I cannot vouch for a Frenchman's opinion on this matter."

He suddenly changed the subject. "It is now essential to scrape a bone with you."

"Yes?"

"You know what it is."

"Can't imagine." I bent a look of English innocence upon him.

"All right then. Why did you not warn me that it is ridiculous to call Sir Humphrey Pumphrey, Bart., 'Sir Bart'?"

"Just getting a bit of my own back, old man. You see, people have been calling me 'Mister Shah' in this country for years. Just as bizarre. I was returning the compliment, albeit vicariously."

Later I met a gracious English dowager who had been at the dinner to which Sir Bart had invited the Kurd. "Such a *quiet* man," she confided, "though I'm sure that he has a dozen wives and believes that women have no souls. Quite spine-chilling, if you think about it. Of course, somebody ought to do something about all that."

I forbore from informing her that the only recorded evidence for a belief in the soullessness of women is to be found in an English source: "Women have no souls, this saying is not new" – *The Oxford Dictionary of English Proverbs* (1970, quoting a proverb of 1566).

"Did you see him burp?" I asked, instead.

"No. I did *not*! But I wouldn't be surprised if he did. They do it as a compliment to the cooking in their country, you know."

I thought I would round off the conversation with a reflection by Lord Halifax, a man of her generation, on the question of foreigners, so I quoted:

> I often think how much easier the world would have been to manage if Herr Hitler and Signor Mussolini had been to Oxford.

"Halifax," I added, "in 1937." But she looked at me rather oddly just the same.

12

Unsuitable for Antarctica

When Their Work is Well
Too much curiosity and tediousnesse (a fault our countrimen be much noted of), that they know not when their work is well.
                    Ariosto: *Orlando Furioso*

BY THE TIME I met the Kurdish sheikh, I thought that I had a fair grasp of most of the peculiarities of England and the English. English people will know better. As with the mysticism of the East, the more of Englishry you learn, the more there is to learn.

What is this indefinable something, this subtle ingredient, which causes English people to say and to do things which seem perfectly ordinary to them, but which can drive foreigners crazy? You have to look at instances very carefully, for they are not hard to categorize, without examination, as deliberate slights. Nowadays, being detribalized, I often miss the nuances myself, and people think I am rude or insensitive.

Here is one example. I was with a French friend, in a library. I was looking for books on England, and he wanted to see some on France.

We inquired at the desk. The librarian, affability itself, at once said, "That's easy. You'll find Britain under 'England.'

As for France, just look between 'Formosa' and 'Friendly Islands.'"

Now, a Scotsman, Welshman or Irishman might well have taken offense at his country being subsumed in "England." I can see that. Especially if he had seen the last paragraph of *High Road to England*, by Sir Richard Faber, which the librarian was reading when we entered his domain: "the British Celt is largely a mythical concept."

But what I noticed more particularly was that the librarian assumed that we would be able to find the "England" classification, but would have to be guided via Formosa to that of France. And, as the Frenchman put it, anguishedly, a France in such minor company, tucked away between some smallish islands. I tried to reassure him, pleading strict alphabetical necessity. But his perfect Gallic logicality immediately pinpointed the weakness in my argument, and laid bare the schemes of the librarian's built-in Albionic perfidy.

"If what you say is true," he hissed, "why were we not told that 'England' is cataloged between 'Enderby Land (Southern Ocean)' and 'Enniskillen (Ireland)'?" I looked in the book he was holding open. He was right.

Is there any connection, any hidden torque in the brain, here, which explains Dr. Robert Ornstein's recent experience at an English store?

Professor Ornstein, over here from America, tells me that he went into a supermarket and asked where he might find the coffee. "The coffee?" said the assistant. "Why, it's just near the tea." It is assumed that anyone in England, unless a complete idiot, can find his or her way to the tea, whatever the store.

"I think that there is some little sub-program in the English brain, implanted by the culture as a whole and activated on certain triggers being tripped." This is how

Professor Gordon Childe, of London University Institute of Archaeology, referred to one English trait which interested him as an Australian.

"I am now old enough to recall perhaps dozens of instances of a certain formerly common form of this. I call it the 'Really? Well, I once had a...' syndrome." He went on:

"At one time, you had only to say that you were from, say, Bosnia or the Galapagos, when someone in the company would say. 'Really? Well, *I* once had a Bosnian/Galapagoan servant...' I remember, too, how foreigners used to tense up at this, just before the riposte, knowing what was to come, but unable to forestall it." My answer, as I now see, was far too English. "Perhaps they always did have Bosnian, or whatever, servants," I suggested.

"My whole point," snapped the professor petulantly, throwing down the copy of *Archaeology* which he had been affecting to read during the conversation, "is that I often knew these people. None of them had ever had such a servant. They had picked the idea up somewhere, perhaps as a part of the role which they were trying to play. Most interesting of all, I have seen dozens, perhaps hundreds, of introductions between foreigners and English people, without the foreigner ever saying, 'I had an English servant once.' And that in spite of the fact that many of them really had had English servants: even had them at the time. The English are not unkind, but they undoubtedly are insensitive."

In England, you cannot count upon anything being spelled out. That is one of its Oriental aspects of life, thought and speech. As a corollary, of course, if something ever is analyzed, one is correspondingly surprised.

I have just caught up with the fact that a professor who is safety adviser to ICI has made a startling discovery, which he duly reported to the British Association for the Advancement of Science. The *Guardian* picked it up:

If every man in the country wore a belt in case his braces [suspenders] let him down, 685 men a year would lose their trousers.

At first, foolishly, I wondered why anyone should care, especially me. I wear no suspenders, it is true. But this does not increase the likelihood of losing my trousers, since the waistband fits over my hip-bones, which must make for safety. At least, so I have just assured myself.

With my customary foreign rashness, I had not read the article right through. This is fatal in England. I found that I had been asking premature questions. I now see that the professor is talking about risks not being what we think they are. Still, as the *Guardian* reporter (Andrew Veitch) continues, "if every man wore a belt and two pairs of braces [suspenders], every five years one man would still lose his trousers."

Perhaps he is a man with less protuberant hip-bones than mine: I hope so. I could always leave the country, of course, to escape this awful English doom. But I am a member of the British Association for the Advancement of Science myself, so I suppose that I should soldier on and rally round, while taking note of the dangers which may beset, if not "every man in the country," at least 685 of the most careful ones, every year.

This opens up the whole matter of caution, which is a great English characteristic, epitomized by Churchill's "What time do *you* make it?" when some wag wagered he would force him to give a direct answer. Yet, even here, you can be left with the impression that something which was done by someone else is somehow your fault.

I recall – how could I forget? – the day when my landlord met me on the stairs with a bundle of letters. "I have a bone to pick with you. This is your mail."

I tried to take it. "Not so fast, now: before you get on your bike…"

Then he told me. The letters were addressed to Snark, Shnorr, Shaw, Shaa, anything but Shah. "If your name's Shar, why doesn't it say so on any of these? Using a false name's not done in this country."

"Look mate," I said, as matily as I could under the circumstances, "I can't help it if that word is spelled SHAH and pronounced, in my country, SHAW."

"Well, watch it. You're not in your own country now, you know," he said.

See what I mean? The accumulated errors of his compatriots were deftly and unhesitatingly laid to my door. And he was (and is) a very nice sort of person: even if he did give me a two-fingered salute with his final admonition. Innocent until proved guilty: but he had, he knew, proved me guilty. Now Dr. Renier, long resident in England and at least partly an admirer of its people, became so annoyed by this kind of behavior that he called it neurasthenia, nervous debility, traceable to the public school system. As a Dutchman, he may claim to be closer to the English than I am, but I have never noticed much debility about them.

Rather than being nervously debilitated, the English are more likely to be, inwardly, excitable. In any case, the figures show that they (or their doctors) think of them as too lively. The desire for calm is so strong that the drugs most often prescribed for them, the figures show, are tranquilizers.

Now, errors like my former landlord's may be bad, but there is (let us be fair) something in the English ear which conveys to the average English person a sound other than that which others hear. This is called "bad at languages," but it is in fact just another evidence of English singularity.

For one thing, in English, all foreign words, or as many as possible, must be pronounced as if the penultimate syllable is stressed. If it has a long "a," so much the better. If not, you put one in. The foreigner has obviously left it out. Hence, the English love the East African Ask*aa*ris. The Saf*aa*ris are even better. And as for the T*aa*zh Mah*aa*l (Indians may recognize the Taj Mahal in this), it is a sort of spiritual bakl*aa*va.

Mind you, there are exceptions. My own name is really pronounced Idd-rees. But everybody says "eyedreez." Television reporters, trying to sound correct, call the Egyptian leader Hosni Mubarak *Moober-ukk*, though the stress should be, as in English, on the penultimate syllable: *Mubaar-ukk*. And you'd think that they'd have no difficulty with the Himalayas; it must be harder to climb them (which they do quite a lot) than to pronounce their name. But the mountain chain is seldom called – correctly – "the Him*aa*lyas." For the English, it's "the Himma-layas."

This kind of thing reached such proportions at the time of the British *Raazh* (Raj) that – and this is not very uncommon – I have met Indian servants who couldn't speak in any other way. After some years with a *Raazh* family, they bewildered their fellow-Indians with their Hindustani. And that wasn't only in the Poonjawb. Ah, the old days in Indiar and Chinar...

The BBC's Pronunciation Unit hasn't managed to triumph over the English Ear, either. To hear an announcer saying *Zimm-babb-wee* (one columnist says "like a demented baboon"), while heroically trying to "talk foreign," will delight some unreconstructed foreigners as much as it gets (I have seen them) some Zimbabweans jumping up and down.

All this happens in spite of the fact, carefully recorded by M. S. Serjeantson (in *A History of Foreign Words in English*) that there are over seventy foreign tongues whose words make up English.

And, of course, there must be a special, secret key to unlock the English ear: the one they use when Dr. Renier's public schoolboys learn all those Oriental languages so well and so rapidly. But nobody knows what it is.

I think it is connected with amateurism. Time and again I have met Englishmen who were not primarily Orientalists who knew such tongues as Persian or Arabic almost perfectly. You could seldom, if ever, say the same about the professionals.

Members of other nationalities can sound strange when trying to speak foreign languages, but the English hold the world record. Their license to this was confirmed as recently as 1951, when Churchill himself announced it. He said, "Everybody has a right to pronounce foreign names as he chooses." Providing he's English, I presume.

Caution is very much an English trait. But, if pronunciation experts can't do much about the English ear, even caution can do little to defend the English against the Afghans. At one banquet, I had been placed opposite my father who was seated next to a civic dignitary. Evidently this man had never been close to an Afghan before, so he decided to play it safe. His first words to my father were, "Are you going abroad this year?"

"Abroad?" said my father. "Sir, I am already abroad."

And caution marked many an approach of the Never-had-it-so-good Prime Minister, then Mr. Harold Macmillan, and subsequently the Earl of Stockton, even though he was a Scot. Unflappability, his other attribute, may in fact be linked with the very caution of which I speak.

He was abroad, himself, on a famous occasion: at the General Assembly of the United Nations. The Russian leader, Khrushchev, had just taken exception to something which had been said. Taking off his shoe, he hammered it on the desk in front of him.

To an Englishman, this action might have meant anything, since it is not a recognized gesture in this country; but Macmillan knew what to do.

"Mr. President," requested the Prime Minister urbanely, "perhaps we could have a translation. I could not quite follow." Macmillan reminisces (in *Pointing the Way*), "This for some reason was thought very witty and effective."

It was for that inspired and very English démarche that I forgive him (thousands wouldn't) for appropriating one of the phrases for which he is best known:

"The Wind of Change is blowing through the Continent."

He used it on February 3, 1960, in Cape Town, almost a thousand years after Al Qasim al Hariri. In *Assembly 21* of his masterwork – the world's first great picaresque novel – Hariri says "Dominion is a Wind of Change, and power a deceptive lightning."

You have to be a linguist to understand, let alone use, the many dialects of English: some accompanied by facial or body movements, or even harsh cries. Special coaching and exposure, sometimes for years, to unfamiliar communities, may be required. In Tunbridge Wells I have to be careful not to use terms picked up from the esoteric, tribal vocabulary of television interviewees. Try saying "At this moment in time," "Basically..." or "I am glad you asked me that" – let alone "My members seek their justified aspirations" – and people will simply turn their backs on you.

We are a full thirty-four miles from London, and that may be one of the reasons. And our village is three and a half miles from the metropolis, Tunbridge Wells itself. If I want service in a village store, I only have to smile and say "Good Morning" or whatever. In the Wells, this is less likely to achieve results. A different approach is needed.

Like a lot of local, retired colonels (and a much greater number who want to be taken for same) I have to start clearing my throat and hawking as loudly as possible, "Ar, ar, ar" and so on, the moment I cross the threshold. The colonel's rallying-honk can get you to the front of a line here as quickly as having the Order of the Red Banner would in Moscow.

So I can handle London, the Wells and the village. Further afield can still be difficult for me. Yesterday at a fairly local service station I heard one mechanic say to another, talking about a man who'd just driven away, "Hard to unnerstand? Ah, well. He's got a *Sussex* accent, ye see." The county of Sussex was all of six hundred yards along the A264.

"The English are not eccentric," a correspondent (*not* Disgusted, Tunbridge Wells) writes, in answer to my inquiry. "They are better described as non-conforming, pending verification."

No fewer than 11% of the world's population use the English language, and that figure is growing. As it does, more and more of us will have to get used to the ways of the people who originated it.

It is a common, though laughable, error to think that speaking and understanding every word is enough to say that you know English. Even idioms are not the chief difficulty. Gesture and challenge, unstudied by even the most zealous of visitors, are often inseparable from – and indeed more important than – mere words. A lot of English people themselves never master this part of the language.

Here is a standard experience, where gesture and challenge are seen at their best:

Whenever I go into a store to complain about such things as a prematurely perished watch-strap, a coughing radio or a book whose pages have molted out of their binding, the Gesture and Challenge technique is frequently brought out.

The assistant – the manager, even, if I have got as far as him – takes one look at me and says, "You've had this in a hot country, haven't you?" The accusatory tone of voice is usually the carrier-wave for this statement, which is intended to be rhetorical. That's the challenge part. The gesture, which accompanies it, involves striking the merchandise against a hard object, such as a concrete floor.

I thought I'd found the solution the day I took back a pair of shoes and pointed to the soles, peeling from their welts. I had my counterstroke ready. As soon as I got the standard response, I drawled, "Hot? You must be joking. No, actually, I've had them in Antarctica."

"There you are," cried the pimply youth behind the counter, with gloomy relish, "extremes are extremes. What did you expect, tramping over all that snow and ice? These shoes weren't made for penguins, you know." He was busy tugging the soles free from the uppers as he spoke.

Limping disconsolately away, I went to rest my poor feet in the public library. There I opened a book and saw a poem by Charles (Manly) Kingsley:

'Tis the hard grey weather breeds hard Englishmen.

This beautiful thought from the *Ode to the North-East Wind* gave me hope that someone from a temperate land would be the ideal choice to take back a shirt which had become bleached on one side and perished on the other after being worn once. Someone from a place where there was not too much heat or cold.

I went to see a friend, Alvaro Lopes, from Madeira: the island which generations of English people have sworn has the perfect climate. I begged him to be a surrogate complainant.

"It's no use," he said, mournfully, "whenever I take, say, a dud watch back, they throw it down as hard as possible on the counter and say, 'Wotcher bin doin' with this, then? Dropped it, I shouldn't wonder.'"

Perhaps he was just trying to slide out of the matter. I have just noticed in the *Dictionary of English Proverbs* that there is a native saying here: "There is falsehood in friendship."

If there ever was a language which was lived as well as spoken, it is English.

It was Arthur Balfour, a renowned statesman of England, who said "Nothing matters very much, and very few things matter at all."

The remark was supposedly about English politics. It may have been employed in that connection, but we are not told the occasion of its genesis. For my money, it came to Balfour as he slunk away from a store trying to make the best of a bad job after trying to get something mended.

This subtle, this indefinable, something which the English have in their language also invades their organising of things. Indeed, it is probably their own form of an Eastern concept: organization without organization. That is to say, it is – or contains – the means of doing things without discernible logic.

Paul Theroux, on the showing of his book about England (*The Kingdom by the Sea*) would perhaps not agree with me. For him, the English are dreadfully inefficient:

> The English were brilliant at running a corner shop, but were failures when they tried their hands at supermarkets... The English do small things well and big things badly.

But I think it depends on whether they really *want* to do something or not. They have some pretty amazing achievements to their credit, even if these were organized without any organization. Theroux has been hard on them in asserting their incapacity. For the sake of balance, I feel constrained to quote a common Middle Eastern proverb which speaks emphatically of English ability:

> The Englishman can do in a day
> what it would take the Devil a year to accomplish.

Does that not bespeak efficiency? Well, in a manner of speaking, as the English put it.

13

All Very Well in Nairobi

The Only Place
London is the only place in which the child grows completely up into the man.
William Hazlitt: *Londoners*

"Fog in the Channel: Continent Cut Off." This headline from *The Times* is supposed to show English insularity and complacency. But I doubt whether the phrase, consciously or otherwise, was ever meant to convey anything of the sort. For the English, the Continent has been cut off since they arrived here, fourteen hundred years ago, and *Times* readers know it.

I think that the headline was put there by a subeditor, as an English joke, and for the express purpose of giving Continentals something to wonder at. After all, English newspapers do not necessarily mean what they say.

Their columns are full of stories about, say, the shortcomings of English people and institutions, and the gentlemen of the Press, by the normal process of feedback and trial and error, must have noticed a good two hundred years ago that their campaigns have very little effect. Given the deteriorating conditions which newspapers feel impelled to report almost daily, it must have become clear long ago that drawing attention to English failings has no effect on English behavior.

But the criticisms and the breast-beating continue to feature in the media, in seeming defiance of the old English watchword: What cannot be Cured must be Endured.

In the space of less than a month in 1986 there were, not exceptionally, three damning indictments reported from elder statesmen alone. The Press reported Harold (Lord) Wilson as saying that, in his experience – presumably as Prime Minister – the security services here "couldn't run a sweet shop." The current Foreign Secretary claimed that Britain was "woefully slow to innovate." Many British companies seemed to prefer living in a fool's paradise to competing internationally. On the same day another former premier, Mr. Edward Heath, said that the British must learn to manage great enterprises (of the size of British Leyland). The lack of ambition in Britain "alarmed" him.

Unable to believe that Press people – and major political figures – need more than six generations to learn a lesson, we must fall back upon an explanation which is contained in another hallowed motto: It is To Confuse The Enemy.

If this seems a very roundabout way of doing things, remember that the English are Eastern not only in the legends of their origins, but in their indirectness.

Perhaps they even compose these items to practice humility, or to counter foreigners, who are known to be boasters. Or it may be that the reason varies from case to case.

This tendency, to be flexible in unexpected things, is a part of their culture which makes foreigners go spare.

I have just read a book by a Frenchman who simply cannot understand the "English inability to devise a system." He thinks the country is chaotic, because the people's minds are full of facts and not with nicely organized pictures of everything in its place. He sees the effect, but cannot find the mechanism.

But the English proceed otherwise: they feed their minds with facts, keep opinions at a low level, and seek an answer as and when one is needed. That is the basis of case-law as opposed to codification, of custom rather than rule – and of the enormous inventiveness of the British.

Our Gallic friend is quite at sea when faced with English esthetics. They have no "proper artists": their painters are no better than the Dutch, he says. An English spokesman, John Hunt, rather uncharacteristically disputes this. "Rembrandt," he writes in *The Examiners*, "is not to be compared in the painting of character with our extraordinarily gifted English artist, Mr. Rippingille." But the ultimate English art is to collect information and only then to see what it adds up to: surely a form of art, even if pursued in unfamiliar areas. The Frenchman I have quoted would, in contrast, have everyone here choose an objective and then work toward it.

He doesn't see that the English will only be understood by a method similar to their own. Just as Freud was confused by women (he couldn't understand, he said, what women *want*) so the outsider, outlandishly, demands to know what the English aim is. Suppose the aim is one which doesn't exactly fit your categories? Collect anecdotal data and then decide what the picture tells you: that is my method, at any rate.

The English have no monopoly of this process: they are just unbeaten in its operation. The Afghan, whose homeland has been called (not by an Englishman: the English tend to like the place) "not so much a country as a disaster," is no mean hand at this technique either. Stonewalling and frozen politeness is another common procedure.

I was sitting one day with the Afghan Ambassador in his study at 31 Princes Gate, London, absorbed in a game of chess. The Third Secretary came into the room and handed His Excellency a business card which identified the caller as, shall we say, Lord Farnes-Barnes. He was waiting downstairs in the hall, studying the black and white marble flagstones, said the junior diplomat.

"Has he an appointment, my child?"

"No, Your Excellency."

The Ambassador motioned to me to make a move, and our heads bent over the board again.

Now the Second Secretary entered, with an identical card and a similar result. He, in turn, appealed to the First Secretary, and he to the Counselor, who brought a verbal message.

"The suppliant downstairs sends his card once more and asks me to remind His Excellency that he is an English lord."

The Ambassador raised his eyebrows and said, without any inflection in his voice, "Tell the gentleman that I have the equivalent of lords, and better than lords, here in this Embassy already, and that they are largely engaged in emptying waste-baskets. If he would care to state his business and the undoubtedly unprecedented chain of events which caused him to call unannounced, it might, however, interest me."

When I left the Embassy a couple of hours later, the Lord had left.

Generalizations about the English, as about anything else, can be risky. The Lord couldn't handle the situation. The Ambassador wouldn't have allowed it to arise in the first place. Of course, as we already know, there are lords and lords. Being a lord doesn't necessarily mean that you know that dropping in on an ambassador is not done.

Sometimes the sang-froid of the English and the Afghans is evenly matched. Not long ago I heard, from my telephone answering machine, a voice I knew well. It belonged to someone I thought was far away: fighting in the Afghan mountains; and it said "Where are you? I'm at such-and-such a number" and no more.

It was Commander (of the Mujahidin) Saif Al Haq, whom I had last heard of blowing up Soviet train stations beyond our northern border, deep inside the national territory of the USSR, as a hint that Russian troops might now care to return to their own country.

I immediately dialed the number, and a Cockney voice answered, "Remington Hotel." I said, "Sorry to trouble you, but I've had a message, in Dari-Persian, from someone, and I wonder if he is there..."

Without a pause, the man said, "Oh, you must mean Mr. Hack, the Afghan guerrilla gentleman. Third floor, room 303. I'll put you through."

And so it was. Haq's name had been instantly Anglicized to Hack; he was, as I have said, an Afghan guerrilla: nothing very odd about that. Why shouldn't an Afghan guerrilla come to London and take a room in a hotel?

Even English people, I suspect, fail to perceive the real workings of this kind of mind when they try to figure it out. This may be because being analytical is foreign. Consider the following passage; I know England well enough to feel sure that most people in this country would characterize it as balderdash:

> The English spirit indeed is like a religion which is only received and can flourish in natures prepared for its reception. It is a seed which requires appropriate soil before it can germinate and take root.

A putative Englishman wrote that. What kind of an Englishman? Well, the words are from *England by an Overseas Englishman* published in London. I came across it after reading some hundreds of books about the English by natives and foreigners, and instantly felt like crying out: "But things don't really feel like that, according to the natives, O Overseas Englishman!"

What has happened to this chap is covered only by the sociological term detribalization. An example of this popped up at the Royal Commonwealth Society where I was having tea and doing some field-work one afternoon.

The place is a resort of expatriates who stay here when on home leave. A huffy Englishman was complaining that the trains were being "unconscionably" delayed. His wife said, "But you always used to say that things were properly organized in England, dear."

"Don't be absurd," growled the husband, "when I said that I was in *Nairobi*."

This dexterity of thought is the instinctive equivalent of repartee, and it can have a very utilitarian application. Not long ago I was dining at a house where some Americans were fellow-guests. One of the Americans had confided in me that he was going to forestall the inevitable sniping at his brand of English, and pretty soon he waded right in.

"Tell me, Colonel," he asked our host, "why do you invite guests to 'wash up,' when you obviously think that that is an Americanism and really means 'wash your hands'? I only ask because 'wash up' as we use it is perfectly good eighteenth-century southern English."

"Oh, that," said the Colonel, "I fear you fellows are always misunderstanding me. I meant that I wanted you to give a hand with the dishes. We don't speak old-fashioned English here, y'know."

In this week's edition of the *New Scientist* there is another example of resourcefulness, although not aimed at foreigners: a case of English against English. After all, the English do not behave as they do just to annoy us. They do these things to one another; they live that way.

Speed humps, "sleeping policemen," built into the road surface to make drivers slow down, had been shown to reduce accidents on the Continent. For some reason, the Department of Transport took against the idea, and fought for years to prevent road bumps for traffic control being introduced here. Then, when they became legal (August 25, 1983) the Department ceased its opposition, as good civil servants should. They simply made regulations about how the humps should be installed.

One year later not a single city had yet provided even one speed hump. Why? Because the Department's requirements were "impossible to satisfy." The chairman of one highways committee put it more energetically: they were "bloody impossible."

This is, for me, the Anglean mentality in full operation: you can make as many rules as you like, but getting them to work is something entirely different. "I'm not going to be put upon," heard on all hands, could be the motto of the country.

The English are more robust than I in describing this remarkable talent. It was an Anglean, I am convinced, who began a letter to the editor of a major London daily paper with the words, "Dear Sir, As an Englishman, I yield to no man in bloody-mindedness..." I would have said, "In my Anglean-ism..."

Yes, the speed humps were from the Continent. And for years, the Continent was indeed cut off.

It's odd how their political masters never seem to learn, in England, that the Civil Service is relentless: after all, both parties are English. An Income Tax demand arrived for Samuel

Pepys, the diarist, in 1967. He had died on May 26, 1703: 264 years before. In 1970, the Dean of Canterbury reported that a letter had been received, addressed to Thomas à Becket, who had unfortunately been assassinated on December 29, 1170, nearly 800 years before.

It was foolishness to attempt to induce such people to adopt speed humps at breakneck speed...

Government by Astonishment, as it should be called, is matched by the sub-program which we could call Stonewalling, which itself sometimes produces astonishment, and more.

Let the Frenchman think that English painting is nothing more than something "like the Dutch." But if it can be considered too vague to have a style, and so can't be easily criticized effectively, that is a safeguard in itself. Nobody can then say, "What I don't like about English pictures is that they tend to have the eyes on the chin," and so on.

The Afghan guerrilla stonewalls by just turning up and being – an Afghan guerrilla. He doesn't bore people with tales of valor, or apologize for being here. The Colonel stonewalls with his "washing-up" gambit. And, of course, the Department of Transport, with their regulations for speedhumps, do their bit.

The English can cause even more than astonishment, as I have many times observed. The procedure often causes people's true natures to be revealed, which can be useful to all concerned: indeed, I have done it myself.

I was in a subterranean chamber of the Alhambra at Granada, clapping my hands in different parts of the place, to test the echo. A serious-looking Continental lady, notebook in hand, came up to me and asked, in good English, why I was doing it.

"Ah," I said, having just arrived from England, and reacting automatically, "I'm insane, you see – that's why."

She gave me a most venomous look, and screamed at the top of her voice, creating some quite interesting echoes:

"You have no right to talk to me like that! You are insulting my intelligence!"

Standing just beside me was an English tourist. When the screaming lady paused for breath he said, "Fat lot've good it is ter 'ave intelligence wot's so easy insulted..."

I have never, before or since, felt the Continent so cut off.

One aspect of the difference between the English and the Continentals is touchiness – or the lack of it. Sir Harold Nicolson, in *Good Behavior*, believes that he has identified the cause. The English are not touchy, he feels, because of a tradition of service and punishment, well exemplified in the public schools:

> And the prefectorial and fagging systems, including corporal punishment, did preserve boys from that sense of "personal honour" ... that has caused so much unhappiness and worry to foreign adolescents.

If you find all this confusing, just remember that England is the sum total of the English, not derived from some abstract idea or system imposed from abroad. The existence of a group-mind which yet produces what seems to be individual choice seems suggested by Charles Spurgeon, the compiler of *Salt-Cellars*.

"England expects every man to do his duty," he quotes. Then:

> England will not get all it expects.
> Every man will do his duty – if he likes.

This is the other side of the supposed insularity and complacency of the English: a sort of rugged independence which evaluates everything and – if it does not get out of control – helps them to endure almost anything.

Americans and Continentals will often say how badly dressed the English can be, even though they have good taste. To the foreigner, to have good taste is to use it and to be seen to be using it; presumably in case people suspect you of having no taste: either that or no money. To the English, good taste is something you not only have, but which you can use or not, as the mood takes you. This conception is not hard to understand – if you come from the East, and are aware of the Sufi teaching "Decide whether you will use something, or whether it will use you."

14

Woadlore

The Problem
When I write "English" or "England," I usually mean the English people and England, not the British people and Britain. After all, the English people, not the British people or the British Empire, is the basic problem to the American people and to Hitler.

D. W. Brogan: *The English People* (1943)

I HAVE REASON to be interested in woad, and even in King Canute and St. George and the Dragon. All of these are familiar to the English; as an Afghan, my interest may be thought unlikely, but it connects with the English from an unusual direction.

The Romans were intrigued to find the inhabitants of southern England, Albion, decorated in blue woad. Although these were not Angles, or even Saxons or Jutes, their present-day successors revel in the idea of this warpaint, and it is mentioned as often as possible in their history books. Indeed, I was informed, with pride, by an English schoolmaster who always refers to the woad-using people of this land when teaching English history, that the matter is more important than one might think.

"You see," he said, "the production of a blue pigment from the woad plant is an intricate technological process, requiring advanced scientific knowledge." He referred me to an impressive passage in a schoolbook, whose author was characteristically proud of the ancient blueskins. It said:

> Woad pigment is obtained by hydrolysis, chemical decomposition or ionic dissociation caused by water.

I rang up a scientist I know and asked him to interpret, if there was any hope of a layman understanding such sophisticated techniques. He told me, "It means 'bung it in a bucket of water.'" Still, those painted people must be the ancestors of some, even many, of the contemporary Britons, as the inhabitants are still called. My schoolmaster friend consciously identified with them, quoting Caesar with gusto: "All the Britons, without exception, stain themselves with woad, which produces a blueish tint; and this gives them a wild look in battle."

In order to test what a British reaction to Romans might have been (the books give few details) I journeyed to a town on the south coast, to ask a local inhabitant.

"What would the people around here have thought when the Romans arrived?" I asked a blue-tinted native. He was a decorator, beefing up the reddish dragon on the front wall of an azure-colored Chinese takeout.

"Died larfin, I shouldn't wunda," he thought, "all them kilts and trying to get them dirty great wooden catapults up the chalk cliffs."

Yes, they might well have jeered, I reflected: people don't change as much as might be expected. The British are supposed to respect Roman civilization; but this may only be a recent development. I had just been reading Samuel Pepys's *Diary* where he spoke of a similar reaction to that of the decorator:

> But Lord! To see the absurd nature of Englishmen, who cannot forbear laughing and jeering at everything that looks strange

he had written. Maybe Pepys was of Roman, or Norman, descent.

English and other British sources are vague about the woad and the painting of the bodies of the people who wore it. Some imply that they were the same as the Picts, the "painted people": but these seem to have been mainly in Scotland, although a number had slipped down south to get a look at the arrivals from Italy.

The Picts and Scots certainly *were* in England later. Vortigern the Briton had brought in the Angles and Saxons to expel them. The Scots, who evicted the Picts from Caledonia, had come from Ireland: and Colonel Blacker's theory has the Irish coming from Egypt, whence they brought the Stone of Scone ("Jacob's Pillow"), the Coronation Stone in Westminster Abbey. These European, Asian and African peoples, though, were beaten to it by the aboriginals who lived in underground dwellings. They came from the "southern Mediterranean."

Just to make things more difficult, some authors think that these were the Picts, "dwarfish and of unknown affiliations." The telling is confused; some believe that there were two lots of them: the Pechts of North-East Scotland, and the Picts, who used the blue dye.

I can contribute only one piece of first-hand information: a piece which may or may not fit. I had seen some very blue-eyed, fair-skinned people – the Blue Men – south of the Mediterranean, in Morocco.

According to the guidebooks, they are blue because the dye from their clothes comes off on the skin. "The dye," writes one expert, "was originally imported from Britain."

Full circle: except for the detail that woad is described in my sources as "a very good dye," which I had always imagined would include being color-fast. Whatever the truth of this matter, it is intriguing to learn that woad is native not to Britain but to the countries around the *Mediterranean.*

The Scottish kings are descended, so says their own traditional lore (and like our own Walis of Swat) from Alexander the Great. He not only hailed from the Mediterranean, but journeyed to my own country, where woad is an important crop: indeed, Afghanistan is the only country which lists woad as a major export. And Alexander passed through Afghanistan, where the people gave him a hard time, their usual robust welcome to would-be conquerors.

Is it inconceivable that Alexander brought back woad, or that the Scots might even have taught the Picts how to use it? The mind boggles: but remember that a lot of the early history of Britain seems to depend upon associations of ideas such as these.

My own relationship with woad, and even with King Canute, is no less direct than many connections, of varying plausibility, found in English history books.

An-nil, or neel, as we call this blue dye, was formerly much used in England, and long after the Picts and woadmen had been absorbed into the general population. The demand became so great in the mid-nineteenth century that prices rocketed and people in the East were growing as much of the stuff as they possibly could.

My great-grandfather, though possessed of considerable lands, was also a spiritual leader and military man, and the story has it that he resisted the pressure of his courtiers and feudal dependants to sow his entire territory with the stuff, during the final woad-boom in Europe. Finally, following extensive representations from the populace, he agreed. Woad was grown in unheard-of quantities. It was harvested and loaded into an unprecedentedly large number of carts drawn by oxen: then it was transported to Bombay, where the keenest neel-buyers were to be found.

All waited expectantly for the return of the caravan and bags stuffed with golden sovereigns. When the day came, however, there was nothing: except the news that *an-nil* was unsaleable. Aniline dyes, made synthetically, had just flooded the market.

As with the tale of King Canute, so the story of the Nawab Mohammed Ali Shah and the woad. Canute shamed his courtiers by letting them have their way and letting events prove them wrong. After the woad débâcle, none of the Nawab's men ever dared to make suggestions as to what the Nawab should do. And they had all been bankrupted, for foolhardily putting their money where their mouths were.

My interest in St. George, Patron Saint of England, did not begin with the Western belief that he was a Middle Easterner, because that tale places him in the vicinity of Beirut, with which I have no plausibly sustainable contact. But we have our own version of the story.

When the British armies invaded Afghanistan in the 1840s, some officers were disconcerted to hear that the snaky fortifications on the mountains above the capital of Kabul were the spine of the great dragon slain by Hazrat Ali ibn Abi Talib, my ancestor, under circumstances which, when the English and Afghan versions were compared, seemed to point to plagiarism on the part of one or the other.

Not that St. George is such a live issue now, nearly a century and a half after the British invasion of Afghanistan. With the English genius for inspired superannuation, the folk-mind seems to have decided that the Patron Saint isn't needed any more. Early in 1985, the *Daily Express* recorded a decision by the Manchester magistrates confirming it. "St. George's Day – April 23 for the uninitiated – was not an occasion to celebrate."

But what will happen to the lady who, with real English compromise and even-handedness, is reported as visiting her church regularly to light two candles: one for St. George and one for the Dragon? Perhaps that is for Rome to worry about: the Vatican demoted the saint in 1960.

Of course, if St. George was not English, or even British, neither was Hazrat Ali an Afghan. My own family have lived in Afghanistan for a somewhat shorter time than the Angles have dwelt in England, and other Afghans sometimes remind us of it, though conceding that we have been "modified by a thousand years' residence here."

Mentioning all this to a native genealogist, Sir Iain Moncreiffe, I was astonished to find that he knew more about such matters than I did. His Press cuttings included an item from fifteen years back, which showed English absorption strenuously at work. First, it recorded that the Yaldwyn family of Britain not only have unbroken male descent from AD 1298, but that they are descended from King Ella, who landed in Britain in the fifth century. He's the one who took over Sussex and Surrey in 491.

"Remarkable, I agree," I said. "Yaldwins, eh?"

"Not that," said Moncreiffe, "look at the last part of the clipping." I was not expecting to find that the correspondent of the *Daily Telegraph* had written that "Sayed Idries lives in Kent" as indeed I do, and "holds the record, of the oldest family in England."

If I were not determined to return and be buried in my ancestral mausoleum, I could now lay claim to something quite unexpected.

I asked my genealogist what this made me. "You're absolutely English," he said without hesitation. "Domicile of origin or of intent is something else. Doesn't affect it in the least."

"Do you have to feel English to be English?" I asked.

"Not at all," he said. "I don't feel like anything in particular, myself, for example." He went to a bookcase and brought out the *Letters of Lord Byron*, turning the pages as he spoke. "England is not only people, it is that and something else," he said. Then, "Yes, look at this. Would you have said that Byron was English?"

"Very much so," I answered.

"Right, now: Letter from Lord Byron to Count d'Orsay, April 22, 1823. His very words are 'Though I love my country, I do not love my countrymen.'"

So that seems to make me an Anglekin, if I wish to be one. Perhaps the fellow-feeling which comes from a common relationship with woad – and an assortment of other factors – could provide a colorable argument, if one were needed.

My trouble is that I sometimes tend to look for rationality, or, at least, for a moral. Such things, in England, can be hard to find, certainly at a deeper than ordinary level:

"Tut, tut, child!" said the Duchess. "Everything's got a moral, if only you can find it."

You see the booby-trap? The assertion that there must be a moral also hints, in English fashion, that you may not be able to find it. And this in a children's book and not – as in the East – in a book of esoteric philosophy.

But if the question of how English one may be is difficult, the family woad legend did do something for me. When the British Government announced plans to restore the United

Kingdom's ailing economy at a stroke, I perked up. When they said that they would do it by growing colossal quantities of peanuts in Africa, I smiled to myself, and murmured "woad." People don't talk about the peanuts project now: not, at any rate, in certain sections of society. Elsewhere, it is known as the Great Ground-Nuts Fiasco of Tanganyika.

15

Carriemoss

Reverence
John [Bull] has such a reverence for everything that has been long in the family, that he will not hear even abuses being reformed, because they are good old family abuses.
    Washington Irving: *The Sketch Book of Geoffrey Crayon Gent*

JUST WHY SAIF Al Haq, Commander of an Afghan Resistance force, should have left his responsibilities to make a flying visit to London was not clear, and he did not attempt to explain. What was obvious was the fact that, within an hour of installing himself in a Kensington hotel and looking out of the window, Haq had become a dedicated England-watcher. Perhaps it was his anthropological background.

At all hours of the day and night, the Commander would call me with significant discoveries. The Continent might be cut off, but Haq never was. "Mr. Hack on the line" became a regular announcement on the extension from my office to my study. And England – and the English – he had taken, reciprocally with the affection of the hotel staff, completely to his bosom.

Hack was constantly finding affinities, analogies, equivalences and the like between the East and this Western land. He seemed fated to run across only those things which reminded him of home: or, at any rate, of the East.

While some Continentals, looking for the essential Englishness of the people and the place, deplore the outlandish and alien derivations of so many things English, Hack positively gloried in them. Just as an American with Scottish roots is said to snap up every garment with a pattern resembling tartan when he arrives on his ancestral heath, so did Hack revel in the Eastern character of England, which he saw on every hand. In his pre-guerrilla days, Saif al Haq had been a leading light in Kabul's university, and though his war-name, Pohantooni, to English ears, sounds like that of a colorful warrior, it in fact means "He of the University."

It was shortly before breakfast, a week after he arrived, that I got the excited call from Haq. "Badshah-Saheb! Komondon Pohantooni speaks. Hear this: you did not tell me of the remarkable presence, in this infidel land, of holy dervishes, parading the streets and calling upon people to praise the name of one of your own illustrious ancestors!"

I had been deep in a book on colloquial English. "Come again?" I said. Because we were speaking our own language, I said it in Dari.

"*Ya-buland!* O All-Highest! I cannot come *again*, because I have never yet been," he corrected me, impatiently.

"Heroic Commander Haq," I said, still finding the transition from Tunbridge Wells to the Hindu-Kush difficult, "did you know that in England there are all sorts of useful and interesting conventions relating to the verbs 'come,' 'be' and 'go'?"

He interrupted me with a harsh Hindu-Kushian expletive related to goats. "I am sure that you have been overdoing your religious exercises, and the overnight strain of them has introduced, as it were, maggots into your brain," he rapped.

"I thought that you were reproaching me for insufficient veneration of London-based dervishes connected with my family," I answered testily.

"Exactly. Now, do you remember the holy chant which one may hear in the streets, in the caravanserais and even on the airwaves, of the East?" He reminded me of it, his voice rising and falling in a semi-musical dirge: "*O Hadrat Imaam Ridaa!*" This is a commemoration of one of the Imams of the Twelver Persuasion, who had died in the year 818, which I recalled was during the reign of King Baldred, here in Kent, just before he was killed, I forgot why, by King Egbert of Wessex.

"Yes, I do indeed, Commander. But my family branched off from the sons of Musa Al Kazim, you know."

That was nearly 1,200 years ago...

"Of course I know. That does not alter the fact that Hadrat Ali Rida was a sanctified personage, and that you share his ancestry."

"What are these dervishes of the Rida Tendency actually doing?" I asked the Commander.

"They are here, in the street, giving their immemorial chant; one, at the reins, guiding a horse and cart, doubtless containing their few simple possessions, the disciple walking respectfully beside it. I can see them from my window."

"Anything else?"

"Yes, people are coming out of the houses and giving them things. And getting something in return. No doubt the Sheikh is, after discussion, bestowing an amulet upon each householder, in recognition of his piety in contributing to the upkeep of the dervishes."

That certainly was interesting; but all kinds of things happen in London, I could not say that I was actually amazed. Except that the English, in general, go in for black cats, avoiding ladders and addressing wishes to shooting stars or birthday candles, rather than following mere superstitions. They are more likely, too, I reflected, to go into the street to confer with rag-and-bone men – "*Commander!*" I shouted, the penny dropping at last. "You've got it all wrong. It's not 'O Hadrat Imaam Ridaa!' at all – it's 'Any old iron or lumbaa!'" The two chants are, in fact, uncannily alike.

"Your faith is undermined," he said, in the words and tone which I had heard so many times from my fellow-Easterners, "for you have dwelt too long in the lands of the unbelievers."

Of course, Haq may have had a point there: not necessarily about my faith, but about the eclecticism of the English. After all, I have heard, again and again, from parachute troops here, that when they jump they shout "O Mohammed!," having adopted this cry from Moslem Indian soldiers in training during the Second World War. If the English can adopt "a Mortimer," as they had from Pakistani immigrants in the North, using the word to mean a meeting, and also the name of the Prophet for their parachuting, why not Imam Rida?

The English have squared the circle or, as they would say, done a hat-trick: three in a row. First, they remain incorrigibly English. Second, they adopt, accept or use a paralyzing range of words, objects and customs which are not at all English. Third, if you seek reassurance that, for instance, West is really East here, you'll get it.

I had now met so many foreign investigators and experts on England and its people, and found so much evidence of their former and repeated missions of inquiry in these islands, that I was able to discern a further ingredient. I suppose it is a variety of what scientists call the Operator Effect.

It may be stated as a rule or principle. "So many and such diverse people come here looking for things that the sum of what they themselves leave behind affects the country itself." And I do not only mean the Kababs in Queensway, the curry in Clacton, the unleavened bread, saris, Chitrali caps, Pakistani shirts, Turkish trousers, Sikh turbans or Chinese slippers. There are many other signs. Naturally, they are adopted in a manner never imagined by their donors.

These earnest inquirers, I felt increasingly sure, were not only taking away bafflement: they were leaving behind a mass of things – unrelated to one another, which is how the English like it – which are allowed to be only transiently outlandish. A Spanish visitor may well have bestowed the Infanta de Castile, but it was soon metamorphosed, some say (others disagree, of course), into the Elephant and Castle. To detail a single, but telling, instance, there is the Luck of Eden Hall.

The tradition in the Musgrave family is that their butler once went to draw water from St. Cuthbert's Well, at their seat in Cumberland, and surprised some of the Little People, who were drinking there. They ran away, leaving a painted glass cup, which he, with proper presence of mind, seized and carried back to Eden Hall. The cup is the Luck (Low German or Dutch *luk*, fortune) of the family of Sir Christopher Musgrave. Longfellow records the pith of the legend in the punch-lines:

> If that glass either break or fall
> Farewell the luck of Eden Hall.

The Luck (now in London's Victoria and Albert Museum) has since been identified as an ancient Middle Eastern goblet, probably Syrian.

Now, with our wits sharpened and all superstition set aside, what are we able to infer? First, that the Little People who ran away were, possibly, a band of small inquiring

Syrians, interested in English ways, who had stopped to refresh themselves on their peregrinations, and were using, quite naturally, a Syrian cup. Although the Cup is said to be "sacred," this is not enough to allow us to conclude that the Syrians in question were tiny but holy dervishes, but it is always possible. But, with English inspiration, an object of mystery, seized from strangers, has almost certainly become the – very English – Luck of Eden Hall.

There is more, much more, in this and similar vein. Sometimes the derivation of a thing is plain and clear: sometimes not. The verandah, complete with Indian name, brought by the English from Calcutta, is one instance. But who brought the camel-striding horse, and from where?

In England, many people spend lifetimes training horses to run in a very unnatural manner. It has been noted, by sharp-eyed oil sheikhs and others, that this training, which makes the ride very smooth, is the specialty of the bedouins of the Hejaz, which was never a part of the British Empire. It is a straight imitation of the leg-stride of the camel of the desert, and camels have never been in general use in England.

So the invisible bequest is there. Even I may, one day, be able to claim that I have contributed to this transmission, though in a minor way. During my early days here, in moments of nostalgia, I used to beat upon a fiber laundry-box (I had no drum) and sing a compulsive song, *Kar-i-maa'st*, which means, in the words of its refrain, "That's OUR work!"

It originates in Paghman, my ancestral home, and has such stirring lines as "O you infidel, don't try to attack us, for attacking is OUR job!" *Kar-i-maa'st, kar-i-maa'st, kar-i-maas'st.*

A couple of friends and I, equally homesick, would beat out the tempo on the box, and repeat the song, hour after hour, in our ground-floor London apartment. At first the people upstairs hammered on our ceiling. Then they wrote us nasty notes; and even threatened to call the police. Ultimately they came down and joined us.

There we sat, night after night, three Afghans and three Englishmen, our voices rising and falling with the beat of *Kar-i-maa'st*, sometimes until the wee small hours of the morning.

And my cup was full when, one night, our neighbors were having a little private *kar-i-maa'st*ing upstairs on their own and a native English colleague of theirs dropped in.

"Whatever are you up to?" he asked.

Without pausing in his inspired beat, one of our English fellow-musicians (his name was Gerald, which means Spear-Wielder) answered, "Why, we're Karimasting: doesn't *everybody* do it?"

So I like to think that perhaps at this very moment, there are people all over the country, crooning, bellowing, or trilling – Karimast. Of course, the phrase will eventually be pronounced something like "Carriemoss," and will be considered an old English air. Probably from the Border Country, you know.

Not, of course, that the English need to nativize something before adopting it. If you look up *Everyman's Dictionary of Dates*, under "Anniversaries of the Western world," you will find:

> January 26, Republic of India proclaimed
> February 4, Ceylon [Sri Lanka] Independence Day
> March 6, Ghana Independence Day
> April 17, Syrian National Day
> May 27, Afghanistan National Day

And so on. The Far East, Middle East, Central Asia, Africa... How Western can you get?

If you know English customs, you are soon on good terms with the English. And, as I discovered, in the case of my *Kari-maa'st*ing – you can share your ways with them.

But there has to be an exchange of some kind, a *quid pro quo*. I once discussed this with the commanding officer of an Afghan garrison fort on our side of the old Indo-Afghan frontier. "There's a language of actions, so to speak, and that's how the British talk to you," he told me. "If you don't 'speak' this language, you get confrontation."

I said, "I thought that the English always begin with a certain kind of standoffish or, well, self-assertive attitude, and you have to match it, to get through that barrier."

The old colonel agreed. "Absolutely right. They once had a British CO, just over there, who came to visit me, wearing a monocle. We exchanged courtesy visits every six months. When it was my turn to go over to his side of the border, I took *two* monocles, ordered from Kabul, and put one in each eye when I spoke to him. After that, he never wore his again, and we became quite good friends. Now, some people would have been annoyed at the supposed arrogance of the man in wearing the eyeglass in the first place, and it would only have ended in enmity."

"How about the present one?" I asked; for this was the time, before Pakistan and independence, when we were eyeball to eyeball with the Brits.

"Well, on my first visit, this chap gave me a brace of pheasants as a goodwill present; which meant that I had to reply in kind. I thought about it for a bit, then I hit on the answer."

"A bigger present?" I asked.

"No, that would have been inappropriate. I gave him what he called the best cup of tea he'd had since Camberley, from a Queen Anne silver teapot, with Fortnum's cake, and so on. Now we play chess, signaling the moves by heliograph."

I am sure that Colonel Azmi would have recommended Haq to look to his courtesy, rather than to words, in dealing with the English.

I found I shared with Azmi a delight in the poem by Saadi of Shiraz, which sums it up. It was Englished by an Englishman, in Victorian times, thus:

> With honeyed words and language soft and fair –
> Thou may'st conduct a mammoth with a hair!

16

Pirates and Admirals

Mere English
Queen Elizabeth I described herself as "mere English." What she meant was "complete and undiluted English."
                      Philip Howard, in *The Times*

I TOOK COMMANDER Haq to the Wallace Collection, to see its fine Eastern swords and armor. These, he remarked, showed how powerfully attracted the English were to such things, as he was; to local customs like the Morris Dancers, originating with the sword-dance of the Moorish, or Morris, men. "Of course," he carefully noted, "geographically speaking, Morocco is not in the East, being distinctly west of these islands; but the Moroccans are quite Eastern, I understand, for people of a Western land."

This put me in mind of the Barbary Corsairs, the Moorish pirates who established themselves in north Africa after the Moors' expulsion from Spain, and this, in turn, recalled a talk I'd had with Earl Mountbatten of Burma.

It was at a reception at India House in London's Aldwych: indeed, he was the guest of honor, as the last viceroy of India before Independence. I found him standing behind a bookcase (the reception was in the library) away from the crowd, nursing a gin and orange. Although we had never met, he took advantage of the convention at parties that no formal introduction is necessary, and began to talk as if we were old acquaintances. "As a sailor," he said, "I have always been interested in the East, so India was not a surprise to me, any more than South-East Asia Command was during the War."

I asked him what aspect of the East attracted him. "Why, the admirals, of course. As an admiral myself, I am intrigued to think that my predecessors in this rank wore baggy trousers and carried scimitars. Our word 'admiral' is, like *amiral* in French and all the rest in other languages, derived from *Amir al Ma*, Commander of the Water, from the Moors and so on."

I bowed. "The Middle Eastern admiral outfit of baggy trousers and curly-toed slippers," I assured him, "would suit Your Excellency admirably." He liked to wear appropriate clothes.

I mentioned the traditional pirate flag. "Yes," said Mountbatten, "that's another interesting one. Because the skull and crossbones are found on old Roman mosaic floors and the like, people thought that that's what the emblem was on the corsair flag, and copied it as such. In reality, the corsair emblem was the Arabic word 'HU' – meaning 'He, God,' on a black flag, the color of the banner of the Prophet, you know. Looked like a skull and bones, if you didn't read Arabic, you see."

Mountbatten was a great reader – he even knew my books – and, speaking in the clipped manner of British sailors, came out with surprisingly detailed knowledge of recondite things. He had investigated, for example, the origins of the gold rings which denote rank when worn on uniform sleeves and epaulets. "They're the only surviving relic of the Amir: the alternating gold and black headbands of the Arabian seafarers."

And there was more, again from the Arabian tradition:

"You know why one is not allowed on the quarter-deck bareheaded, and why you must salute the quarter-deck?"

I told Mountbatten that I could not imagine. After all, the mysteries of English maritime etiquette and ritual were beyond me.

"Then they shouldn't be. They're part of your own tradition. The Mediterranean was formerly the highway of the Fatimites of North Africa. This Arab dynasty claimed descent from the Prophet. Their Emirs commanded the ships and represented the Caliph himself, do you see. To be bareheaded in the presence of the ruler or his deputy was insulting, in your culture if not in ours. And the quarter-deck, in turn, represented the Apostolic Throne of Arabia. Naturally you would salute it, in token of homage."

"You mean," I asked, "that, centuries later, the seadogs of Britain, called infidels by the Fatimites, perpetuate the homage to the extinct Caliphs of Egypt imitated from their sea-lords?"

"Now you're getting the idea," he assured me.

"But why?"

"There's this legend that's supposed to account for it. Seems that some old dervish, full of sanctity, gave one of the ancient caliphs an assurance that seamen would salute his memory till the end of time. Only forgot one thing when he accomplished it, though. Forgot to include in his spell, or whatever it was, the request that there should be an Arabian caliph in power till eternity."

He knew that polo was a Persian game: "They still show the original stone goal-posts in northern Iran, you know..."

Connections, however tenuous, mean a lot in England: just as they do in Afghanistan. In line with Mountbatten's rapid association-of-ideas way of thinking, I realized that I could trace a connection with the gallant English successor to the

Arabian sea-wolves. Our daughter Saira had as nurse Sister Rowe, "Rowie," who had looked after both Prince Charles and Princess Anne. Later, in 1964, Rowie went to nurse Mountbatten's twin grandsons. Having a nurse in common, in the East, always produces a close bond. Although this custom is nothing like as strong in England, Rowie regarded all "her" children as her own, just as any Eastern woman in her place would have done.

Her loyalty to Mountbatten was as fierce as anything I have seen, as was her attachment to the Royal Family, perhaps equaled only by her detestation of anything German. How, I wonder, would she have reacted, if she were still alive, to Paul Hogan's words in *Punch*, on March 20, 1985? To him, Mountbatten was

> perhaps the greatest Englishman of the century, and all the more so for not being of English blood.

I wanted to get Haq's views on bonding between nurses and the families which they served, and also the possibility of becoming English in one generation when Afghans were not always willing to accept thirty-three ancestors born on their soil as unequivocally establishing naturalization: but he wasn't listening. What fired his imagination was Mountbatten's store of Eastern information, and he struck fist on palm excitedly when I recounted the Admiral's words, on our way home from the Wallace Collection.

"There *must* be more to it than that," he said, "there will be connections with the East in that family, the royal family of England, you mark my words. If there were not, Prince Louis would never have become so interested in such matters. Besides, *everything* here has an Eastern aspect."

So, next day, we spent hours in the British Library, at the British Museum. Finally we found it: Commander Haq was right. The book *Blood Royal*, by Sir Iain Moncreiffe of that Ilk (the man who had shown me the newspaper item about my own descent) proved that, and abundantly. Haq shook my hand in delight as he pointed to the passage where the Albany Herald (and genealogist extraordinary) traces Her Majesty the Queen's descent from King Mohammed of Seville. "She is married," he pointed out, "to Lord Louis's kinsman, Prince Philip." And he, in turn, stemmed from another Eastern family, the Mithradites, ancient royal house of Iran. Moncreiffe had shown that, too.

"I know," I said, "and, by the way, were you aware that Sir Iain himself comes from the family of King Pharnabuzuz, monarch of the Iberians, who was around in 326 BC: and the Iberians are said to originate in Asia, too?"

Haq slapped me on the back. Since he was six foot six inches tall and large in proportion, this unnerved the eager but fragile-looking library assistant from whom the Commander now snatched another book. It was a bound volume of the old *Strand Magazine*, for the second half of 1892. It was open at an illustrated article featuring Queen Victoria, and Haq became more and more animated as he perused it.

The piece excitedly discussed (and embellished the point with illustrations) the Queen's great knowledge of the Urdu language. But that was not all; there was also a sample of a Persian poem by the Sufi mystic sage Saadi, copied in Her Majesty's own hand. The English Empress of India had delved as deeply as that into the spirituality of the East. For Haq this was a real discovery: he was a follower of the same spiritual brotherhood as the one to which Saadi had been affiliated.

Now he had a common bond with Queen Victoria.

Then he pointed out something more of the Eastern connection: the Queen even kept a diary in Urdu. Under the dateline of Windsor Castle, July 4, 1889, she writes, in that language, how she entertained the Shah of Persia and some of his ministers to luncheon there.

"As you will know," ventured our librarian, "Queen Victoria was German, Guelph by name – originally Welfe – and so was her husband, as were the Georges before them."

Commander Haq shook his head violently, with eyes closed, as if to banish such irrelevancies. But the British Library man was well into his stride, leading up to a fresh piece of Anglo-Eastern information. "When the German Emperor Wilhelm, kinsman of Victoria," he shrilled, "visited Damascus, he placed his sword, in token of respect, upon the tomb of the great Sultan Saladin. And the German Hohenstaufen rulers of Sicily, known as the Baptized Sultans, were allies of the Normans who fought at Hastings. The single-and double-headed Eagles, proud emblems of Europe, were copied from Middle Eastern originals. Heraldic texts show this, and even trace the Middle Eastern origins of the Fleur-de-Lys."

Haq looked at me in triumph. Before I was able to drag him away, he had also found out that, after the landing and during the whole night before the decisive battle for England, the Normans had piously stayed awake in prayer: while the Saxons under Harold had roistered the night away, being very drunk, or at least hungover, on the fateful morning of October 14, 1066.

"That also means," I told my compatriot, "that both sides must have been exhausted even before they started the battle. For my part, I incline more toward the Anglekins. I like their English spirit." So Haq, though he tried, did not manage to drag me to Battle, in Sussex, to inspect the field of honor, where his fellow Easterners' allies found victory.

As I told Haq, sternly, and as every Englishman knows, the English spirit so absorbed the Normans that neither their Norseman nor their Latin background is ultimately considered equal to an English one. "This country, Commander," I reminded him, "Norman propaganda notwithstanding, is called *England*, not New Normandy."

Instead of Hastings, Haq settled for Leighton House. A stupefyingly miscellaneous collection of Eastern tiles, prayer-niches, pillars and other loot, accumulated with true Victorian collection-mania, is lovingly assembled there, plastered on walls and generally jumbled around an Eastern fountain-court. It was almost as good as the Brighton Pavilion.

I steered Haq away from the Eastern undertones of the Phoenicians alleged to have been in Cornwall and even the Saracen origins of Gothic writing and architecture as shown in such books as *Miras i Islam* – a copy of which he carried everywhere. This proved to be a Persian translation of a standard English work, *The Legacy of Islam*, edited by Sir Thomas Arnold and full of articles by learned Western Orientalists. Haq seemed almost offended that Sir Thomas was no longer alive. "I would have visited him, you know," he said gloomily.

On Haq's initiative, we spent many happy hours reading the Arabic and Persian graffiti which bespatter the London Underground, and in conversation with dozens of the men who thronged the Regent's Park Mosque and the London streets dressed in Eastern costume. There were so many of these in and around Harley Street that the district looked almost like a suburb of a Gulf city: some of the patients, after their consultations, even sat on the sidewalks, relating traditional tales and enjoying the sunshine.

In conversation with many of these people, Haq discovered that they lacked a deep interest in their own Eastern culture, but were fascinated by advanced Western medical equipment, which they insisted should be used indiscriminately upon them.

Hack put their attitude down to the fact that these poor people were sick; though he waylaid as many as he could, and gently tried to instruct them in English thought and customs. Each tradition was, he knew, derived from the East.

Many an ailing camel-driver who has been rushed by chartered plane from Kuwait, Bahrain or the United Arab Emirates, knows England only as the London Clinic and from what he has learned from Commander Haq. The guerrilla chief did not attempt anything too advanced. Among the facts he imparted were that an Indian Summer is the finest part of the year, that a brave youth is known as a Proper Little Turk, and that it is good luck for a person of dark complexion, or a chimney-sweep in lieu, to kiss the bride, or to cross the threshold on New Year's Eve.

"The English word for Money Changer," I heard the Commander inform one dazed bedouin, as he pointed to an illuminated sign saying SARRAF (designed to entice Middle Easterners), "is the same as ours, as you see."

This reminded me, irresistibly, of the day when my children came home from their English prep school, lisping about their teacher who had just been on a pilgrimage to the Holy Land. "Children," she had gushed, "you will be surprised to know that the Arabic word for 'Welcome,' which I myself heard in Jerusalem, is the same as ours, *Welcome*! They all said it!"

My daughter Safia had been admonished when she asked, "Then what does *marhaba* mean? I thought *that* was the Arabic word for 'welcome.'"

Saif Al Haq, having finished his mysterious business in darkest England, is now back in Afghanistan. I expect that, when he is not taking potshots at Russians, he is explaining to bemused Pashtuns that such is the affection of the English for the Afghans that they have both a Cabul and a Candahar road, named after our two largest cities and within a stone's throw of one another, in south-west London. And that the Inglizi Royal Family stems from some of the noblest Eastern stock, on both the male and female sides.

I have a fresh nugget of information for him. Lord Gore-Booth, President of the Sherlock Holmes Society of London, has noted that Sherlock Holmes's Dr. Watson was in the 1880 Afghan campaign. It's the kind of link that will please both the British (since Watson is a sort of English folk-hero) and the Afghans (because they won the Battle of Maiwand).

Like the good academic he is (when he is not a guerrilla), Haq strove to put some balance into his studies. Among the voluminous notes which he left with me for safekeeping is a page headed "negative characteristics."

"In addition to the numerous indications of Eastern influence," he had written, "we are obliged to note that English culture still presents a somewhat patchy appearance.

"Sententiousness is rife, and seldom clearly recognized as such; but this will be dealt with in its proper place.

"As for day-to-day experiences, field-workers will encounter some surprises. This observer, for instance, recorded that, to obtain such common commodities as *jalghoza* nuts (here called 'pine kernels') and seedless green raisins, it was often necessary to apply to crank food stores."

Commander Haq is our nation's greatest expert on pickles, so I was not surprised to see that he had allowed personal feelings to intrude upon his otherwise scientific work: "It was often difficult," he continued, "to obtain pickles of reasonable quality and satisfactory range throughout the territory investigated.

"In an entirely different area, it was found that the wanton exposure of human flesh and a strange bodily-decoration proclivity, traditionally regarded by anthropologists as inseparable from a primitive culture, went unremarked even in supposedly civilized circles."

Haq concedes that more than one visit would be needed to form anything like a complete picture of the people:

"In spite of some considerable effort, ably assisted by local Afghan residents (to whom my thanks are due), it was not found possible, on such a short reconnaissance, to verify the conclusion of a previous worker in the field.

"I refer to Voltaire's *Description of the English Nation*. He says: 'Froth at top, dregs at bottom, but the middle is excellent.'"

I was expecting Haq to add the customary piece of Eastern wisdom here, but he did not. So I have annotated his text with the Afghan saying, "Everyone thinks that his own country is a Kashmir."

And yet, and yet... Re-reading some of Haq's notes, I wonder whether the joke may be on me. The Afghans, it is well known, love pulling your leg. They love making fun of intellectual pretension. Some of them have specialized in exposing the bizarre association-of-ideas thinking which historians of all countries use to establish and maintain their arguments.

Haq may be showing just how over the top is his obsession with the Eastern influences in this country – or he may have left a clue by overstating his case – in his section on the military.

"Turning to the matter of the Queen's Own Highlanders, as not untypical of the army as a whole," he writes, "astonishing and exciting links may be descried by even a short study of the British *Army List*, published annually by Her Majesty's Stationery Office.

"This élite military unit is stated as having no less than five emblems, all of them with Eastern associations: Queen Victoria's cipher (we have noted her interest in, and connections with, the East); together with the Garter (reputed to be of Eastern origins or affiliations); and the Sphinx and the Elephant, which need no comment. Also the Duke of Edinburgh's cipher: and he, of course, is descended from an Iranian imperial house, as noted by the genealogist Sir Moncreiffe."

There is much more. The Highlanders are affiliated to an Eastern regiment, the Gurkha Rifles. The Colonel-in-Chief is none other than Prince Philip. And this unit has close connections with our own country: 1879, Kabul; 1880, Kandahar; 1878–80, Afghanistan: not to mention Chitral...

I looked up the *List*, and found that Haq has his facts, if not his extrapolations, right. Not only that, but the Highlanders had been at Sidi Barrani and Tobruk, in the Western Desert. And at Cassino. That, I could add as a footnote to this learned monograph, coincided with the North African and Italian service of my cousin, Colonel Ibne-Hasan Shah, a hero of Cassino.

If Haq could extract that much information from page 163 of the *Army List*, who knows what he might have discovered if he had had more time, could have dug deeper...

17

Xavier Turlough is My Name

Importance of a Name
A name? If the party had a choice, what mortal would be a Bugg by choice, as a Hogg, a Grunn or a Chubb rejoice, or any such nauseous blazon?
            Thomas Hood: *Miss Kilmansegg*

A JAPANESE GENTLEMAN living in England sent me his translation of a novel published in Tokyo. It might well, he thought, become a best-seller in England. "And, hopefurry," as he said on the telephone, in the USA as well. Could I recommend the London publisher who might most suitably be entrusted with its publication?

It was a thriller, and the Japanese reader might well be chilled to the marrow by the horror of its opening paragraph:

"Gentle Mr. Yamamoto looked mildly up from his meditations. There, in the garden, framed by the unbelievable beauty of the apple-blossom he saw, with mounting horror, that he was being watched by a pair of sinister *blue* eyes!

"They were not only blue. They were absolutely straight! They were set in the brutish, florid face of Johnny Smith, the villainous Englishman. A round-eyes, Mr. Yamamoto realized with adequate perturbation, here to disturb his immemorial tranquility, his poetical raw-fish dinner..."

Smith: a real villain's name... Recently, my son Tahir Shah had reported, with some puzzlement, a confused exchange over names which had taken place the week before at his English public (which means private) school. The master, during a lesson, had said:

"Now, many English names come from the occupations of our ancestors. Examples are Smith, Wheelwright, Tanner. Now, what do you suppose your forebears were, Shah?"

Tahir Shah, not imagining that there might be adverse consequences, had at once replied, "I suppose they were kings, sir."

This innocent remark was inevitably taken as very bad form. One does not boast, neither does one speak lightly of names, in public schools. You certainly can't get away with saying "I'm descended from kings."

The rule here is similar to that which is observed in the matter of pornography. The information must come out implicitly but inseparably from the narrative. Tahir, as I advised him, should have said, "I don't really know, sir; but I recall a tradition that one of my ancestors had just declared war on the empire next door, when..." Or something of that kind.

Or something on the lines of a fragment I heard the other day at the Club:

"We were all in rather a flap, not least me, at the impending visit of the General. After all, I was only a lowly Colonel at the time..."

Even then, Tahir Shah might not have got away with it. The new Berlitz guide to London warns, "In Britain, children are not really integrated into general life..."

The Japanese novel and the problem in the classroom provided the final impetus for some consideration of the mysteries of English names. I'd had a slight but recurrent desire to go into the matter before: whenever (which was often) people called me Shar, Shore, Snore, even Swarm. In America, for some reason, they always get it right; but the English versatility in spelling and speaking my name is quite impressive. The Irish, whether of North or South, usually manage to render it as Andreas Shaw; less inventive than one would have expected: but reassuring in its consistency.

A major English dictionary enabled me to get to grips with the question. What, after all, could be more promising for the investigator than its list of "The More Common English Christian Names"?

Common perhaps, but with that essentially English quality of being unsuspected until revealed in print. Right at the beginning I wondered why I had never met anyone with the common English name Absolom. Even Almeric had passed me by. I have never known an English Siegfried or even a Sancho.

Christian, no doubt, are both Luther and Xavier (even if the latter does come from the Arabic); but Abraham, Israel and Cyrus? When were they Christianized, and where, among the English, are they common?

Did you know that Igor is a Common English Christian Name? And Casimir (Polish) and Tabitha (Aramaic)? And that Monica, archetypical name of the Head Girl of a myriad school stories – or of the school itself – is "possibly African"?

How Aneurin (Welsh) crept in is easier to guess than the case of another common name: Huldah (Hebrew for a weasel). But how many people are called Maida (origin "obscure")? Incidentally, Australian readers tired of the English criticising their habit of calling a woman a Fair Cow can find some ammunition here. The Common English name Rachel (Hebrew) means "ewe"; and "cow" may well be thought less uncomplimentary than "weasel," which the same dictionary calls active, furtive and bloodthirsty as applied to humans. Cows have, for instance, much nicer eyes.

Desmond is Irish, of course, and Basil is Greek, just as Cordelia is Latin. I admit they are commoner, even if only in Mills and Boon romances, than another common English name listed here: Turlough – pronounced Turlo – a variation of "Rory." It means, I see, "like Thor."

Still, Andreas does mean "manly..."

In case I am giving the impression that the English steal their names from other peoples, let us note that there are four in this intimidating list which are unique to England. Pamela, Vanessa, Lorna and Wendy were all invented by various fiction writers, and have no meaning.

Initially under the impression that the English are casual about the meaning and use of names, I was impressed to find that another source-book, Hadyn's *Dictionary of Dates*, invokes immemorial tradition. It begins its treatment of names by establishing the fact that "Adam and Eve named their sons – Genesis iv. 25, 26." This confident beginning led me to hope that I would now find a weighty, authoritative and detailed treatment of the subject in the succeeding text. Alas, like so much in Englishry, the article soon begins to peter out in what looks like padding – though it may only be Protestant propaganda:

> The popes change their names on their exaltation to the pontificate, a custom introduced by pope Sergius, whose name till then was Swine-snout, 687.

One recalls the English idiom, defined by the great Dr. (E. Cobham) Brewer, LLD: "*To call a person names. To blackguard him...*"

And my search for clues to the English through their names by means of scholarly research ran into the sand with the assertion by a further dictionary: "*NAME*... fictiousness without reality."

The casual English attitude toward names should be more widely understood in the Middle East. I wish I'd had hot dinners as often as I've been assailed with questions on this subject. They generally run: "Are the English illiterate or insulting when they constantly misspell and mispronounce Eastern names?"

Some of the most famous foreign correspondents, and even eminent Orientalists, do not seem to know that there is no such name as "Abdul." It is one half of an always composite name. In desperation, having been held responsible for the "stupidity of the English Press" by three Abduls in one day, I wrote the Editor of *The Times* about it. I got a breezy letter back, "We have taken note of it here." You may be able to guess what has been done in the intervening twenty years.

It is generally believed abroad that an English name can always be recognized as such, by a certain indefinable something. An Indian who wanted to go up-market with his curry paste, renamed himself Thrub Crumblelldon. He told me that people in Bombay scrambled for the delicacy as soon as they read the label, and the "English thudding consonants" hit their ears.

My good friend Nertian Blibian, of good Armenian stock, celebrated his acquisition of British nationality by a change of name. "I have achieved a typically English-sounding name, without losing everything of my own," he told me, proudly displaying his card. It said: "NERT BLIB, British Citizen." Even to me, that sounded less English than the Germano-Celtic Andreas Shaw, or even the Arabic-Irish Xavier Turlough. But I can't explain why.

Talking of Nert, I was interested to discover that he had got at least one thing right. He had shown that he was more English than many a British-born citizen by limiting himself to a single first name.

I learned about this from the *Evening News*, in which a famous columnist wrote, earlier this century:

> A man has never need of two names to make him his Christian name; this is a custom brought in from Germany; it has been custom here but a hundred and fifty years at most.

Not for the real, traditionalist Englishman the solecism of Edward G. Bloggs, or even Edward George Bloggs, for, says the article, "Our first batch was born in the eighteenth century."

I have only one forename myself, which gave me an English advantage long before I was old enough to appreciate it: let alone able to read the *Evening News*. And the subject is of great moment, for the writer goes on to say, "These are important matters, very proper to be debated in any English household that has a baby to be christened." Understood; though the debate in households with babies to be named can cover a wider range of subjects than single or plural naming.

I discovered this when I overheard Mrs. Coggins talking to a fellow-conspirator about a new infant which had appeared in her neighborhood.

Somehow she finds my telephone easier to use than her own. I think it's because I haven't yet splashed out on a shiny new pushbutton one such as everyone who is anyone on Mrs. Coggins's housing development already has.

"And she says, 'What do you think, like?' she says, just like that; and I says to her, I says, 'Well, I'll tell you what I think,' I says, 'that's what I'll do. I'll tell you.' So I says, 'If it was me, I'd know what to do, I would, I don't mind telling you,' I says. And what do you think she says? She says, 'Well, then, what would you do?' she says, just like that, she said it. And I says, 'Well, now you've asked me, and I wouldn't interfere for anything, as you know, I'll tell you what I'd say. I'd say something to the Vicar, that's what I'd do. I'd say – I would – "Vicar, I'll have him baptized, I will; but I'll not have him christened. He'll just have to make up his own mind when he's grown up, when he's ready, what religion he wants to be."' Just the same as what I told them at Harry's school; I said, 'He can learn scripture but I'll not have him taught religion, pore little soul.'"

As she was so busy, I did not have the chance to clear all that detail with Mrs. Coggins. But, looking at the figures, I was not surprised to see the effect which a multitude of Mrs. Cogginses has had upon the christening figures of the Church of England. According to the published records, dissent reached critical mass in 1960, when only a minority of babies were christened in the Kingdom. By 1981, less than 37% were being baptized. The *Evening News* seems to have had little effect upon the encroachment of Germanic habits, since most babies, baptized or otherwise, still have more than one given name.

An Eastern friend dropped in to complain about the unabated use of Abdul in the media while Mrs. Coggins was still on the line: he had been unable to get through to me, and thought I'd taken the phone off the hook. "I'm listening to my research assistant on the subject of English names," I explained, trying to mollify him by letting him read *The Times*'s by then ancient assurance that they had noted the complaint.

"They're not like us, you know," he said. "I've just realized something else very strange about them."

I invited him to elaborate.

"They *need* a sense of the bizarre. They name their children all right: but then they suddenly abbreviate their names, like we do with animals."

"Incredible!" I cried.

"Yes, I thought that would surprise you. I can go further, though it may stretch your credulity. Edward, here, is 'Ted'; Albert is 'Bert,' and Henry is 'Harry.' Whether christened or not, there are hordes of people called such things as Fred, Ron, Don, Bill and Chas. They contract words and use slang."

"They must be crackers and no mistake," I said, "but belt up, Abdul. I'm peckish. Let's go have some din-dins down Ted the Paki's."

Abbreviations had interested me since I received a letter headed "Dear Fellow Life Member of the B Ass" from a member of the British Association for the Advancement of Science. And the mention of slang put me in mind of Peg-Leg. The following day, wondering whether my own name could be successfully Anglified, I went to see him. He was an old acquaintance, Colonel (Hon. Brigadier-General) Peter Winser, a devout Moral Re-Armer, who carried on expert researches into recondite names from his headquarters, a cluster of farm outbuildings north of Oxford.

"Anglification," I said, "as I have determined from the *Oxford Dictionary*, means 'the act or process of making anything English, or conforming to English modes.' Could this be done with my name?"

"My dear chap," he answered, quick as a flash, "nothing could be easier. You see, it's already been done."

"Already done?" I stammered. "That's impossible. I'd have been the first to hear of such a thing myself."

"Why? D'ye imagine you've heard of *everything*?"

"Not everything: just my name. Why did someone do it, then, without telling me?" I felt quite affronted.

"All in good time," said the Hon. Brigadier-General. "First of all, I'll tell you what it is."

I had once met an Englishman whose name had been rendered in Chinese as "Little Circular Lemon Chime," which had a certain charm (if nothing else) but I was not prepared for the war-horse-etymologist's next words.

"Your name, in English," he declaimed, "is NOBCID ENOCH CHECK CHAM." He leaned back on his Ashanti queen's stool, with a benign English expression on his face.

"I won't be called that!" I shouted. "It sounds like some kind of Eskimo Tibetan Lama half-converted by a fundamentalist missionary." Not that I had anything against such a person, as I assured him, but we all have our feelings about things, especially names.

Then he explained.

"Your full name, as I understand it, may be expressed as Nawab Sayed Idries Shah, Khan. That's with various titles front and back."

"Well?"

"Well, where does the word 'Nob' come from?"

"Eighteenth century. Nawabs of India were so rich that people who made their pile there were called, in England, 'Nobs.'"

"First part of your name, do you see."

"All right; but Nobcid?"

"Cid is the Western form of 'Sayed.' Came here via Spain, under the Saracens. El Cid and so on."

"Sounds a bit inelegant, General."

"You might say the same about Witherspoon, for instance. But it's a perfectly good name."

I said, "I have always known that my first name translates as the biblical 'Enoch,' and I thought that was quite enough."

"It is not enough if you want your full name."

"And 'Check'?"

"The Persian word 'Shah' became 'check' in English through the phrase 'checkmate' – *Shah-mat* – literally 'the king is dead,' used in chess."

"And 'Cham'?" I asked, weakly.

"'Cham' is, naturally, what people here called 'Khan.' Genghiz Khan was the Grand Cham in our parlance. Figures in plenty of books, as do all the other names you have."

"General, what if I don't want to use my Anglification?"

"Then, old feller, I'd just stick to the native version if I were you."

At that moment I heard the sound of a car pulling up outside. Rather than be introduced to the General's visitor as Nobcid Cham, I fled, through a side door.

As my train left Charlbury far behind, I comforted myself with the words of Taverner:

> As I say in our Englyshe prouerbe:
> Set the heres head aginst the gose gyblet.

What wisdom there is in these ancient sayings of England.

The trouble is that one always thinks of the ideal riposte when it's too late. I now remembered what hare's head I might have set against the goose's giblet. Only *one* of the words in Nobcid Enoch Check Cham is in fact a name: Enoch. The rest are titles. My actual name, I reflected, is Idries al-Hashimi. I use "Shah" as a surname because I once thought it would be easier for people in the West to pronounce.

I wonder which style the General would advise me to use? In his version, I seem to be a mixture of an East India Company magnate plus, Spanish grandee, together with an Old Testament figure, a board-game and a Mongolian warchief. In my usual name, I seem less unfamiliar in England. "Shah" nowadays offers the choice of a Persian monarch, a newspaper proprietor or an Indian small shopkeeper.

It probably does make a difference, as Nert Blib believed. Would King George VI have seemed so suitable if he had continued to call himself Albert? Would Oliver Cromwell have sounded so redoubtable under his other name? Lord Protector Oliver Williams hasn't, to me, quite got the right ring to it. Like Johnny Smith, the villain of the Japanese novel.

18

Stands to Reason

English Traditions
Nine English traditions out of ten date from the latter half of the nineteenth century.
      C. P. Snow: *The Masters*

HIS HIGHNESS THE Nawab of Chotapur had been told that the English, and especially former public schoolboys, were masochists. He had learnt of this peculiarity from a friend of ours, Sir Hassan Suhrawardy. And Sir Hassan was not only a doctor, but a governor of London University's School of Oriental Studies. And a Member of the Council of the Asiatic Society of London. Surely, if anyone knew, he did.

"They *like* being beaten?" asked the Nawab, hardly able to credit the report. His Highness then offered the sum of £1,000 to each and every Englishman who would visit his state to be "lashed and like it." There were no takers. When the Nawab told me his plan, I had referred him to the Latin: "Do not get your slaves from Britain." The reason which the ancient Roman had given was that they were unreliable and surly, and obviously not delighted at being enslaved. They were not typical masochists. "Demonstration is better than reading," the Nawab said; but, although he waited eagerly for weeks, nobody volunteered.

"There are distinct impediments to the investigation of the English," the Nawab warned me, as if hinting at some Whitehall-inspired plot to prevent him furthering his scientific interests.

Another Nawab, my grandfather (he of Sardhana) found a similar tiresome constraint upon his never-ending curiosity about the English Mystery, as it was sometimes called by us. He used to mull over its significance: the English seemed logical up to a point, and then suddenly reversed their behavior.

One such paradox, so the story went, involved a man who arrived at our domain from London, soliciting orders for a bulletproof vest. He took the next elephant out when he received a note: "The Nawab will be pleased to shoot at you in the vest, to test it, tomorrow at six a.m."

At the Nawab's Durbar the following day, the matter of the Englishman's disappearance was discussed in detail. Nobody had ever questioned that the Great Nawab was a crack shot with a hunting rifle and high-velocity ammunition. The man could not, therefore, have feared the bullet going off target and hitting him, say, between the eyes.

"Perhaps he did not like it here; we may be too far north for him," suggested the Racing Uncle, who was trying to work the discussion around to the need for him to take his horses south for an important meeting.

"Can't imagine who wouldn't like it," said the Military Uncle, "there's plenty of shooting."

"Perhaps he sought our ancient talisman for success and against impotence, and funked it at the last moment," ventured another grandee.

But this was just the warm-up period. Everyone knew that, after the tentative opinions, my grandfather would speak.

The signal soon came, as the grand old man cleared his throat with a sound locally referred to as not unlike boulders rolling down the slopes of the Hindu Kush.

"Stands to reason, *malumdar ast*," he said.

"Yes, Highness. Stands to reason," came the chorus. One does not disagree with a Nawab in full durbar.

"The English actually *like* Nawabs, don't they? Look at that fellow Pataudi, cricketer. Cheer him to the echo."

"To the echo, High Presence."

"Use the name for themselves, too, to denote power and magnificence. Of course they mispronounce it 'Nabob.'"

"Mispronounce it 'Nabob,' O Point toward which the Compass Needle Turns, O *Qiblagah*."

"Exactly. You see what I mean. It wasn't dislike. It must have been that the vest was no good."

"The vest was no good, *Sahib-al-Siyada*, Lord of Princeliness."

A generation later, two of the Nawab's grandsons, my cousin Mirza Aqil-Hussain Khan, The Barlas, and I, walked into a gunsmith's in the West End. The old man in charge of the place suggested that we might care to be measured for shotguns while we were in Town. We weren't in the mood for it, and I idly asked about the padded garment displayed on a dummy.

"There's a story about those," said the gun man, "which concerns an Eastern potentate who doubted the efficacy of our bulletproof vests." He closed his eyes, as if praying for forgiveness for even quoting such a heresy, and pursed his lips. Then he told us the story of his partner and the Nawab of Sardhana, our grandfather.

"My partner," he said, "had to make it plain that an Englishman's word could not be questioned without some sort of reaction, so he left at once."

The Mirza's eyes met mine, briefly, and then he asked, "Do you think that this potentate, whatever his name was, really registered the rebuke?"

"Oh, I should think he did, sir."

As the Mirza and I strolled through the mysterious streets of London, and past the Jermyn Street tailor whose window proclaimed that he was By Appointment to His Majesty King Amanullah of Afghanistan (who hadn't been King since 1929, half a century before), I said, "Penny for your thoughts, Aqil."

"I was only thinking," he said, "what a terrible waste it is: all these amazing people, now without an empire."

I intend to ask Aqil Khan next time I see him whether this thought was prompted by his public-school background or by his own ancestral traditions. Aqil, you see, is, on his father's side, of the Clan of Barlas, from which sprang the great conqueror and empire-builder Timur the Lame, known to the English as Tamerlane. Did Aqil just believe that everyone should have his own empire, or was it nostalgia for the British Raj? And I'll tell him that the Empire is still in business.

This recollection was prompted by a television documentary film shown in England. In it, the young and promising English producer argued that the Empire was itself a manifestation of English masochism. What would the Nawab of Chotapur have thought of that? Perhaps that the British were too busy torturing themselves with imperial responsibility to take up his munificent offer to be lashed in the cause of science.

I repeated the bulletproof vest story to an English authority for comment.

He was Brigadier Sir John Smyth, holder of the Victoria Cross and formerly head of extensive, if locally unwelcome, operations on the North-West Frontier. Oddly enough, he looked and talked rather like my grandfather. When he started to talk, he cleared his throat in a similar alarming manner – and he even used the same phrase:

"Stands to reason," he growled, "stands to reason. There were quite enough Afghans shooting at the English without our seeking it, without some damn fool of a London boxwallah accepting further invitations. The British Resident warned him, shouldn't wonder."

It gets easier, in some ways, as you go along, this English thing: it's a matter of putting yourself into the right frame of mind. Until you do, you'll be a prisoner of assumptions; missing the point of what you're doing, like the roast-meat vendor on a pilgrimage to Mecca, in the Afghan legend. He spent all his time calculating how many kabobs could be made from the meat of his camel.

19

Smoke and Frozen Tiger

English Happiness
An Englishman is never happy but when he is miserable.
    Archbishop Whateley: *Commonplace-Book*

SOME OF MY best friends are French, I have first to say: but eating in England may well be safer for the uninitiated. I base this claim on my escape from a culinary incident, when I was invited by a friend to lunch at "the best restaurant in Paris."

My host and guide was Russell Page, the English landscape gardening architect; he not only had an OBE for his work on the design of the Festival Gardens, but was accepted in Europe as a Perfect English Gentleman. In England he was better known as an authority on France.

Page was sure to be right, so I went with him. After an hour recovering from the British Airways breakfast, we were seated, toying with our napkins, when the chef de cuisine himself was brought out by the *Patron* to discuss the precise origins, content, preparation and presentation of the meal: an extraordinary touch of graciousness, I thought. It also had the advantage of taking so much time that I was ravenous.

When we were served, it seemed only a moment before the hors d'oeuvre plates were whipped away, as the head waiter whispered, "We cannot keep the Chef waiting," and my steak was brought in, with great solemnity.

The perfection of the procession of waiters was marred only for a moment by one of them who offered me a dish from the wrong side. Fortunately, decorum was restored by the head waiter's hissing "Hypocrite!" at him, elaborating to me with a conspiratorial smile and the words, "To call himself a waiter is assuredly the act of a hypocrite, *m'sieu*."

I had been living in England and naturally, though I forbore from asking for ketchup or Worcestershire sauce, I automatically said, "Some salt and mustard, please."

It was then that everyone within hearing shrank from me as people in a Bateman cartoon do from the solecist of the era. After a *sotto voce* consultation, someone scuttled into the kitchen, to be greeted almost at once by a Krakatoan roar and out leaped – the Chef himself. Waving a long, thin knife in the air, he snarled, "*OUT, je vous en prie, m'sieu!* OUT! That it should come to this: someone claiming that MY steak should lack anything required by a discerning palate!"

Yes, it really did happen: otherwise I might have stayed in Paris. The English had predisposed me in its favor; for reasons of their own, perhaps to get rid of us foreigners, they constantly rave that it is "the only place to be." When they are at home, that is.

My Paris experience has a bearing on the English question. It shows how a limited exposure to a nation can condition one's whole attitude toward it. I don't know how long you need for France. In the case of England I can testify that it takes a full quarter of a century before the amazing experiences, mostly triggered by your own behavior, begin to become less frequent.

I am fairly sure that the great English proconsul Lord Curzon must have spent only a short time in France. This would account for one of his more memorable utterances, which has caused some puzzlement both here and abroad.

When told that the Egyptians were showing a preference for the French language over English, he immediately, and magisterially, replied:

"French is good enough for the Egyptians."

Even Sir Harold Nicolson cannot help remarking that the patrician Curzon spoke with a Derbyshire accent.

Of course, eating is not all plain sailing in England. There is a law, for instance, which forbids fish and chip shops to sell fish and chips on Sunday – though they may sell other things. And, although chips are a favorite item of diet, someone recently published the uncomfortable fact that the chips (and deep-fat frying) were introduced from France.

There is even an underground movement to make coffee more popular. I have the following from a coffee-importer, who insists that I put it in my book. Tea has been the national drink for only a short time, a couple of hundred years or so. Samuel Pepys noted, in 1660, that it was "Tee, a China drink which I never drank before." Worse still, when it was first introduced, English people ate the leaves and threw the liquid away.

Food is not only a nutrient, in England: it is also part of the national activity in which words are given multiple meanings, and the word concretized into the thing. As with other areas of English life, this dauntingly philosophical concept is internalized throughout the community. Everyone does it. Elsewhere, to give a thing a name and then to change the thing accordingly is done only by advanced metaphysical masters. In England, for example, the verb "to cook" means both "to prepare as food by heat" and also "to falsify, concoct, ruin, spoil."

The matter of eating is complicated by the English habit of giving as many things as possible foreign names. I have seen an Indian foaming at the mouth with rage, if not with duck, at being offered a dried fish, the bummalo, known as Bombay Duck. He was from Bombay, and had eaten real duck there. He seemed to think that the dish as known in London was some kind of insult to India.

(I feel that his chauvinism was exceptional. My reason for saying this is based on an experience of my own in Bombay, which seemed to show a lack of touchiness on the part of the Indians which an old-time Rajite would have called Very English. I had been introduced to a large gathering as the man who had quoted, in a book, the words of a Central Asian poet, sweltering in the heat: "The ways of Allah are wonderful. He had Hell, yet He still created India!" There was tremendous applause.)

When I made it known, in London, that I was interested in reactions to English behavior, I found myself almost besieged by foreigners with grievances relating to misnomers. There was perplexity at the term *French leave*, deserting one's post; at *Dutch* – alcohol-induced – courage; at *German*, imitation, silver.

There was Iberian outrage at the description of a jellyfish as a *Portuguese* Man-of-War; and consternation at a certain breed of rabbit being called a Belgian Giant. Why, I have been asked, should *American* cloth be the name for such an inferior material?

All I could do in the interests of Anglo–other relations (which, inexplicably, I found myself obliged to assist) was to murmur that it was the English who liked to call the less attractive young members of their own community "Street Arabs." But that annoyed an Arab, too.

Much of this kind of talk took place in England at meals. In the East, of course, we generally eat in silence. On the Continent, more often than not, food is the occasion of declamation and debate. This may be the reason why foreigners got so hot and bothered, while eating, as they brought up matters of English "vulgarity." But the supposed tactlessness of the English is often due to sensitivity on the part of their observers.

Careful study convinces me that very few of the things they say or do are intended as deliberately insulting. I did not, myself, feel affronted at the discovery that *Afghan* Bands, sold in conjurors' stores in London, are mere rings of paper which burn easily. Afghan dogs are what *we* call Arabians, *Tazis*: so that can hardly count. And, of course, an "Afghan Salaam" is our word for the throwing of a home-made grenade at would-be conquerors, mostly Englishmen, during the less felicitous days of our relationship.

Another, innocent, reason for renaming as many things as possible only makes things more complicated. The English sometimes adopt random names for things, because they seem more exotic than would "Liverpool silver" or "Little Puddleton cloth." The English, too, often seem to have an inspired or poetic, as distinct from a Continental-systematic, attitude toward words and what they mean. After all, it is not uncommon to hear quoted the phrase "words mean what I want them to mean."

Sir David Ross, then Vice-Chancellor of Oxford University, no less, once did that to me. Indeed, he did more. He was a considerable scholar, who could live, to a degree, in the past. I had known him for some time when he invited me to tea and handed me his Greek-keyboard portable typewriter. "You mentioned, I believe, that you were an Afghan," he said. "Excellent. Greco-Buddhist civilization. Just type a few words in Greek on this for me and get it to work better, will you? I think it needs repairing."

He was right about Greek being known by Afghans: but he was about two thousand years out in his dating. As for being a Greek-speaking typewriter mechanic: some foreigners would have had a short fuse about this; Turks, for example, might have wondered what Sir David was implying.

Associations have more than a little to do with this. After all my own father, a hundred per cent Afghan in mind, was apt to refer to someone he didn't much like – irrespective of his name – as "that fellow Galbraith" almost certainly because of some ancient association.

My amazement, recklessly expressed in print once or twice, at the relaxed work of some English (and other British) Orientalists, has at times generated powerful hostility. But that was in their own fraternity. Non-academics knew instinctively that these "chaps were being rather unEnglish because scholarly competitiveness is an import of European mainland habits." I got many letters of commiseration.

That the behavior of some pedants may stem from a very unEnglish sense of inferiority is vouched for by no less an authority than Prince Philip, Duke of Edinburgh, who has publicly stated that academic institutions are brilliantly designed to make people feel inadequate. I have not the temerity to disagree.

This is exactly the accusation leveled by foreigners at the behavior of the English. The difference is, of course, that the Continental import called education here *is* designed to put people down. The English one is more of a honing device, aimed at sharpening your perceptions and forming you into a sturdier product. It is intended, primarily, to be used by the English on the English.

Fortified by His Royal Highness's statement, I quote the extraordinary performance of one major English dictionary. The etymologies advanced include Persian words confidently labeled Turkish, Urdu or even Sanskrit. Arabic words are ascribed to the Persian tongue; Pushtu ones may be called "Indian" – though whether Blackfoot, Cherokee or other is not specified.

This louche attitude toward words may have implications in the culinary sphere: if it has no deeper, instructional, meaning. Its influence on the Indian (often, in fact, Pakistani or Bangladeshi) eating-places in England has to be experienced to be believed. If you add to the easyrider attitude of the English toward meanings the wedding of Hindu-Muslim-Turkic-Afghan cultures which had already occurred in India, you have a recipe for vertigo.

Let us now enter your typical Indian restaurant and chance our luck. Addressing yourself to the menu, especially when told by a timid guest to "choose because you know the lingo," you soon find enough familiar Persian or Central Asian words to feel that rush of self-confidence which will precede your downfall. Yes, they are all there: *pilau/pilao*, spiced rice; *murgh*, chicken; *kofta*, meatballs.

Then it starts to penetrate. *Tunduri?* This can mean "thunder." *Sag?* Persian for dog. *Tikka*, for heaven's sake, *tikka* is a lump or a torn scrap. *Pasanda* (favorite) is spelled Pursida, "questioned."

One day Abdus-Sattar Khan, an Afghan diplomat, and I went into an Indian restaurant in a university town in England and ordered, from their Mogul cuisine, and in impeccable Mogul dialect, the following: "Smoke, torn thundering dog and frozen tiger." We were served with the equivalent in the Indian-English convention: milk, baked spinach and ice cream. The "Question" dish, which we also risked, indeed turned out to be pasanda, the "preferred, favorite."

Yet eating is not the only important thing in life, and some of the English have shown that they are as conciliatory toward their former enemies as the Afghans can be. I offer this interpolation because this is just what I was told when I mentioned the food question to my host while dining at the House of Lords. Maybe you can see the connection.

"Take the case of Lord Leatherhead, speaking of the Battle of Waterloo in 1972, a hundred and fifty-seven years afterward," my host said. While I was struggling to find the link, he started to quote Lord Leatherhead:

"It is somewhat tactless to print on the back of the £5 note a picture of British gunners blowing the French army to blazes and accompanying it with a large portrait of the Duke of Wellington."

Twelve years later, perhaps as a result of Lord Leatherhead's high-level gesture of conciliation, the President of France visited England. Although there were rumblings from Scotland Yard when a member of M. Mitterand's suite brought some explosives with him, he did, after all, bury them in the garden of their Ambassador's own residence. Accustomed to eccentricity at home, the London newspapers tended to treat the matter lightly, with both cartoons and lampoons.

My host went on to recall how Lord Hailsham, the Lord Chancellor, welcomed the distinguished visitor with appropriate courtesy in the Royal Gallery at Westminster. He even went so far as to appropriate, in his speech, the Roman conqueror of England, C. Julius Caesar, as one of the great things which France had given Britain. The other benefits included roads, walled towns, plumbing and the French language. Further, he cried, in French of a sort, "Long Live France! Long Live the French throughout the World! Long Live Western Civilization!" For good measure, he added, "Long Live the Christians!"

A few days before, a correspondent in *The Times* had been regretting the disappearance of the French text from the labels on bottles of a well-known English proprietary sauce. This day, however, someone else wrote to say that this may have been because English sauce disguises the taste of food, instead of improving it. Perhaps that, too, was a sign of goodwill toward Gaul from Albion on this auspicious occasion.

Of course, it takes time to modify history. The gunners firing at the French on the £5 notes, alas, remained. And, as Godfrey Barker recorded in the *Daily Telegraph*, the huge murals covering the walls of the Royal Gallery were still there. The assembled legislators, unable to understand the French speech, looked reflectively around them, and noted that they "tastefully depicted English soldiers trampling the French under horse at Agincourt and Waterloo and bloodily slaughtering them." The Angles couldn't have done any better.

Things take time, as they say over here. The English, though, have forgiven the Indians their rising of 1857, and the Pakistanis their withdrawal from the Commonwealth: and eat their food in large quantities.

As to the Commonwealth itself, the largest association of states in the world other than the United Nations, there is another mystery to point out. The most intense research, even in England, has failed to determine exactly what the Commonwealth – called, even by *The Times*, a "curious organization" – really is.

I have checked this out, on behalf of my foreign readers. Contriving to obtain an introduction to John Kenneth Thompson, CMG, Director of the Commonwealth Institute in London, former diplomat and Governor of the Centre for International Briefing, I asked the question forthrightly: "What *is* The Commonwealth?"

Naturally he did not answer in similar terms, but referred me to the Common Ideas agreed by Commonwealth leaders during his directorship. They are:

World Peace and Order
Equal Rights for all Citizens
The Liberty of the Individual

Opposition to Colonial Domination
Opposition to Racial Oppression
The Resolve to Achieve a Fairer Society.

Both Marxist and United States ideologists, unfortunately, claim primacy in all these concepts, whether they practice them or not.

For a time, with the increasing interest in food over here, the English seemed to be moving, slowly but steadily, toward forgiving the French their horsemeat and frogs' legs. Then, quite recently, things accelerated, so this area is worth watching. France is getting closer.

Philip Howard, in *The Times*, stresses that genealogists have traced the Huguenot, French Protestant, ancestry of the Princes William and Henry through no less than fifteen lines of descent. He draws the obvious conclusion:

"Next time you are tempted to make some irritable chauvinistic remark about the French, remember, we too are French."

Are they planning to take over France? I have decided, in any case, to forget the incident in the Paris restaurant. And yet I confess that I do feel safer eating in England. A gourmet, indeed, would quickly place me as one of those barbarians who would never understand the inspired words attributed to the Savoy's Escoffier: "I would a hundred times rather risk Devil's Island or even the guillotine than live on the alleged food of England."

Escoffier, of course, died some years ago. If he had lived until the 1980s, he would have learned that the world championship for snail-eating – 3 minutes, 45.78 seconds to consume a kilo of them – was held by Peter Dowdeswell, from Earls Barton, Northamptonshire, in England. And that the English, though late starters, can win at most things, if they put their minds to it.

England teaches, above all, the curse and folly of expectations. Why, after all, rely upon dictionaries? Why expect an Indian restaurant to name its food correctly? Why assume a cook won't chase you away with a knife, that German silver comes from Germany – and all the rest?

One form of this teaching is carried out through hoaxes. The English do not need foreigners, for instance, because they can manufacture them when desired. Eldred Pottinger was a spy in Herat, and nobody realized that he was English. The Afghans, looking at his turban and noting that he knew nothing about Islam, took him for an Indian horse-dealer from Kutch. Another Englishman, it is alleged, became a high-ranking officer in Hitlerite Germany; Sir Richard Burton posed as a Middle Easterner when he felt like it; Cyril Hoskins of Plymouth became Lobsang Rampa, the Lhasa doctor with the third eye. "Dr. Emil Busch, colleague of Professor Freud" was in reality an English undergraduate, George Edinger: and he completely fooled Oxford University. The greatest hoaxer of them all, Horace de Vere Cole, became the Sultan of Zanzibar's uncle and took in the Royal Navy...

Odd, somehow, that English hoaxers so often revert to the Germanic or Eastern roles, characters of the lands of their penultimate and ancientest forebears.

The trouble with us foreigners is that, in the words of the fool in our own proverb, we jump to conclusions, or try to comfort ourselves (or both) with the phrase "*Tomorrow there will be apricots.*" Not so the English.

20

Demons of the Upper Air

The Americans are English, Too...
Be proud of those strong sons of thine
Who wrenched their rights from thee!
    Tennyson: *England and America in 1782*

THE SAD, ANGLOPHILE Dane asked me, in his cups, why the drunken mate on a ship in a storm, who treacherously threatens the English captain with a Swedish knife in English fiction, is so often a Scandinavian madman called Larsen.

His interest, unlike mine, was not entirely objective, since he was himself seldom sober, carried a spring-knife, was from one of the Nordic democracies – and was called Larsen. I could see why he was interested, but could think of no answer.

But the question nagged away in my mind, for I had been in England long enough to know that things here are seldom what they seem. Then, one day, I saw it all in a flash. *Things are not always what they seem*: indeed they are often intended to be the exact reverse, or as much so as makes little difference.

I rang Larsen in Copenhagen to tell him the great discovery – that of Reverse Reality. I explained to his wife, who had answered the telephone, that when the English wrote about mad Danish mates attacking English captains they really meant that mad English mates attacked sane Danish captains, or something.

I am not sure that the tidings got through to Larsen. He was, so the lady told me, under arrest following some fracas involving a switchblade and the master of a ship registered at Liverpool.

Still, that did not necessarily invalidate the point. The English, when closely and correctly studied, emerge as the most Oriental people this side of the Orient itself. And more Oriental than some in the Far East, come to that: I saw plenty of very Westernized people in Singapore.

Following the Reversing Law, you look totally Oriental when you say, in London, "Of course you mustn't dream of running me home" when you desperately want to be delivered there in the blinding rain at three in the morning.

You say "Quite frankly..." when frank is the last thing you are going to be. You say "Thank you so much" when you do not mean it. And you say "Sorry!" when someone steps on *your* foot. Just as your master the tax-man calls himself *your* obedient servant.

This theory explains a host of anomalies previously classified as baffling to science. Of course it plays merry hell with the world of learning: but it has the merit of showing that you have to be a genius to appear as stupid as the expert who labeled, for instance, the Sheffield Coin.

In this celebrated affair, an object in the museum at South Shields, England, was labeled "A Roman Serstice 135–138 AD."

A nine-year-old, among the visitors to the museum, was able without great difficulty to show that this venerable relic was no coin but in fact a *plastic* free gift originating from a soft drinks firm. See what I mean? The child was relatively uneducated, had not yet learned the law that things have to be presented as their opposites if possible, and if not possible at least as something other than they are.

This tendency is especially marked in the case of drinks of all kinds, among the English. Perhaps, therefore, the clue to the mystery of the coin which was not a coin at all may be sought in the fact that it was issued by a drinks firm. Students may care to note that, for the English, Root Beer is not beer at all; Hungary Water is not water; Red Biddy is not a lady but a powerful alcoholic drink.

The English taste for debunkery and their inexplicable way with drinks is underlined in the matter of the famous Earl Grey tea, which some are said to regard as a pure and elegant tea. H. J. Weaver, however, in his *Seeds of Change* (London 1985) makes it clear that Earl Grey, despite its name, originated as the very reverse:

"The bergamot-flavoured Earl Grey, now regarded as a 'great tea,' started as a standard adulteration to spin out a shortage."

There is a weaving and ducking, a feinting and a display of fancy footwork among the English which cannot but command admiration. Intricate, shot through with learning and sophistication, as stylized as a ballet, this way of thought and action can, surely, not be excelled by the most complicated Oriental...

But why do it at all, why be so Oriental? I found out by asking a Chinese gentleman why *they* do it. He was a Hong Kong sage visiting the country. After nodding sagely, he took me to a Chinese wedding. Here the minister (a Methodist) gave a long address in which he averred that the couple who had just been joined would have short, unhappy and penniless lives. This, explained the Chinese professor, was traditional. It was intended for the ears of the malevolent Demons of the Upper Air, who, believing that havoc was already scheduled to be wrought upon the pair, would then fly contentedly away to seek a more promising target for their activities.

Feel free to use my method to determine why, for instance, a Welsh Rabbit is not Welsh or rabbit, but bread and cheese, toasted. The Chinese gentleman was convinced that it is because people in England had a superstition that demons would try to attack, consume or otherwise interfere with, toasted bread and cheese. If they were to attack a *Welsh rabbit*, however, what Englishman would lose sleep over that?[4] And perhaps, by the same token, these demons are so fond of restaurant food that The Athenaeum and other clubs have found it prudent to label their restaurants *coffee* rooms. Evidently demons don't like coffee...

There seems to be an element of not tempting providence (a well-known English adjuration) here. How otherwise can we, as mere foreigners, explain the following passage in an English educational book which I consulted to find out why the child refused to accept that "A Roman Serstice, 135–138 AD" was the correct description of a plastic token. I reproduce the paragraph in full; for the incredulous, it is from *Reading Without Tears*, Longmans, Part I, London, July 1936, p. 9:

> Happily, children are generally too inattentive to derive injury from learning; but when, through a docile, studious, or ambitious disposition, they follow their parents' wishes, and apply with diligence year after year to their studies – too often health, mental power, and even life are sacrificed.

---

[4] They've done better than that: they have renamed it "rarebit": "*Welsh rabbit*, melted cheese, with or without ale, &c., poured over hot toast – sometimes written, 'Welsh rarebit' by wiseacres" (*Chambers Twentieth Century Dictionary*).

Most people, if asked to date this extract, would place it in the nineteenth century at the latest. But it comes from the enlightened nineteen-thirties.

Don't work too hard, then, is the message, diligence can damage your health.

Hence, Dutch courage is not courage at all, Westminster Abbey is not an abbey, it is a church, turkeys do not come from Turkey, the West Indies are not in the Indies, a Young Turk is hardly ever young and, in England, he never is a Turk.

Of course, not all cases which appear anomalous to outsiders (which is also an English word for "one not considered fit to associate with," my dictionary says) can be attributed to deliberate anti-upper-air-demon work. Sometimes the demons seem to have made a breakthrough. Look at a few reports in the London Press.

A machine which was believed to have helped patients by means of electro-convulsive therapy was found not to have been working at all; an inn near Tavistock, whose purpose was to attract customers, was deemed "too popular" by the parish council; a dog caused a lamp-post to explode by lifting its leg against it; and a police constable's belief in God was killed by a flood of pious leaflets through his letter-box.

The English, their institutions and even at least one of their electroshock machines, will perform contrary to expectations. Why, why, why? cry the foreigners. The *Guardian*, though one of their most "concerned" newspapers, has called "the British disease": "our predilection to advise, evaluate and judge rather than actually [to] do anything."

I trace this behavior to the deeply embedded characteristic first noticed by Professor Kenneth de Burgh Codrington of London University.

"The 'Need to Disagree'" (he told me in a letter), "so marked among us English, is actually at the root of our

English discovery of the Principle of Compromise: the famous English tendency to compromise."

I had told the Professor that I was going to write a book on the English or, at least, about experiences in their country. This had produced the reflection that, since the English are always doing so much judging, evaluating and advising, many of them must disagree – and the Principle of Compromise was born out of the need for peace.

Codrington expanded his theory in relation to my project:

"If, in your book, you mention well-known people, some will love it. Others, for no better reason, will say that you are name-dropping. If you don't identify the sources of your anecdotes, some will lose interest. If you go into detail, some will say that you are tedious – others will love it. If you don't, you'll be called a skimper. Be critical and they'll say you have a chip on your shoulder. Praise us, and we'll fear you're fawning. It is this kind of mind which made us literary critics, scientists, a pluralist society and a great, if impossible, nation. We are rather like the Afghans."

Codrington, I reflected, must know how alike the English and the Afghans are; he spent years in Afghanistan, speaking the language and becoming a member of a Sufi fraternity.

A reputable churchman of my acquaintance, upon whom I tested the Chinese demon theory, to check whether English people believed in such things, agreed at once. He averred that "much of what we nowadays call research is inspired by the Devil." He went on a lot longer in this vein, and what I gathered from it all was that the things which disappointed him were always diabolical in origin. As an Englishman, heir to the Law of Reverse Reality, he had theologized the secular, just as English laymen had, naturally, secularized theology.

Certainly, if we were (wrongly) to assume that the English have sacrosanct beliefs, we would still find a great number of them in the debunking business. They seem to delight in showing how things can't possibly be what they seem or are thought to be. Woe betide anyone who tries to confute an Englishman's beliefs by casting doubt on any of his traditions. The Englishman will be able to carry off the game, set and match by showing that some Englishman has already done so. And this is, I think, their great secret: *it is almost impossible to find out what will undermine them*. They are in a sense in league, at least in part, with the Demons of the Upper Air.

King Canute was not foolish, as formerly taught, the experts now swear, but wise, giving an object lesson to his foolish courtiers. The National Anthem? It's not an anthem, it's a prayer, as Patience Strong once explained. King Arthur "probably never existed." The Crusaders? "A bunch of ruffians. Look how they sacked Christian Constantinople." The English really came from Schleswig-Holstein? "Well, what about it?" Is the weather/climate terrible? "Doesn't stop tourists, political refugees – and you – from coming here, does it? AND without it we would never have invented the electric fan or central heating, would we?" The Celts may hiss at them; some of the Welsh even burn down their vacation cottages: but the *English* are running the show. "Not really, some of my best friends are Scots, Irish, Welsh..."

Then, what about Napoleon's Perfidious Albion, eh? Ah, it's not even original:

"It was said earlier by Bossuet. And he said, in any case, 'La Perfide Angleterre.' Attacked the country, you see, not the people."

And, still on matters military, I see that General F. M. Richardson for years insisted in his lectures at Camberley Staff College both that British regiments are not old and that some of the finest officers and men in Scottish highland regiments "have been, and still are, English."

And I, I have just realized, seem to have caught the British disease identified by the *Guardian*: to advise, evaluate and judge rather than actually doing anything. But what, exactly, *can* one do?

Not a lot, as the English would say. Their advising, evaluating and judging can devastatingly demolish almost anyone's beliefs.

Most Americans are friendly toward the English. At the same time, they all know that their forefathers fought a war of independence against the British. Or did they? According to one stream of thought in the United Kingdom, the Americans did *not* fight a war for their freedom against Britain. It was the *British* who won that war. How so? You may well ask.

The matter is quite obvious, as I have been straightfacedly informed: the American colonists were of British stock, fighting a German king, George of Hanover. And his troops included thousands of Germans, Hessians. Naturally the Real British, the Colonists, won.

As one among many, the best-selling novelist and historian Charlotte M. Yonge, puts it, in her *Christian Names*:

> In speaking of England we include not only our colonies but America.

Do I hear someone mutter "just try telling that to the Yanks"? Well, you might do so with impunity. The British have even got the Americans to believe it. Just look in Ralph Waldo Emerson's *English Traits*:

> There [in America] and not here [in England] is the seat and centre of the British race.

No wonder Larsen the Dane was confused about whether the British liked his countrymen or not: things are never as simple as so many good Scandinavians feel entitled to expect. In England, it seems to me, people have the attitude of our own sage Jalaluddin Rumi, who wrote, "The life of this world is a truce between opposites."

So the Americans were British. But now, surely, they are fully independent, no longer a colony, and certainly not subject to British manipulation? So it might appear to some people: the British know better.

According to an article (WESTWARD, LOOK, THE LAND IS BRITISH runs the headline) of October 28, 1984, "the US is still our first colony." Its author, Sir Alastair Burnet, in his closing words, explains why this may still be news to you: "After all, isn't it our business to keep quiet about how we're still manipulating the place?"

Things, as I tried to tell Larsen, are indeed not always what they seem. That is why I recommend inquirers to try my secret formula, the procedure I always use in England when I feel that I can't handle things anymore.

I go out on to the roof, praying that it is not an overcast night. Then I search the skies for some familiar sight. If I can then see, say, the Big Dipper, in its right place, I am fairly certain that I am still on my native planet.

Then I go to my calligraphic copy of the *Quatrains of Omar Khayyam* and read

> All bewildered, 'tween certainty and doubts
> The people are pondering about belief and sect.
> Suddenly, a herald from concealment shouts:
> "Ignorant ones! The way is neither this nor that."

Yes, Khayyam, you have to use a specialized approach all right.

21

Just Before Albania

Goddam
In spite of their hats being very ugly, Goddam!
I love the English.
                Pierre Jean de Beranger: *Les Boxeurs*

HATS were first manufactured in England by Spaniards in 1510... Every person above seven years of age to wear on Sundays and holidays a cap of wool, knit, made, thickened and dressed in England by some of the trade of cappers, under the forfeiture of three farthings for every day's neglect, 1571.
                Joseph Hadyn: *Dictionary of Dates*

IT IS NOT difficult to journey from the center of London to the seat of the Mother of Parliaments of the United Kingdom, but I nearly missed it. Parliament is British, not English alone, because the country is a sort of federation. Lots of foreigners do not know this, but then many English people don't, either.

The *Oxford English Dictionary*, invoked – and accepted – as an authority in a thousand law cases, actually speaks of someone being "Naturalized English," though this is a legal impossibility. There is no English nationality. The London

Library, which I had just left, places books about the history of the United Kingdom, including the Celtic portions, firmly under "England." Just as decisively, I noticed with a shiver, it says, under "Immigration," that one must "see EMIGRATION."

I was not surprised when, asking a policeman the way to the British Parliament, I was directed to the British Museum for information. "Or you could try the Commonwealth Institute, in Kensington." At the time I was standing almost in the shadow of the Parliament's century-old, Victorian-Gothic pile which tourists naturally imagine to be of immense age. Nobody thinks of it as British: why should the local policeman? English is the word.

But, once over the tricky question of the English Parliament, I found the local police well informed. "That's the Commons, sir; it's called the House of Commons, but they haven't actually got a house."

"No House? Then where do they meet?"

"Where I said, over there. Only it's called the Palace of Westminster."

"Why can't they have a house of their own? Common people in a Palace?"

"If I were you, sir, I'd ask *them* that. None of my business."

This was probably sound advice. A lord might have been unable to help, if Lord Maynard was anything to go by. Someone mentioned the House of Commons in his presence; his reaction was "Is that going on still?"

Iceland and the Isle of Man, to name but two of dozens, dispute this assembly's claim to be the oldest democratic institution in the world. Members of an Afghan *jirga* would consider even these two as rather modern, and assert a primacy dating back thousands of years. But that sort of thing is for specialists: as, I believe, is any reference to what I saw and heard of a debate from the strangers' gallery.

I sent my name in to the Member who had kindly agreed to see me, and looked at my notes, prepared by an English friend. "Although essentially the house of the Common People, Parliament in England is the last place where you should ever use the word *common* to refer to its Members..."

As I waited, in the lobby, I heard a visitor asking questions from an old hand. "But if it's called 'lobbying,' why don't they allow all these people into the lobby?"

"Oh, they'd only be in the way. Just a term we use, you see."

"And the petitions? Surely they realize that nothing can be done at this stage of a Bill, so why do they hire motor-coaches and swarm about outside?"

"Well, they like it, you know. They really understand that nothing can be done to stop the new highway. But they like to know that they have done their best. Makes them feel that they are taking part in the democratic process."

I recalled three phrases chosen by Ms. Sofer, in *The Times*, to represent English thinking: "Live and Let Live"; "Best of a Bad Job"; "Better Luck Next Time..."

These could very well be the mottoes of the British electorate, I thought: and very probably were. The voting patterns of the people defeat the forecasters. In spite of the supposedly rigid class-system of the country, masses of workers regularly voted for the Conservatives, who were, at the same time, well known for grinding the faces of the toiling masses.

Perhaps this was because less than one-seventh of the electors, when the matter was investigated, could be found to have working-class characteristics.

In between elections, over half of the voters switched loyalties, so that no party could really tell what the people thought or what they would think, almost from one moment to the next. Does this reflect cynicism, I wondered, or wisdom:

the fact that when you ask people in England what they think of the political parties, most of them say, "Well, they're all the same, aren't they?"

Certainly, here in the House of Commons, one could not tell Labour Members from Conservatives, unless (as was unusual) they were wearing red or blue ties. In England, I had noticed, there were more and more people saying that candidates only stood for Parliament as a means to gain power of some sort; pointing to the number of Conservatives who seemed uninterested in their constituents: or to the Labourites who were singing the Red Flag at one moment and turning up the next as members of the peerage, and buying farms in the agricultural shires.

Or was there some deep-seated, unperceived, Anglean or Saxon logic working its way through the electors and elected alike? "Load not upon a day the burden of a year," I counseled myself with the old Afghan proverb, and sat calmly until a messenger, every inch an old sweat, called out, "Your Member should be coming now, sir, if you'll pardon the expression." A perfect ex-NCO's double entendre.

My Member, it turned out, was a volatile Welshman, who represented a constituency which was largely Anglo-Saxon. I asked him if many Englishmen were elected by Welsh electorates. "Never: we wouldn't stand for that kind of nonsense in the valleys, boyo," was his reply.

He refused to discuss anything Saxon, let alone Anglean. The thought of a Saxon Witenagemot as precursor of Parliament only annoyed him. When I mentioned the Tudor sovereigns of England, however, he brightened up. "The proper name is Tewdwr, and don't you forget it," was his only stricture. "Good Welsh name, before the English mucked it up. But," he continued reflectively, "mebbe they did it themselves. Any fool would know that the English would never allow themselves to be ruled by Celts whose name was pronounced Tewuddwyr."

With neo-Gothic determination, the architect of the building had made the main hall of the place so cavernous that one felt absolutely dwarfed. Guides showing people around speak in hushed tones, alluding reverently to the ancient traditions in a way which quite unnerves transatlantic visitors, who seldom register that it is a Victorian building whose first stone was laid in 1840.

One day such a party was being shown around, and feeling suitably impressed, when Lord Hailsham appeared. Waving to a friend, Neil Marten MP, he called out, "Neil!" As soon as they heard the word, the entire American group obediently knelt.

"There's a group of American lawyers," my Member said, pointing to a self-consciously serious clump of craning figures, "on their way to Runnymede, near Windsor. I wonder what they would think if they knew that the final confirmation of Magna Carta, the basis of their freedoms, has been repealed: and then only in a schedule to the Statute Law (Repeals) Act, in 1969? But it's unlikely they'll ever hear of it. Hardly anyone in England has, look you."

We strolled on the terrace before my MP had to go, to prepare a question for the Prime Minister. He was an expert in the artifice which is necessary to get questions asked when questions are not to be asked, as it were.

This is what he told me. First you have to ask the Prime Minister an innocuous question (through the Speaker), usually, "What are the PM's engagements?" Then, as a supplementary, you slip in your prepared shaft: "Does the PM, in the course of these engagements, propose to visit the scene of the horrors of mismanagement caused by the Government's decision to rename all cats fish and all fish cats, in accordance with the latest directive of the European Economic Community?"

The answer always goes something like this: "No, Mr. Speaker, because HM Government is entirely persuaded that they were misnamed in the first place."

Which of the speakers was known as The Speaker, I asked him. "The only one who does not speak, of course." Of course. Now, why hadn't I thought of that? In other countries he would be called the President of the Assembly, or perhaps the Chairman. As *The Times* has just reminded us, "Next to the Monarch, the Speaker is the highest dignitary in the land." It goes on, "The Office is something of a mystery" – and I would not have expected less from the Angleans – and, even better, "such it should remain."

My Member did not seem to want to go further into the mystery, but switched the conversation to another part of the legislature, the House of Lords. I felt that I could contribute my mite. "Lord," I said, "so they say, comes from Loaf-Ward, the Man with the Bread, and Lady from Loafwardie, the Female Loaf-keeper or Kneader."

"That's nothing," he said, "did you know that, although people will do anything for a simple knighthood today, it wasn't always like that? By the law of 38 Henry III, 1254, anyone who had £10 a year was forced to be knighted or pay a fine?" I did know it, in fact; and also that that was only twenty-one years after the first use of the word "gentleman" recorded by the *Oxford English Dictionary*.

He'd handed me an opportunity to take the initiative. "Strange," I remarked, "that you should have had to pay at all to be made a 'lad,' which, according to the dictionaries, is what 'knight' means."

He giggled. "That's worth knowing. To think that I was one myself, for years, without knowing it."

Steering the topic back to the Commons, I asked something which had puzzled me for years. "If the democratically elected Members of Parliament come here to represent the wishes of the people, why do they pass various laws which – opinion polls show – the people do not want at all?"

He was equal to this one. "Funny, isn't it," he replied, "how you foreigners always ask the same questions?"

I apologized, of course. "That's all right," he said, generously, "we'll say no more about it, then, shall we?"

After all, the system does work, even if nobody knows how or why.

By now it was twelve noon, nearly time for luncheon, though I missed the opportunity of reminding my Member that "lunch" is recorded as being Welsh for "a gulp," and that it had formerly been known as dinner. Indeed, it still is, in many circles: a custom which effectively cuts off whole sections of the country one from another. Factory managers here are alleged to say to workers, "I am going to lunch. You go off and get your dinner."

The English have, for centuries, displayed a curious tendency to name and rename their meals, and to move them about during the day with a restlessness which one would not at first associate with such a steady people. Deep research rewards us with some, naturally, baffling information.

Breakfast has moved from five in the morning, as I have noted, to any time before eleven-thirty. It has thus overtaken dinner, which in Norman times was at nine in the morning, moving to eleven by the fifteenth and sixteenth centuries, then to noon, and finally, as now, to something like one to two-thirty, when it is often called luncheon.

Supper, for Chaucer, was at four p.m., which is now teatime: although tea (not to mention High Tea) can be at five. High Tea crept down to six o'clock in the evening in the sixteenth century, and it can now take place, renamed dinner, at seven-thirty or eight. And supper may now be taken after dinner.

The times now apparently stabilized, for the three main meals in England are almost exactly similar to those observed since early recorded history in the Middle East. Naturally, I am not sure – as I have hinted – exactly what to think of this, but I have fed it into my unconscious, or English, mind.

There it joined a native's statement of outstanding English characteristics:

> Though... we may entitle ourselves to the pride of the Spanish, jealousy of the Italians, wantonness of the French, drunkenness of the Dutch, and laziness of the Irish... yet our ancientest carte is for the sin of gluttony.

Perhaps Thomas Fuller wrote that (in the seventeenth century) following the long trail down the centuries when the English finally fixed their mealtimes after eating their way through the day.

They experiment with names of foods. In many households, if you are served ice-cream, jello, trifle or fruit after a meal and do not call it "pudding" – a completely different thing – you will not be invited again.

These thoughts were in my mind as I sat eating my luncheon ("lunch" is defined by one important dictionary as "a restaurateur's name for an ordinary man's dinner") at a chop-house, just after my parliamentary expedition. They were prompted by an exchange with the head waiter, busily cold-shouldering two foreign tourists, who were suffering from the delusion that one could get chops at a chop-house. I took pity on them.

"Those people at the next table," I said, "seem to want to order."

"When I have time, sir." But there wasn't anyone else in the place: and I said so. He leaned forward and spoke in a stage whisper.

"Did you hear how they talk?"

"How?"

"I heard one say to the other, 'If we can't have the chops, I'll take the fish.' The other answered, 'I like the idea of the steak.'"

I motioned to him to go on.

"In good society you do not say 'the fish,' 'the lobster,' 'the soup.' It is bad manners. All you say is, 'I'll have steak, or partridge, or shepherd's pie' and so on. There is, in fact, no such thing in English as 'the flan': there is a flan, or a portion of flan, that's all. Anything else is French."

"But French is the language of the cuisine, surely."

"*Mais certainement – but* only if you are speaking French. The definite article is not to be employed in the French manner in English. It is common to do so."

My mind raced back to another expert, who had rebuked me about a steak, in London. He was a butcher. I had said to him, "What's your steak like?"

Instantly, drawing himself up to his full height, he had responded: "This, sir, is ENGLISH steak."

A Scotsman might well have taken that to mean that the meat was inferior to the Caledonian variety, and would have been able, unlike me, to tick him off.

As the waiter glided away, I overheard that one of the foreign tourists was an aviator. He was saying, "English pilots! Do you know they won't take off if the inventory shows that they're one plastic spoon short? Call it 'operational difficulties.'"

The associative mechanism brought me, this time, a picture of the only English pilot that I'd had any truck with. I was in a plane, which was crossing the Red Sea toward Cairo. Unknown to me, the British Ambassador in Saudi Arabia had informed the airline that I might be carrying important papers: although in fact I was not. Suddenly, the stewardess came out of the pilot's cabin and signalled to my secretary to follow her.

When he came back his face was ashen. "The Captain was sitting at the controls," he told me, "and, fixing me with a steely gaze, said, 'Tell your master that I've heard from HBM's Ambassador in Saudi that I am to look after your papers. Be good enough to inform him, further, that since this is an ENGLISH aircraft, no such facilities exist.'"

I smiled at the memory, for my comeback to that one helped me dispel the feeling of uneasiness which the head waiter's remarks were doubtless designed to engender.

I had read enough letters from the Foreign Office to equip me to essay something similar. I motioned to my secretary to get out his portable typewriter, and dictated:

> The Captain, Flight 666, Over the Red Sea.
>
> Sir: I have the honor to say that your verbal message relating to a communication between you and HBM's Ambassador at Jeddah has been safely received: and I beg leave to state that its content leads me to suppose that it should more properly be transmitted to the Ambassador, who – I am confident – is capable of defending himself, without my assistance, on matters English.
>
> Your most obedient Servant...

Of course you hardly ever stump an Englishman. Soon after the message was delivered to the man in command, I noticed that he had left the public-address system switched on (AOP, the English call it: accidentally on purpose), and I could distinctly hear him in converse with the co-pilot:

"Who's that chap in the back, chucking his weight about?"

"Some kind of an Afghan, from Afghanistan, you know."

"Afghanistan – where's that?"

"Oh, you know, in stamp albums it's on the page just before 'Albania.'"

It is at times like that, I have been told by other outlanders, that the red mist may start to rise before the eyes. Slow breathing and relaxation dispel it. As it happened, I had recently been sitting in the *Diwan* of King Abdul-Aziz ibn Saud at Riyadh. With His Majesty was the Arabian explorer Abdullah St. John Philby, father of Kim Philby who defected to the Soviet Union. They were talking about lineage; the venerable English traveler had trotted out his old claim to be "Eastern": that he was of gypsy origin. "The gypsies are Indian, Majesty: their language has been identified as such, and proves it. And just look at me: I once had dark, wavy hair, I have a long nose, big ears and gypsy eyebrows."

"Gypsies are not much like us, O Abdullah," said the King, "and if I were you I would stick to being English." Then he turned to me and added, "The English are not much like us, either: except in love of horses and in patience. And in the fact that among them, too, excitable people are always looked upon as failures."

Remembering this, I sat back in my seat and took one or two slow breaths, inwardly repeating the wisdom of the mystic Junaid of Baghdad:

None attains to the Degree of Truth
Until a thousand sincere ones
Have declared him an infidel.

The pilot and co-pilot had sounded calm: Junaid's words calmed me. As to the horses, I liked them, too. For their connection with this tale you will have to wait until the last line of this chapter.

Meanwhile, I had better clear up why the British Embassy at Jeddah should have claimed that I was carrying important papers. This is a crucial matter. In most countries of the East, possessing documents about which a British ambassador is known to be concerned can still be the kiss of death. Why, I agonized, had the Ambassador said such a thing? Did he want me reviled, even arrested, as an infidel agent? If so, what did the British have against me? A fellow Easterner had shown me, not long before, what he thought of people like me, armed with a Frankish identity.

He was the immigration officer at an airport. He took my passport, looked at my Middle Eastern name on it, pointed at the Lion and Unicorn coat of arms and said, "And what did you have to do to get one of *these* things?"

Try as I might, I did not discover what lay behind the "important papers" matter until two or three years later. Talking to a senior Foreign Office man in London, I told him the story of the imaginary papers.

"My dear fella, you've got it back to front," he said at once. "It's quite obvious; the Ambassador was just trying to get the airline to give you special consideration."

"I see," I said, with as much English aplomb as I could manage, while thinking, "Well, the old fool's idea didn't work, did it?"

He knew what I had in my mind, and looked at me with amusement. "Of course, you can take a horse to water, but you can't make it drink, what?"

A horse... I had made a note of the pilot's name in my pocket diary, with some vague idea of making a complaint, or sending a set of Afghan stamps for the co-pilot's album. Now I remembered it, and a whole panorama of Englishry swam before my eyes: English clairvoyance, stocking up on recondite information, the ability to make tremendous puns. And how well briefed these Foreign Office people are.

The aviator's name, you see, was Captain Bertram (Bright Raven) *de la Mare*.

22

Mouse in Milk

English Rights
Within the boundaries of the City of London, stolen goods may legally be sold between sunrise and sunset.
   Reader's Digest: *You and Your Rights*

ALTHOUGH THE CITIES of England teem with unusual people, have many excellent libraries and generate some of the most exciting information on the Kingdom, the countryside is essential as a counter-balance.

Indeed, the ease of life attributed to the city-dwellers has not always improved their ability to absorb and retain information in an undistorted form.

I was put on the track of this important fact by two items in *The Times*, of London, which appeared on September 27 and 28, 1982.

The first was a letter from a lady in Cambridge, saying that when she was a child her mother had been advised to dose her with a mouse boiled in milk as a remedy for whooping-cough. The mother, however, was "a little distrustful of country remedies."

But what is almost certainly an original, country, form of the recipe – indeed, two of them – was given the following day by a *Times* columnist. He noted that two *herbs*, both called "mouse ear," were recommended for the treatment of whooping-cough in country districts. The transition from the country to the town seems to be the cause of the change from leaf to mouse, from vegetable to animal.

Hardly had the thought occurred to me than I came across another important clue. Rustics had always been regarded as stupid: and at some time in England's past some townee chose what seemed to him a particularly weird example of this imbecility. It became a catchword in London: "Tenterden Steeple be the cause of the Goodwin Sands." Ultimately this phrase took on a life of its own as the answer to anyone who said anything where cause and effect could be questioned.

And yet... was there, perhaps, some little-known scientific principle whereby a church-tower could create a treacherous sandbank? The church was in the county of Kent, and the sands are located off the Kentish coast. That was all I knew about the matter – at first.

I was beginning to think that the yokels were indeed idiots, when something in a history book caught my eye. It said that the dangerous banks "consisted at one time of about 4,000 acres of low land, fenced by a sea wall. William the Conqueror bestowed them on the Abbey of St. Augustine."

Delving deeper, I found that a certain Mr. Moore had "gone into Kent" to find out what could have caused the sands in the first place. Believe it or not, although this was centuries after the rich soil became sandbanks, one of the countrymen could give an explanation which linked the ships' graveyard and the church. Money raised in the county for keeping the sea-walls in repair had been used instead by the then Bishop of Rochester to build – Tenterden steeple. The sea broke through, according to the records, as early as the year 1100, and some blame the Abbot of the monastery. Be that as it may, the folk-memory of the accusation was still accurate after several hundred years.

I headed, next, for the West Country to continue my inquiries and observations, and to attend a lecture at Bath. The speaker, a distinguished scientist, described placebo therapy, whereby thirty to forty per cent of people recovered from ailments if given therapeutically inert substances.

Two farmers, one of whom seemed to be hard of hearing, were sitting in the row in front of me. After the doctor had finished his very involved discourse, the deaf rustic shouted to his companion, "Wot ee be sayin' Jaarj?"

The answer, a masterpiece of compression without any loss of lucidity, was "Nothin' much you doan' areddy know, Jack. Just that doctorin's loike a scarecrow, or bodies are, rather. Just put up any old thing, and you can fool one in three."

"Nard's uz goodaza wink to a bloind aars," said Jack, nodding in agreement. Yokel lore is worth listening to. It can save you listening to an entire lecture.

As I traveled beyond Bath, I spotted a gas station by the road, and drew in for a refill. And there, standing with a can in his hand, was a figure wearing – an Afghan cap, such as the guerrillas have adopted from the people of the high Nuristan mountains. In his other hand he had some money and a piece of paper with writing on it.

I exchanged a few words with him, and he told me that he was working for an oil-sheikh who had bought the big house hereabouts. We parted when it was my turn to be served, and as the tank was being filled, I picked up the paper which the servant had dropped. On it was written, in an Afghan hand, "4 liter *tel-i-khak*." Now, I knew that *tel-i-khak*, "earth oil," means paraffin: but did the West Country pump attendant?

"Speaks English, does he?" I asked.

"Not a word, me dear."

"Comes in for paraffin all the time, does he, then?"

"Never seen 'im in me loife, bless ee."

"Then how did you know what he wanted?"

"Well, ee 'ad a paraffin can, and smelt of it, too, dinne? Generator run out, if y'aaks me."

The townee uses words, but the countryman is not limited to speech for communication.

I remembered that an English countryman, and an aristocratic landowner at that, had once told me that "Nobody in the *country* would read a Sherlock Holmes story. You need town people for that, people who've never learned how to observe things."

He practiced what he preached. And he was a very forthright man. With a charming smile, he handed back a book of mine which I'd just tried to present to him, and said, "Thanks, but I'm not much of a readin' feller. Can't teach an old dog new tricks, what?"

Not all countrymen, of course, are like that. Many, with little book-learning, can hold their own well enough in the face of literature. My next stop was at an inn where I had bread and cheese in the open air where a drover, having parked his sheep, was sitting pulling at his pipe. I was immersed in a book, but he leaned over with the informality of the countryside and said, "Woss in thaat, then?"

I said, "Well, it says here – it's a book written in 1881 – that 'Dancing was invented by the Curetes in 1534 BC.'"

"When wuz thaat, then?"

"Three thousand, five hundred and sixteen years ago."

"Reckon it's older than thaat, though. Wonder ow they reckon to know to the year, loike?"

I had to agree with him. I wondered, too.

"Ow old's the earth, then?" he gestured toward some tilled fields.

I looked it up, under "Creation."

"It says here that the creation of the world could have been in 4004 BC, but that about 140 different dates have been assigned to it, varying from 3616 to 6984. And that Dr. Hales, whoever he was, 'gives 5411.'"

"They know more about the daancin' than about the makin', then? But oi reckon it be older than thaat..."

Perhaps I had been too long in London, but I began to feel, irrationally, impatient with this man, even if he was, as I knew, right. I took out a newspaper clipping and said, "Did you know that it was discovered in 1981 that mice don't really like cheese?"

"Oh, ah," he said, before I could go on, "nuts, fruits, fat, that be what they loike, loike..."

I looked down at the printed report of the great new discovery which had made the national newspapers. It said that it had now been determined that mice preferred "dried fruits, nuts, lard..." Just what this yokel had known all the time.

For some reason, I started to giggle.

"Oi loikes to hear a man laaf," said my friend, "that be a soyne of..."

I missed what he said, but I'm going back one day, when I've collected myself a little.

Meanwhile I'm studying Omar Khayyam's poem about who and what he is. If he'd ever met an Englishman, or read books about these people, I'm sure he would have put it in their mouths:

> If I from wine am acting like a drunk, I am
> and if I'm an infidel and idolator, I am:
> Everyone's got a theory about me –
> But I'm mine, and what I am, I am.

23

Government by Astonishment

> *Governing*
> Britain... is naturally not over-fertile of men able to govern justly and prudently in peace.
> John Milton: *History of England*

I WAS IMPRESSED by the long and erudite article. Written by an English lady, it seemed to show, with chapter and verse, quotations from a dozen ancient manuscripts, that the French had got their French all wrong. And the English were right.

It appears that, when a citizen of these Anglean former dependencies of the Normandy duchy says something in French without a gargled "r" or a nasal "n," without dropping the final "t" or "s" – he is speaking French just as the French used to do. The accent, still in full flow in the Channel Islands, and typically associated with English schoolchildren, the dreaded *Parlezz vooze Fransays*, is exactly how the Normans used to talk. The modern pronunciation, this lady assures us, is just that: a recent affectation. Even today the Parisian French themselves have to fight hard to maintain it, and the people of the south don't go in for it at all.

Yes, I was interested at first. Then, checking the new information against my mental data bank of Englishry, I suddenly realized that the very concept was alien because scholastic. To become obsessed with something, to tease out its meaning, to pound that meaning into others, these are the marks of the more tiresome Schoolmen, those tedious Latinate Middle Ages people credited with debates about the pinhead (some say pinpoint) accommodation available for angels.

No, a true Angle or Anglo-Saxon will either not care at all how anything is pronounced if it is in a foreign language, or else he will give it a name and in some miraculous manner induce the foreigner to adopt it.

Take the word Wales. Welsh was the name given by Saxons to foreigners, especially the inhabitants of Gaul. "Welsh" means "foreign." And yet I have watched an international football match in the Western Principality where more than half the crowd were shouting, in English, "Play up, Wales!" – Play up, Foreigners. They were Welshmen, of course.

The dictionary makes it clear enough that the word is from "Angl. and Kentish *welisc*, a foreigner," and also the Anglo-Saxon name "for Britons, &c." A Turk called Ozbeg, whom I met in London, and who rather badly wanted to be English, might have found a way of passing himself off, as an alternative, as Welsh, which is generally now considered only to mean someone from a part of the United Kingdom. After all, very few people, especially the linguistic purists who are not uncommon here, could deny that by the dictionary's definition a Japanese, Hottentot or anyone else could, in a sense, be considered Welsh. Living in Kent, where the word was once common for any foreigner, I suppose that I could also claim Welsh origin myself, in that sense.

While on the subject of Welsh, there is a further interesting fact. The name of the county of Kent is Old British: *Cant*, a corner or headland. This, itself, is a Welsh, or foreign, word; but the Kent people, now Teutonic, retained the name while changing the population. In good Angle fashion, they vanished the population, merging into – Kent, the colony of the Jutes.

But they went further. More than a thousand years after they arrived on these shores – in Elizabeth I's time, in fact – the people of my adoptive county seemed to be holding out against any facile identification with the rest of the country or the culture. Jutes, Angles, Saxons, whatever they were, they had put their stamp on the place. I quote Taylor's *The Water Poet*, from 1630:

> Some bookes are arrogant and impudent
> So are most thieves in Christendom and Kent.

To be a Kentish Man: a resident of Kent, I would have to be born west of the Medway. This would make me "A Kentish man: a Resident of Kent." I might not be allowed to style myself what the dictionaries term A Man of Kent, for to be such you must be born east of the Medway. Ah, but how far east? I am not quite sure whether the lower Himalayas counts, but then in England (and Kent) anything is possible.

I am not clear whether the writer of the English-French thesis is for or against the Norman Conquest of 1066, or whether she is herself a Kentish lady. But I do know that the people of Kent were very nonchalant in their treatment of Duke William.

The motto of the County is *Invicta*, which means Unconquered. The origin of this device dates back to the Conquest: except that, in the case of Kent, conquest there was none. The Invicti, as they called themselves, were not vanquished like the rest of the English because they went out "with green boughs to meet the Conqueror and obtained in consequence a confirmation of their ancient privileges from the new king."

The man who explained this to me, and who gave me the references to confirm it, was a local journalist, who had called to interview me. His first words were "Are you a Man of Kent or a Kentish man?" On the subject of the motto, he said, "If you haven't much Latin, the meaning of *Invicta* is 'If you can't beat them, join them.'" And it was he who directed me to Caesar's *Gallic War Commentaries*: "By far the most civilized of the natives of Britain are the inhabitants of Kent."

The Battle of Hastings was a long time ago. But yesterday my daughter Saira overheard a conversation between two local policemen outside our gate. We were having a garden party. One said to the other, "Who are all these people?" The other answered, "I don't know, but that one over there has come all the way from Middlesex." Middlesex is less than thirty-five miles away as the crow flies.

But the remoteness of Kent does not mean that I cannot drive the whole thirty-four miles to London and sip of its linguistic and other sophistications.

I once drove up to a policeman in Piccadilly Circus and asked a simple question. He took one look at me and instantly concluded that I could hardly understand a word of English. And his pidgin ("right handee, savvy?") almost floored me. "Near, soon get there, savvy? Go topside, right handee, no?"

I said, "Yes, I think I understand, many thanks. It was only that I wanted to know the best route, because of traffic restrictions."

He wasn't daunted: he knew I was a foreigner and couldn't understand a civilized language. So he repeated it all, this time in a very loud voice, ending it with a paraphrase of my first words, "No goodee only *thinkee* savvy. Must proper savvy, savvy?"

I don't quite know how to fit in one fact with the undoubted perceptivity of the English: unless it be that certain kinds of training (scholastic and police, for instance) lends an evanescence in their understanding. The fact is that a policeman only has to see me coming to decide that I am a tongue-tied foreigner...

"Savvy," I said. There didn't seem anything else I could say at the time, though some expletives have occurred to me since.

I related this experience to a former British envoy to Afghanistan, Sir William Fraser-Tytler, not sure whether he would believe it. Several English friends who have heard it refuse to credit it, although it is absolutely true. But Fraser-Tytler only said, "That's nothing unusual: what about Wellington Koo?"

Dr. Koo was an eminent diplomatist and Ambassador of China. The story was that he was at a banquet in his honor one day when the English lady who had been seated beside him, noting his Oriental features, graciously said, "You likee soupee?"

At this, Fraser-Tytler said, the Chinese gentleman only nodded and smiled, as he did at various other equally ingenious linguistic sallies by the lady.

Finally the Ambassador rose to speak, and did so in perfect English. When he sat down, he smiled at the lady and asked, "You likee speechee?"

"Of course," said the British diplomat, "Dr. Koo was a Christian and had had some contact with English ways." So had Fraser-Tytler, I realized, even though at least half of his name was Scottish.

Reverting to the theory that French should really be pronounced with what we call an English accent, I have the feeling that French people hearing this may well agree and give in through sheer astonishment. This might, indeed, be the secret weapon, the Trojan Horse feared by some Continentals when the British first threatened to join the Common Market.

There are precedents for Government by Astonishment in which the English have been involved. When the chief of an African people saw an Englishman advancing toward him with an ostrich-feather in his hat, he immediately placed himself and his territory under British rule. Asked why he did not fight the Great White Chief, he answered, "Because I reckoned that anyone who wore such a valueless trifle on his head must despise all outward show, and have great power."

Near-royalty have been involved as well. In the eighteenth century, the American colonials were getting restless, and Queen Anne sent her cousin, Lord Cornbury, to be English Governor in New York.

This worthy man, dressed in female garb, over corsets embracing his bulky frame, governed the astonished Americans for no less than seven years. He did things in a big way: his shoes were of satin and he wore diamonds in his hair. When questioned about all this, he riposted, "I represent a woman, and in all respects I ought to represent her as faithfully as I can."

It is a sad commentary on the understanding of his compatriots, though, that when back in England – having overspent on dresses – he found himself confined to prison for debt.

Perhaps we have a useful clue here. Is English apparent preposterousness just a means of gaining ascendancy over others by the use of the astonishment weapon? Did the good people of Kent so amaze William the Conqueror by calling themselves Unconquered that he gave them all those concessions? Think about it.

I have thought about it; and more: I took the problem to the most expert Englishman I knew, Professor L. F. Rushbrook Williams, of All Souls College, Oxford. His was one of the longest entries in *Who's Who* (12 centimeters: though easily beaten by Lord Mountbatten's 24.5 cm) and he had done everything, from being a Minister to an Income Tax authority, to running the Middle Eastern Department of the Ministry of Information, to "Special Duty" all over the world. He was a mine of every kind of information, a former confidant of the Duke of Windsor, a Fellow of All Souls, and I do not know what else. He was not only a staunch friend, but he had done me many a kindness without apparent reason.

Naturally, he was also slightly unusual. He drove all over the country in an ancient car with an illuminated blue frosted glass eagle on top. He was the perfect adviser on Englishry.

"Not long ago, Respected Professor," I began, "an English friend told me that he had been received by the ambassador of a country on the Indian subcontinent who was clipping his toenails at the time. This appeared revolting to my friend, who was English.

"But the Englishman added, 'Of course, if the chap had only been *British*, one would have put it down to mild eccentricity…'"

I looked at Rushbrook Williams to see if he wanted any further information, but he did not.

"Your question is, then, 'How do English people get away with things, and even find their repute enhanced by them, when foreigners in the same position would find themselves blackballed?'"

"In a nutshell," I agreed.

"Because," said the Professor, "the English take note, wittingly or no, of two things that others tend to ignore. First, timing: when and where. Second, they do not limit themselves to a single eccentricity: they bombard you with them. Signals come at you from all directions."

So generating astonishment, which is the English strong suit, was a result of manipulating the emotions of the opponent, or vis-à-vis, or whatever? I wanted to know.

"Well," he said, "it takes two for someone to be impressed. If the foreigner were not vulnerable to influence, the English would not be able to affect them, would they?"

I sought basic data on the English in what seemed like the most promising source, a real treasure. Professor Sir Ernest Barker had edited, for the Oxford University Press, a book of two hundred thousand words, composed of essays by twenty-seven redoubtable contributors, under the title of *The Character of England*.

"The aim of this book," says Barker, "has been to describe the spirit of England, rather than all the varied material in which the spirit works." Excellent, just what I wanted. He emphasizes that the book is concerned with England, and not Britain. Even better.

Barker and his associates freely admit the very miscellaneous origins and traditions of the English, which he poetically refers to as "many strains and many treasures." Their behavior – as he concludes in his summing-up – has undergone tremendous shifts and changes throughout history. How, then, are we to isolate those things which can be called typically or uniquely English?

"What," he asks, as I read on with mounting excitement, "is really 'in charge'?"

Exactly my question. Well, in spite of the changes (fierce to mild, colonialist to liberationist, dirty to clean, and so on interminably, many outsiders would feel), Barker isolates the magic ingredients: there are no fewer than six. These are the "constants," for "even in speaking of change we have seen that the more the Englishman changes, the more he remains the same."

At last we can list them:

1. Social homogeneity
2. Amateurism

3. The figure and idea of the gentleman
4. People doing things for themselves
5. Eccentricity ("the Englishman is governed by the weather in his soul")
6. Youthfulness ("a trait which the Englishman shares with the ancient Greeks... the joke").

Barker includes the joke as a constant in the face of the statement by one of his own contributors that humor in England is a transitory thing. For centuries, says H. W. Garrold, the Anglo-Saxon had no humor. He believes that a sense of fun is one of the things that keep on disappearing, sometimes for long periods, from among the English. Perhaps, though, it is a constant in the sense of its persistence against odds. It all depends on what you mean by "constant."

But what strikes me most about this analysis is that, not only as an Afghan but as one who has lived in several countries, I can hardly think of *any* people who would not claim almost all these supposedly English characteristics as their own. I have also shown the list to English people, who have contested its reliability.

No, Barker, I don't think it is the mixture, or the constants behind the mixture. It is the way in which the constants are used, when, where and how. So it boils down to a skill, as near as you can really define it. And where is *that* located?

If outside observers of the English cannot quite make them out, even a galaxy of English experts gathered under the aegis of the dreaming spires have little better to offer. It is not the experts who are right, it is Professor Rushbrook Williams when he says, "First, timing, when and where."

That's what causes the astonishment. So, if you want to learn about the English, begin with yourself. Learn how not to be astonished by anything, not even by a huge, authoritative book about the English, by the English, which is often wildly off the mark. Avoid scholasticism, even if it Englishly proves that the only real French is spoken by the British of the Channel Islands.

And don't limit yourself to the matter of French, even though I have emphasized it here. The Germans may well have rumbled the British astonishment weapon. A diplomat in Bonn told me a current anecdote about the time when the British were applying to join the Common Market. A Special Negotiator was in West Germany, sounding the Chancellor on whether his country would support London's application.

"Yes, come into the Community, by all means," said the Chancellor, "but there is one proviso: you must leave your astonishing beer at home, for we are not accustomed to extreme astonishment, here in Europe."

Nobody can read English books and newspapers, let alone have conversations with English people, without learning that the Island Race seems to attribute its doughty characteristics to freedom from foreign invasion. During some discussions on British membership of the Common Market at which I was present, someone said, "The British have been as unpopular as anyone in Europe, you know..."

"How do you mean?" asked an English diplomat.

"Well, I know that you have this sea-girt fortress and so on," said the Continental, "but people have tried to overrun you, just as they have us."

"Not really," yawned the diplomat, "you see, people quite like us. We've only had to deal with the French, the Spanish and a couple of Germans, apart from the Dutch."

"Well," said the other man, "that's enough, isn't it?"

The Englishman shook his head. "You simply must understand," he said, "that it wasn't as if their *people* wanted to do it. It was just two Frenchies, a couple of Germans and a Spanish king. And even then, only one of them, since the Normans, ever really *tried*!"

Astonishment might even make a would-be invader think twice. Suppose, for example, you were a foreigner and came upon this in *Who's Who*, the bible of the Great and the Good in England – the way Mr. Christopher Logue summarizes his military career:

> Private in Black Watch, two years in army prison, discharged with ignominy, 1948.

You would surely look in vain for any comparable statement in the most reputable reference-book of any other country in the world. It's terrifying.

But master the causing of astonishment, and it will probably get you anywhere. This is so vital, and yet so subtle, a fact that I offer no apology for quoting the saying attributed to the medieval dervish Sheikh, Haji Bektash:

"A hint sufficeth the wise, yet a thousand admonitions profit not the heedless."

24

Guerrilla at the Palace

Have It!
Have at it, and have it! One might add many capital English proverbs of this kind, all so characteristic of the activity and boldness of our forefathers.
                      E. Fitzgerald: *Polonius*

A THIRD WORLD Expert had adopted me as a friend. Like all experts, he was always on about something, and I was therefore not surprised when he came to see me with a newspaper cutting in his hand. As he waved it in the air, I called for coffee and resigned myself to yet another tirade about how viciously the media manipulate the news to the detriment of developing peoples, minorities and so on.

At first I thought that I had been right. Holding the tiny scrap of paper in his hand, he declaimed:

> Peasant Utambu, 25, beats the urge to smoke by eating creepy-crawlies, like ants and woodlice. He said at his kraal: "They're better than cigarettes, any day."

He was about to say more, but I knew what he usually wanted, so I silenced him with an imperious gesture. "You would be quite right to complain," I told him. "This is too obviously a plant, a story concocted by the fascist lackeys of the international Wall-Street plutocratic running dogs of imperialistic chauvinism and their allies, the..."

But he stopped me dead in my tracks. "No, *no*! You don't understand at all. It's not like that this time."

Looking into his wild eyes, I realized that this was no ordinary visit. I snatched the piece of newsprint from him and read:

> THE SNAIL CURE (*Daily Express*)
> Gardener Clive Johns, 25, beats his urge to smoke by eating creepy-crawlies like ants and woodlice. He said at his Devon home: "They're better than a ciggie, any day."

"What is all this about? Why the deception?" I rapped, in my best Anglekin voice.

"Don't you *see*?" he retorted, waving his arms. Then he explained.

"People think that only reports about the Third World are pejorative or dismissive, and that that is what makes people look down on the developing nations."

"Well, that's what you are always telling me," I said, "so why the change?"

"Some fool told me to paraphrase any newspaper story from the West," he said sulkily, "and I'd find that people here laughed at themselves as much as they do at anyone else."

"I could have told you that myself," I said; but he wasn't listening now. He had got into his stride. "I gave you the first version *as if* it had been from Asia or Africa, changing the name and place. But, as you yourself have read, *it was not.* A tale like that, reported from a Less Developed Country, would reinforce the anti-Third World mental stereotype. When it is shown that the English are just the same, nobody turns a hair."

"But surely," I ruminated, "it's good enough for a laugh, isn't it?"

"There it is again!" he screamed. "Why should people be laughed at, and how can they be made the object of amusement and still remain serious?"

"Well, they can't remain serious if they are laughing..."

"Serious means, as in the dictionary, 'not to be taken lightly.'"

"How do you know Gardener Clive Johns doesn't *want* to be taken lightly?"

"Well, all I can say is that *I*, for one, do not want to be taken lightly. How do the English do it? Even abroad they don't care. A British Ambassador, an Englishman, once dressed as a mailman for a party in Asia attended by grandees, none of them attired as anything less than a duke."

"Was it a costume party?"

"Yes, of course it was!"

"Well, then, I don't see what you're on about. And, if this party was in the Third World, why weren't they spending the money on social uplift?"

He has never spoken to me again, but he did help to start a train of memories about diplomats.

One of my early experiences in this area was hearing an English former Minister Plenipotentiary illustrate, most graphically, his people's mentality, at dinner in our house.

"I once lost my pocket-book when I took out my cigarette case in St. James's Park," he said. "It must have dropped on to the grass, and I didn't miss it at first.

"I sent some secretary fellows out to look for it, but they reported that someone must have carried it off, and I gave it up for lost.

"Then, several months later, I got a letter. Badly scrawled, it was, and addressed to me at my club. It was from the finder, who'd found my card inside.

"The letter said something like this: 'I found yer wallit and the munny innit. Remawse is norin me, so heres ten shillings. Wen it nores some more I'll send some more.'"

There was a tremendous laugh, but the Foreign Office man continued, "I always think that that illustrates the English character perfectly. You see, we are a people of moderation. That fellow felt remorse, but he did not let it get out of control. Ten shillings' worth at a time was his idea of things."

It was reassuring to reflect that the two and half million pounds a day disbursed by the Foreign Office was in such financially realistic hands.

Since so much of their time is spent in testing the water and feeling out thinking, both good Foreign Office terms, UK diplomats must maintain a fund of good stories. They must always keep their end up, too. This is because, in winning a position of personal ascendancy, the Head of Mission does the same for the Monarch (whom he represents) as well. So it is not boasting to promote oneself.

At the same time, it is often difficult to show one's importance, expertise or other impressive qualities without a feed-man, as all good entertainers know. In an embassy, the job of feed-man is held by a Second or Third Secretary, the lowest positions on the totem-pole. It is not true that the job is confined to breaking in the Head of Mission's new set of false teeth: the junior diplomat has to help keep the ball rolling.

I was present at one interchange not long ago. It went like this:

AMBASSADOR: Went around the new multi-million, automated, high-tech – you know the kind of thing – factory out here last year, just before you came to us, Pitherthwaite...

PITHERTHWAITE (Second Secretary): I understand that they had a lot of West German and Japanese efficiency experts to check it out, sir, so it must be efficient. Did you manage to suggest any improvements?

AMBASSADOR: Only one, I'm afraid. (Short replies are the signal to the feed-man to offer the line for the clincher.)

PITHERTHWAITE: Did that save them much, in terms of money, sir?

AMBASSADOR: Best they could manage, with my suggestions, was a saving of an extra twelve to twenty million pounds a year, I believe. I think that's what the Minister of National Economy was rabbitin' on about the other day...

It has even been alleged that preferment in the Diplomatic depends upon skill in this area. I do not for a moment believe that, but I had an opportunity of seeing this ambassador in action in the field. And in connection with a costume occasion in a Third World capital city.

I was to be the featured guest at a masquerade, got myself up in a leopard-striped guerrilla battle-suit, and carried a Russian assault rifle borrowed from the Presidential Guard. I even sang, *sotto voce*, the stirring anthem, "We are the Sons and Daughters of Kalashnikov," for verisimilitude. Naturally, I hoped to get the prize for Best Costume.

The British Ambassador lived next door to the State Guest House where I was lodged, and did not see why he should not come along with me, in the limousine which I had been allotted, to the party. He was attired, as he told me, to resemble the great Caliph of Baghdad, Haroun El-Raschid of the *1001 Nights*: gold-filet headdress, curly-toed slippers, shiny black beard, disemboweling knife and all. I felt a momentary crisis of identity as I remembered that the Caliph and I were from the same family. It was, no doubt, to help me control my vanity that the Ambassador made light of my role. "Run out of people to invite, have they?" he said.

We were still some way from the Presidential Palace when the car was stopped at a roadblock. Absolutely nobody could proceed further. All roads were closed, because our host, the Great Leader, was holding an important function...

This is what the driver retailed to us through the communicating window. I told him to say that we were going to the masquerade ball, but the police just stood there, fingering the triggers of their guns, right in the middle of the road. Everyone, it seemed, always said things like that to try to get through roadblocks.

The Ambassador sat quietly, regally, the tips of his fingers together, as if in prayer. I remember thinking what an old fool he seemed, how lost without a fawning underling to straighten things out. Well, it was time for me to make a command decision, take decisive action. "I'll sort this out in short order, Excellency," I said, crisply. He smiled.

"Here!" I barked at the elegant police major in charge of the roadblock, through the car's open window. He pranced up, snarling, and I thrust my invitation into his hand. He flashed a flashlight on the huge, gold-edged card. The wording read, below the seal of the Grand Chamberlain:

> I am Commanded by
> HIS EXCELLENCY THE PRESIDENT
> To Invite You To
> A MASQUERADE BALL

At Which The Guest of Honor Will Be IDRIES SHAH...

"I am that Idries Shah," I said, smugly.

He looked at the card reflectively, turned it round and round, tore it into four pieces and threw them back at me, with an uncomprehending and insolent grin.

Now it was the Ambassador's turn. First, he reached past me and rolled the half-open window right down. Then, in the local language, be barked, "Colonel, if those sons of dogs and their infernal barrier are not out of the way in half a minute, I shall have their flesh fed to unclean animals. Take heed, for it is I, the King, who speak!"

It was hardly constitutional, and I had a vague sense that it must be illegal. But then I thought of the words of the great constitutionalist Walter Bagehot, "An Englishman whose heart is in a matter is not easily baffled."

Somehow this reflection seemed to calm me as I watched, as on a film, the police contingent come to life under the tongue-lashing which the Major now gave them. Some snapped to attention, others rushed to remove a log, festooned with barbed-wire, from the highway, and one even inadvertently knocked the Major down as he shouted, again and again, arms flailing, "Instantly, Glorious Majesty!" In no time we were through.

At the Palace, the British Ambassador, now being called Resplendent Majesty by the chauffeur, with both of them thoroughly into the skin of the part, was admitted with every courtesy and consideration. His Excellency won the first prize for his costume, too; accepting the prize with quiet dignity. "Courtesy to a visiting monarch; they always get preferential treatment," was how he modestly put it.

If this true story leads you to suppose that the English always get their way by exceeding others in arrogance, let me put you right. Attitude, to an Englishman, is the servant of his objectives. There is no odium attached to servility, for instance. As William Makepeace Thackeray shows, in *Vanity Fair*, one adjusts one's behavior to suit the conditions:

> Whenever he met a great man, he grovelled before him and my lorded him, as only a free-born Englishman can do.

Lord Young, Minister Without Portfolio, has said that "there is something about the British character that equates service with being servile" by the way. But I advise you to keep an eye on this. For some years now, the English newspapers have been full of suggestions that the Service, not the smokestack, Industries are the ones of the future. They point to tourism, financial and social services, and several other areas as the points of economic growth.

You may be sure that this is the infallible instinct of the old Anglean, guiding the Island Race toward yet another baffling change of character. John Lyly may have said that the Englishman can "suffer no stranger to be his equal." That's right: so he'll yet display a form of service which will be so good that it'll leave *you* lost in admiration – and maybe even feeling inferior yourself.

25

Security, and So On

Temptations
But in spite of all temptations
To belong to other nations,
He remains an Englishman.
          Sir W. S. Gilbert: *HMS Pinafore*

EVERYONE KNOWS THAT England is full of spies, both native and foreign.

Foreign spies are always being expelled; but naturally, when dealing with spies, as with anyone else, the Brits inject their own, distinctive flavor into the matter. When Sir Alec Douglas-Home threw out no fewer than 105 Russians for spying, he announced that he had done it "to improve our relations with the Soviet Union." Where else in the world would you have heard such a phrase, under such circumstances?

Native spies and traitors have included some of the country's most senior officials. One Conservative government minister, even, has been alleged to be a Soviet agent. Skim the London Press and you will not lack cases of people accused of breaking the Official Secrets Act.

You would imagine, after decades of this sort of thing, that people would become inured to it, or somebody would put a stop to it. Not likely. Every time there is a fresh espionage revelation, people are amazed. They find it hard to believe that anyone could do such things. They gape at pictures of Old Etonians, civil servants, or military personnel involved in spy-work.

There is a paradoxical quality about all this, if compared with experience elsewhere. England is full of spies and people know it but can't credit it. Other countries (especially where there is nothing to spy upon) are full of people who constantly say "Spies are Everywhere." I have myself been treated as a spy, or near-spy, in three different countries. And only because spies, there, are deemed to be Everywhere.

This may only be a manifestation of my Law of Displaced Assumptions, which says that the accuracy of human beliefs tends to be in inverse ratio to the facts. After all, for most of human history, people assumed that the Earth was flat, in exact opposition to reality. This even defies the Law of Probability, which is supposed to predict that some would say "Flat," some "Round," others "Don't know," and so on.

The British (though more expressly the English) admit that they are surrounded by secrecy; yet I cannot find anyone here who claims to be secretive. It's always the other fellow.

I once read (in the *Daily Express*, London, June 11, 1971, page 10, column 1: I feel I must document it) something interesting in this connection about *Calendula*. A woman had been required to sign an undertaking under the Official Secrets Act before she was allowed to deal with them. Nothing of her work was to be divulged, except to someone who had also signed.

The meaning of *Calendula*? Marigolds. The nature of her job? Temporary thinner-out of the plants, in a garden.

I quoted the report in a radio interview, and got a letter from a man who insisted that this precaution was "quite proper." I am afraid I forget his argument, but it was closely reasoned. The letter was headed SECURITY AND SO ON. "And So On" covers almost anything in England.

Secrecy seems to be in the very bones of the people. My father once told me about a walk he took in Soho, when on a visit to England in the nineteen-thirties. He saw a large party of men assembled on the sidewalk and wondered why they were there. So he crossed the road and asked, "Excuse me, gentlemen, what are you doing here?"

Some looked belligerent, others edged away from him. Then one of them answered, "Wouldn't you like to know?" And they all laughed.

"Soho had a name for sin and vice at that time," he said, "as well as having excellent restaurants and plenty of honest people. If I had not persisted, I might have gone away with the impression that I had seen an organized crime family up to no good. But I withdrew to a strategic distance and continued my observation. Before long a motor-coach drew up and the men got in. Plastered all over it were stickers saying 'Arsenal Football Club Supporters.'"

Only recently I overheard the following exchange at Charing Cross Main Line Railway Station, one of London's most important termini:

> WOMAN TO TICKET COLLECTOR: When is the next Hastings train?
> TICKET COLLECTOR: Can't tell you that.
> WOMAN: Why ever not?
> TICKET COLLECTOR: If I did, everyone would want to know, wouldn't they?
> WOMAN: Well, if they did, I wouldn't mind telling them.

Having lived for quite a time in England, I decoded the man's message easily enough: unlike the intending lady passenger who was, I think, American. I translate for the benefit of foreigners.

The man was saying, elliptically of course, that it was not his job to give train information. It is normal practice in England not to answer anything directly. Standard practice, too, is not to ask direct questions: it is considered aggressive to assume that the other person can, should or will answer at all. The correct form, if compelled to approach another for help, is to start with "Excuse me, I wonder whether..."

On no account should anyone, on being asked absurd, quasi-rhetorical questions, answer them lucidly. An automatic answer to the ticket collector (but one which would only occur to a foreigner) would be:

> Everyone, surely, would not wish to know what I have just asked you about the Hastings train. Such information would tend to be sought only by those who had some legitimate interest in the matter. Of their number, only those who lacked certain information – the time of the next train – would be seeking it. Naturally, I exclude the frivolous or insane; but they are not "everybody," constituting, as they do, a minority. Admittedly, the proportion of psychologically underprivileged people is alarmingly high. For your information, and while we are on the subject, I may say that the figures show that one person in twelve is, has been or will be, required to undergo treatment in an institution for mental problems. As to the frivolous, statistics are not available, but I do not think that they can be very numerous in situations such as this, since their attentions would, in the nature of things, have to be distributed among a wide range of encounters, diluting their effect.

The same would apply, too, in the case of the intellectually impaired.

Systematic Thinking was originally a European, clerical import during the Middle Ages which the people of this nation are individually and collectively still trying to shake off. In some European countries, by the time you had finished such an address as the one which I have outlined above, you would be surrounded by a respectful crowd, and addressed as Doctor. You might even get a small round of applause.

Even in parts of the Middle East, the ticket collector would fall back, abashed at your eloquence, giving you a perfect lead-in to a theological exposition or homily. It has happened to me. At the end of a long tirade, when I was reproaching an official for negligence, he took my hand in his and murmured, to cries of assent from the crowd, "Beautiful Arabic, but I am afraid that I did not understand a word."

Intellectuality, in England, gives sure grounds for suspicion, and people dislike it intensely. It is the complete reverse in the Eastern Bloc. In a Letter to the Editor of *The Times* in 1966, Mr. John Moore shared with his compatriots his revulsion at being thought intellectual and highlighted the Russian attitude.

At a Shaw centenary luncheon, the Soviet Chargé d'Affaires asked Mr. Moore, his neighbor, if he was an intellectual. "Like any Englishman worthy of the name, I hotly denied the distasteful accusation," the offended Mr. Moore records. Then "The Russian brooded darkly. I could see he was deeply troubled. At last he turned to me and demanded: 'If you are *not* an intellectual, why are you here?'"

No doubt the Russian was wondering whether Mr. Moore was some kind of security man; at all events, he shared with the ticket collector a reserve which is so marked in England that, when I first went to the United States, I felt that the

Americans must be out of their minds to talk so freely about so many things that normal people would automatically hide.

No Englishman worthy of the name is an Intellectual. This does not mean that he has no intellectual life. Whatever it is, most of us foreigners will never learn about it, as Thomas de Quincey has made clear. In his *Confessions of an English Opium Eater* (Penguin, 1975 edition, page 78) he unequivocally states:

> I honour the Barbarians too much by supposing them capable of any pleasures approaching to the intellectual ones of an Englishman.

I checked the Hastings Train experience with an Englishman I know (half Spanish, half Welsh, born in Scotland, educated in Sussex).

Without hesitation – Sussex University is less secretive than most English seats of learning; I was actually told where my lecture-hall was when I went there to speak – he said that the custom was a hangover from the Second World War. From 1939 to 1945, he told me, *everything* in the United Kingdom was a military secret and the habit of caution had persisted. He got quite stroppy when I remarked that the people in France, say, or Finland, seemed to have got over it. Many of them will cheerfully tell you the time of the next train to Grenoble or out of Helsinki, especially if they know it. Failing that, they may even tell you where to find out.

There may be something special about the English which has conditioned them, alone, to retaining, and passing on through the generations, the lessons learned during the war. This would involve, though, an infraction of Occam's Razor and a sort of Anglo-Saxon Lysenkoism. Putting that concept on to the back burner, I approached a Scot who had lived here since well before the Second World War.

He said: "Laddie, when I arrived in London back in 1928, long before the war, I stopped a man and asked him the way to the YMCA. He replied, 'Why would you want to know that?' Their attitude's as old as the itch. The last war only gave them new horizons."

Perhaps knowledge is precious, and must not be given out to the unworthy. There could even be a fear that the Anglean secret, of how to succeed without trying, and how to make foreigners climb the walls in frustration, might leak out. Some English people have even glimpsed this caution at work, and recognized it.

They tell the story of the Member of Parliament who bet a colleague that he would compel Winston Churchill to give him a straight answer. Then he buttonholed the Prime Minister in the lobby and asked, "Could you please tell me the time?"

Churchill got out his watch, paused, and said, "What time do *you* make it?"

Psychoanalytic theory has a different explanation for the prevalence of spying among the English. It holds that they are reacting against secretiveness: as an unconscious revolt against their fathers (or uncles-in-law, I forget the exact context). They are determined to find things out, says another school, simply because it is so difficult. A third school (they are all European ones, so perhaps equally inapplicable to English conditions) holds that the English become spies simply because they *are* so secretive. To be a spy is seen as the ultimate in attainment: secrecy is of the essence in spying.

The only British spy whom I am conscious of having known was, oddly enough, not secretive at all. He kept telling me that he was in "the Secret Service," even when I begged him to stop, as I don't like knowing too much about such things.

Now Egbert (Sword-Bright) Peartree, as I shall call him, could have done with a little of that very same caution:

because the lack of it nearly caused him to lose face one day in my apartment.

Peartree, in addition to being a professed spy, was very well up in English literature; especially if you asked him about current writing immediately after the weekend reviews came out with their riches of trendy critiques. After midweek, though, Peartree used to languish a bit, and by Thursday evening he was often desperate for a cultural fix.

It was late on a Thursday when he came to the house, with that strained look which my alcoholic housekeeper used to call "the want." He asked for parsnip juice; I believe because it was the right thing for health at the time. I didn't have any to give him, and sat waiting to do my Hampstead duty, putting up with bores, making them like me instead of themselves, in their own interests.

Peartree said, in the quasi-academic interrogative manner of his kind: "You know Robert Graves, don't you? Wrote a foreword to one or two of your books."

"Yes, Peartree. But he doesn't like parsnip juice."

He ignored my levity, didn't even try to score off me on that one. I looked at his eyes and saw that they were pleading: he was in a bad way. It could not have been easy, having to apply to that philistine Shah for cultural refreshment.

"You've spent several summers in Majorca as Graves's guest?"

"I have."

"Tell me, have you, by any chance, got anything he's written but which hasn't been published?"

"As a matter of fact," I said, remembering some poems which Robert had given me in Deya, "I have."

"Please, please, let me see it," he entreated.

At that moment I felt a call of nature, and withdrew to the appropriate place. While I was in there, I realized that it would be a tiresome job to find the poems, which I had shoved into a book somewhere. So I took a piece of paper, from the roller handily mounted on the wall: and wrote, inventing a Gravesian poem:

> Her cruelty, ever crouching, yet straight-aimed
> Stabs me through and through
> And yet the oozing blood will write a masterpiece.

I reckoned it would do: estrangement, with as few Latin-based words as possible. Graves's trademarks. Good enough for Peartree, anyway.

Returning to where Peartree sat, I handed him the paper. His eyes gleamed as he read it. "Marvelous. Superb. How I wish I could write like that... the economy, the imagery, the Goddess." He was a man renewed.

I could not resist saying, "Now look, Peartree, you're a real phony. You may care to know that I wrote that myself, a minute ago, in the loo. And yet you're always telling me that I'm no writer, or I'd attempt the Great English Novel. And you might as well know that I don't believe that you are a spy, either."

For a moment he stared at me, wide-eyed. Then, in a rush of words, he shouted, "If *you* wrote that, then *you're* a true genius!"

So what am I to believe? I can see that, if he did not believe in my genius, Peartree could get out of his dilemma only by discovering it. On the other hand, it is tempting to think that I might take up poetry some day. Or dare to write that novel...

Peartree has never visited me again. Perhaps he is too busy with his spying.

Churchill, with his caution, even about what time it was, would never have allowed himself to be trapped as Peartree was trapped by me.

Of course, he *was* head of the Security Services, and would never have called himself an intellectual.

You don't have to spend time with spies to know a great deal about them. The media, novels, and even books on the English language, tell you quite enough.

Most of their spying seems curiously unsystematic, almost to have come about through an impulse. They do it when they can. I can explain this in the words of the English schoolman, John of Salisbury, Cardinal and tutor of Henry II of England:

> He who will not when he may
> May not when he will.

In the Middle East the equivalent is the saying, *I'laqi al asal wa la tasal* – "Lick up the honey and ask no questions." And I see from his biography that this prelate was deeply interested in heresies and the like: which may have been the twelfth-century equivalent of our modern-day espionage, for theological lovers of illicit thrills.

These native spies seldom show remorse, for they feel they have made a Step in the Right Direction. I looked up this important English phrase in *Roget's Thesaurus of English Words and Phrases*, a sensible precaution before using such idioms. I found it listed under *Utility*, usefulness. And bracketed with *subservience, etc.*, and with *Common Weal* and *Public Good*. It is also in the same section as *worth one's salt*, and *pro bono publico*.

How do they carry on their trade, these spies? Roget knows: they

> Inquire, seek, search, speer, look for, scan, reconnoiter, explore, sound, rummage, ransack, pry, peer, look round.

Compared to the words listed for spying, those for *secret* are very sparse in English, as we see from Roget's listings. So they don't even talk about it very much. If they did, they'd have to keep using the same words again and again. As even foreigners know, it is considered poor English composition and even bad form here to repeat words too often.

It is probably the mania for confidentiality which produces its opposite, just as over-religiosity stimulates fanaticism. In England, even monarchs can find themselves constrained by the national need to conceal, and even to conspire.

King Charles II once saw a thief, disguised as a courtier, steal a snuff-box from Lord Arlington's pocket. Seeing that the King was watching, the thief tapped his finger on his nose, winked, and quickly made off. Charles said nothing.

Later, when Lord Arlington was looking for his snuff, the King said, "You need not give yourself any more trouble about it. Your box is gone and I own myself an accomplice. I could not help it; I was made a confidant."

Something which is hidden, secret, and so on, has glamour. Even if it lacks it, glamour soon surrounds it. But the romance of espionage seems to be getting the English treatment at last: being stripped of its mystery. Mata Hari is the archetypal exciting Oriental spy, is she not? Books and films about her have established that image. But Nigel West has written (in 1984) a book called *Unreliable Witness*, about spies, in which she figures. That's how I now know much more about this lissome, Eastern, fascinating, hedonistic creature. But, guess what? She was really only a "bored Dutch army wife," middle-aged and, in fact, was at one point simply Mrs. Marguerite MacLeod by name.

As with everything else, the English get the last word on this subject. The playwright Alan Bennett, speaking of treachery in a television program, has explained a fundamental point: "You only have to survive in England and all is forgiven you," he says. "If you eat a boiled egg at ninety in England, they think that you deserve the Nobel Prize."

Discounting the flippancy of the last sentence, the matter of surviving long enough interests me. Is it a hint that all English turncoats are really double-agents, and only time will tell?

After all, everyone had become thoroughly accustomed to seeing MI6 represented as full of blundering idiots and Russian agents when, in 1985, it was revealed that Mr. Oleg Gordievsky, a senior KGB spy-chief, had been a British agent for periods variously stated as ten, fifteen and nineteen years.

Or are they like Lord Nelson, who, although a national hero, was described by Lord Fisher in his *Memoirs* as "nothing if he was not insubordinate"?

If insubordination makes some of them spies and some of them heroes, there is no doubt in my mind that the English will always come out on top because of the tremendous range of their language, Oriental in its multidimensionality. Its subtlety and nuances makes it perfect for spies; unlike, for instance, French.

Guy de Maupassant wrote something about the use of language, quoted again and again by literary critics, which could not possibly be applied to English:

> Whatever one wishes to say, there is one noun only by which to express it, one verb only to give it life, one adjective only which will describe it. One must search until one has discovered them, this noun, this verb, this adjective, and never rest content with approximation...

Imagine someone who believed this trying to get to grips with English.

As our proverb has it, "Whoever tries to explain the inexplicable is generally suffering from an illness."

26

The Secret System of the Angleans

> *Gratification*
> His gratification at being English is not based on an accumulation of gratifying facts about England, but on being English.
> D. W. Brogan: *The English People*

THE ANGLES DID not emphasize leadership or principles: certainly they are not reported as having a lot of either. But they did know how to get results. By combining, they triumphed, like the old Roman infantry shield-bearers or the new Japanese car-making teams. The English, those Anglekins, when establishing their Empire, were rarely beaten. Look at the combining of these latter-day Romans, in the form of the British Square, that unbeatable military formation.

Yet it was once broken by the Fuzzy-Wuzzies, at the Battle of Omdurman. Determined to find out how this was done, I traveled to a Hadendowa village when I was in the Sudan and asked the headman how they had achieved it. He had no specific knowledge of the event, but his answer was illuminating. He said, "I am sure that our ancestors did it because we didn't know that the British Square could not be broken." This is exactly the kind of answer I would have expected from an Englishman. In other words, the Angle mentality, fleetingly reflected here in the Sudanese warrior, did the trick.

Telling this story, I have generally observed intense enjoyment on the faces of my English hearers, coupled with a thoughtful expression which I have come to know and understand. They are filing the information away for future use. This is the second, the empirical, characteristic: the one which made the Empire, and the one which produces so many inventors and initiators of the useful, the strange, even the frightful.

Sir Henry Newbolt knew how to turn the defeat of the impregnable British Square to good Imperial account:

> The sand of the desert is sodden red.
> Red with the wreck of a square that broke.
> The Gatling's jammed and the Colonel dead –
> And the regiment blind with dust and smoke.

How many times have baffled foreigners heard, or read in a book, words such as these: "We didn't *want* to have an empire – we wanted trade, and the Empire just came about"? This is almost certainly true in part, whatever some may say about perfidious double-think.

I went further, and tested it. The last time someone said this to me, I asked, "Then why didn't you drop the whole thing, instead of making it bigger and bigger?"

The answer proved the instinct of the race and confirmed just how they must have been thinking as their Empire began to grow: "Well, that would have meant not taking due advantage of the situation, wouldn't it?"

And another Englishman pointed out to me that the English word colony was derived from the Latin *colonia*, "merely a word meaning 'an estate in the country'." And who doesn't want one of those?

Taking advantage of the situation, exploiting possibilities to the full, is an intriguing, and not solely military, concept. I used to know General Sir Ernest Swinton, the inventor of the battle-tank. A man of great distinction and charm, he was gentle and smiling in manner: only occasionally did his furious inward energy surface. One such time was during the Second World War when his bank manager suggested he might buy Defense Bonds. "*Defense Bonds*, you fool?" roared the General. "*Attack* Bonds, that's what I want!" He was not only a 24-carat Englishman, but always thought in terms of "full exploitation of every opportunity." It may have been his insistence upon Permeation and Penetration as a golden rule in life which gave me my first inkling of a secret English ambition. It goes something like this:

"There'll always be an England," the General had said, quoting a popular song. Then he added, mysteriously to me at the time, "Wherever it may be."

Now, decades later, I have allowed that input to surface in my mind. "Wherever it may be" as applied to England could provide the clue to the genesis of the Empire. After all, we know that it came about by accident. We also know that wherever English people go they demand hot-water bottles, China or other preferred tea at the right time, and even plum pudding in temperatures of 100 degrees plus. What are they (or were they) actually up to?

Going to other countries, and making them, or parts of them, as like their own as possible, even settling in very large numbers, speaking only English. Those are the clues. Now add the fact that the early English, of Schleswig, did not stay at home, but took over another country, Albion, and made it into England. What other people have moved their entire country, as well as its whole population, abroad? What does it mean? Probably that the Greeks were right when they named the Scythians, from whom the English claimed descent – "Nomades."

Whether the English actually pulled it off in America, Rhodesia, or anywhere else is not the point.

They moved in and started altering things to their own taste. I know English people who have their apartments or houses on leases and don't refurbish them much because "after all, it's only on a fifty-year lease, reverts to the landlord, you see..." But the British Embassy building in Kabul looks as though it was built to last a thousand years.

One English book, explaining the massive emigrations of the Spanish and Portuguese to Latin America, says, "their urge can only be explained through their seven-hundred-year history as outposts of the Arabian bedouins..." If them, why not the migratory Angles?

The Germans, Scandinavians, Poles, Irish and others who went to the New World were driven, according to English books, by hunger and the desire for a better life. But you rarely, if ever, hear the English emigrants so described. Why? Presumably because the English desire to move around at will, even to create new Englands, is an integral part of their heritage. No wonder they feel hurt when people call them colonizers. Very likely they were just trying the place on for size. The chance occurs: so you take advantage of it.

Similarly, Fleming did not throw away the polluting culture which led to penicillin and other antibiotics: he took advantage of it, just as Watt did with the principle of the steam engine, or Jenner with the cowpox. Of course, I want to assure my Greek readers, I have heard all about Archimedes' inspiration when he was in the bath and worked out how bodies displaced water. I have even tried that one out on an educated Englishman, and his reply is fully illustrative of the mentality, the self-confidence and the relevance of the *modus operandi* of these worthy descendants of the Angles.

He said, "First, an Englishman would have done it, if we had been in the habit of bathing at the time; second, that chap Hiero, the Tyrant of Syracuse, was worrying about the adulteration of the metal in his crown in *Greece*, for heaven's sake, not here. He asked Archimedes to work it out. Third, we need an input of foreign words, like 'Eureka,' to keep up the vitality of the language: sort of gene-pool..." I stopped listening at that point, though there was quite a bit more. You will, however, see what I mean. Similar arguments are used to cover the Scottish and Irish contributions.

Scattered inputs, expediency, combining together, and doing nothing until the time is judged ripe: that is the recipe. It was an Englishman, Sir Arthur Eddington, who wrote:

> There once was a brainy baboon
> Who always breathed down a bassoon,
> For he said "It appears
> That in billions of years
> I shall certainly hit on a tune."

It's that old idea of enough monkeys with enough time and typewriters to write the works of Shakespeare. Take another look and you will see certain interesting depths of meaning. Eddington chooses a baboon, not an Englishman, who would not waste so much time, knowing that he does not have billions of years. English punctuality is based on knowing that time is limited. Second, the bassoon is Italian and not the favorite English instrument. Certainly there have been, and are, very good English bassoonists: but it is not the national musical instrument; hence a pejorative is perhaps intended. Third, the baboon was acting in a thoroughly un English way: not unnaturally, since he was a foreigner. His attempt to achieve something by long-term planning is directly opposed to the Anglo-Saxon mentality.⁵ Some would say that his attempts expose the uselessness of long-term ambition.

A perfect example of this attitude was given me by the man (a member of the European Parliament) who quoted the limerick. He used it in relation to the Commission of the Common Market, where Britain is a Member. When I had written it down I said, "Bert, that may sum up your feelings about the Market, or even the Commission, but what's to be the British role in the whole thing? After all, you've been in it now for years."

"Ah," he said, "we'll just have to wait and see, won't we?"

Wait and see: the phrase repeatedly used by that redoubtable Englishman, Henry Asquith, Earl of Oxford. "A wise and masterful inactivity" is another much-loved English political term.

It will not have escaped you, in spite of the fact that I have stated it systematically, that this book is conceived and executed on almost entirely British lines, assisted where necessary by Afghan Oriental cunning and a few other odds and ends. But now we may come to a further question, one which has long baffled foreigners, and to which I think I have found the answer: by indirect routes, of course, which means – mainly – studying Mr. Coggins when I remember to do so. This is usually when we meet at the bus stop. The interactions can take as little as two minutes (when the bus comes on time) or as much as two hours (when it does not, which is usually).

Foreigners, as I know from many a long diatribe by the sons and daughters of Germania, Tuscany, Arabia Felix and elsewhere, have ambivalent attitudes toward the English. First, they recognize that the English will always come out

---

⁵ The English word "plan" is – of course – French, and from the Latin.

on top. As soon as you start to watch them, you get that strange feeling which comes after observing the three-card trick. It shouldn't happen, but it does... And, second, as with the trick, there is an ingredient of greed. Not for money, but to know how the blazes they do it. It's greed just the same. And there is another, a third point, to me equally important: how the secret can be acquired.

Starting with the last item first. I am convinced that it can indeed be learned. Take the instance of my recent visit, on an educational advisory mission, to a certain Third World country. My colleagues and I were sitting in the office of a high-flying "educator" and asking how, when and where he carried out his courses, aimed at enriching the potential of his Civil Service students.

He gave us a long account, which sounded impressive, but which we three specialists in this area simply could not follow. And he did it in almost perfect English. Then my associate, Professor Carapace (I use my English dictionary to rename him temporarily), tried another tack, and the following dialogue, according to my tape-recording, ensued:

> CARAPACE: Can we actually attend one of your courses?
> THIRD WORLD CIVIL SERVANT: That would take too long.
> CARAPACE: Then perhaps a part of one.
> TWCS: Still too long.
> CARAPACE: Perhaps just look in on a single class, for an hour?
> TWCS: They are very far away.
> CARAPACE: I see from the brochure, which you handed me when we came in, that there is a class at the end of that corridor, there. I think we can manage the walk.

TWCS: But unfortunately not at this time.
CARAPACE: The brochure says that there is a lecture in progress at this very moment, eleven-thirty. Shall we just drop in, gentlemen? [Looking around at the rest of us.]

At that point, two fateful and terrible things happened. The tape ran out, so I have no record of what was said; and the Professor took his eyes off those of his vis-à-vis.

All I remember is that we did not get to see that class. What happened? I do not know. How did the Third World Civil Servant steer us away, or make us forget, or otherwise pull off the trick? Again, I cannot for the life of me understand. Carapace and our other colleagues can't remember, either.

But I do know that this man, defending his territory with the greatest aplomb, charm and success, against any potential inspection, had been trained in the British tradition.

So the art of coming out on top can be learned, at least by some.

You will note that the civil servant was an educator, and trained as an academic in the British dispensation. The unpopularity of scholars is widespread: academic work has been styled, by an eminent Englishman, as "study by those who can't of that which doesn't need it." This has led some unreflective people to imagine that academics are therefore duffers. Far from it. They learn, if not wisdom, what Oxford calls New Guinea Politics: skills of no mean order. Since this is England, we always have to be on the alert for the possibility that what they are really doing is not necessarily what the label says. The analogy of the Learned Establishment of England may well be with the Holy Roman Empire: which was neither holy, Roman nor an empire.

Naturally, as fellow foreigners will be only too ready to believe, there were sources from which to learn the higher mysteries of politics, government, and administration, which were reserved for England. I gleaned something of this only today, from *The Times*.

Sir Anthony Parsons, London's United Nations ambassador and formerly HBM's head man in Tehran, has alluded to the arrangements. According to *The Times*, he spoke of the days of Empire thus: "Our education system [of the dependent territories] was used to produce junior clerks; Nehru had to go to Cambridge."

How do they do it? We have already seen that they follow the recipe already discerned by me: involving scattered inputs, expediency, combining together and waiting for the right moment.

Why then, have they not taken over the earth?

To me there can be only one explanation, the one which some of today's Eastern and other enthusiasts are fond of including in their category of Spiritual Pollution. Not exactly the spiritual side of the pollution, but rather the mistaken ideas side, and the part which refers to cluttering the mind with irrelevancies. The pragmatist, no less than the systematist, is always at risk here. He may have the data, he may have the timing: he may even have the judgment. But is there inaccurate – or just too much – data in that cranial treasure-house?

This is not intended as a criticism, but I have been forced to the view (which is English, currently, for "opinion") that this is the area which needs close, nay urgent, attention. There are just too many things, here in England, which mislead people, and fill their minds to such an extent as to paralyze foreigners and even to handicap the English themselves.

Had I stumbled across this circumstance elsewhere, I would have kept my trap shut: anyone may be sensitive when told that things are not what they seem in his or her country.

This may be why so many well-meaning people have had to blaze the trail, or pave the way, by couching such assertions in metaphysical terms. Even Shakespeare, in his own land, was not foolhardy in this respect, with his "More things in heaven and earth..." But I am a reckless Afghan.

First, however, I must modify the boast inherent in the last sentence. I have found that English people, on the whole (unless insecure characters, which means that they are abnormal), do not resent new information or the correction of fallacious beliefs. Books on popular fallacies sell by the thousand.

A member of the aristocracy will often say, when subjected to my explanations, "I say, jolly good, what!" Someone from the middle class is sure to mutter, "Would you believe it?" And the stalwart manual worker is liable to prefer "Do you reckon?" In each case he is taking fresh data aboard, and he will make use of it. Either in the pub, at coffee-time, or in the club, he will repeat it. He might even invent the modern equivalent of a steam-engine out of it for all I know, once he's got around to it.

The attentive reader will have noticed that, here in England, the most difficult thing to do is to get a rise out of an English man or woman. They are specially trained to resist this, whether in the home, in school, in the army or at work. The training might be called bullying, but is really a sort of rite of passage, a test, which hones the special part which other impacts cannot reach. The bullying system produces an attitude miscalled, by foreigners, "the menace of imperturbability." So secret, or so automatic, is the system that it has no name.

These days, you'll give few British Generals apoplexy by talking about loss of Empire, country full of immigrants, the menace of the EEC. Major-General F. M. Richardson, for one, is ahead of you:

Now our Empire no longer exists. We are a multiracial society in an offshore island of the Continent of Europe.

Thus his words in *Fighting Spirit*, a book about morals. They always get in before you.

That is the real secret of the system. A foreigner states that he cannot stand the English: only to find that Lord Byron has said it first. You don't get a rise out of your target Englishperson. Every time he or she hears anything critical, out comes the mental book of quotations. If you want to acquire the art of the English, you have to master this. And, as they say, what's the betting you'll never manage it?

And never forget the English proverb, proudly quoted in many a book since at least 1732: "He is not laughed at that laughs at himself first."

Do you think that the people are badly behaved? Fine, see William Hazlitt, in *Manners Make the Man*: "Ill manners make the Englishman," he said in 1829. Do you feel like calling them inefficient? They just say, "Yes, we do rather tend to muddle through."

In order to credit what I am about to say, you may have to verify it by looking at Stevenson's *Book of Quotations*. Take a deep breath and read there, listed under, of all things, "ENGLAND: HER FAULTS," yes I said *Faults*, these words:

> I will not cease from mental fight
> Nor shall my sword sleep in my hand
> Till we have built Jerusalem
> In England's green and pleasant land.
> William Blake, *Milton*, I, 13

So, if you come to England armed only with such pallid and hopeless criticisms as Ausonius's *Epigrams* ("Nemo bonus

Brito est/No good man is a Briton") to challenge the natives with – forget it. They have heard it all before. Ausonius wrote in the fourth century AD.

They are not like us, you see; they do it to each other. I have just been listening to a political speech. The speaker was heckled by another Englishman who demanded to know whether he was a "man of principle." The answer:

> "Yes! I shall tell you whether I am a man of principle if you can show me that you know what principle means. And, if you do know, you will not have to ask the question, sir!"

This sort of situation can be described thus: "If you don't win, you lose. If the other fellow doesn't lose, he wins."

Poor Professor Brogan, more than once almost exasperated, summarized, in *The English People*, the strength and irksomeness of this product of bullying-training thus:

> One of the most valuable and irritating English qualities is indifference to outside criticism. Even the most acute foreign exposure of native vices or native weaknesses is normally met with complacent indifference, or with an even more eager acquiescence, and emphatic assertion of the view that the foreign critic doesn't know the half of it.

And, of course, the English catch-phrase is "If You Can't Beat Them, Join Them."

Brogan's conclusion is that the English answer to Kipling's "What do they know of England who only England know?" is:

"Quite enough."

They don't mind in the least – indeed, they gave Brogan a knighthood.

27

What He's Really Like

Good and Bad
The fondness for rural life among the higher classes of the English has had a great and salutary effect upon the national character.
       Washington Irving: *Sketch Book*

In the country... for want of good conversation, one's understanding and invention contract a moss on them, like an old paling in an orchard.
       John Aubrey: *Minutes of Lives*

ALTHOUGH MANY FOREIGNERS' beliefs and complaints about the English are unjustified, one of them is perfectly accurate: it is hard to establish oneself with them.

But this goes for the English themselves, too. "Do I know you?" is not a request for information: it means "I don't know you," or even "I'm not sure that I want to know you." Incidentally, you should avoid people who say "Are you anybody?" They are nobodies.

Once established, of course, you can do no wrong. How is it done? How long does it take? What are the criteria? These are hard questions, but we must do what we can.

In my (quite small) village, in Kent, I am as well established as I can be with some of the people; others have hardly heard of me. How does this come about? In one store I am as regularly forgotten as I am remembered, welcomed, even, in another which is not thirty yards away. All this has little to do with time put in as a Man of Kent.

I went to have a pair of shoes made in metropolitan London, at a store I had never entered before, and in ten minutes they had brought out the records of my father's and grandfather's feet: though I am still not quite sure why they did it. On the other hand I spoke to someone I know in the village, and he did not know me at all. Perhaps I had better explain.

For years I walked, as I still do, down the main street of the village, and got to know several of the natives, waiting for buses, walking their dogs, or shopping. One day I strolled the fifty yards to the post office and met Herbert (Army-Bright) – someone I had talked to many a time before. "Morning," he said, and then: "here – you're from the big house, aren't you?"

I said that indeed I was. We were quite near our driveway leading from the main road, and various cars marked BBC TELEVISION were going in and out. It was during a break in the filming of *One Pair of Eyes* and I had been talking to-camera all morning.

Herbert screwed up his eyes and pointed at the cars.

"What they doing, then?"

I said, "They're making a TV documentary, life and thought, that kind of thing."

"Ah," he reflected, "I've always wondered what he's like, him up at the house. Never seen him, though. What's he *really* like?"

So I was established as a local resident: but not as me.

And yet the Afghan guerrilla, Mr. Haq, had taken only a day or so to become Mr. Hack, known and even appreciated at his hotel.

Recognition, of a sort, is possible through descent and also, perhaps it should be called, decision. My former newsagent was something of a bibliophile. When he first saw my name on the list for the paper-round, he said, "There was once a man with a name like yours, famous author and philosopher he was. Got one of his books. Name of Sirdar Ikbal Ali Shah. Haven't read it, though. Never had the time. But I've got it."

"That was my father," I said.

"Thought so."

I started to give him books of mine; in fact, for three or four years I gave him a copy of each one I wrote, and I was writing two a year at the time. He took them without a word, and we never discussed them.

During my visits to his store, whenever anyone of importance in the Middle East died, he would say, "Saw that king of whatchemacallit died. Your dad knew him, I suppose?"

He would stand erect, run a hand down the front of his neat buff warehouse-coat, and close his eyes, eyebrows raised, lids quivering, until I said "Yes." It so happened that most of them were indeed people that my father had known.

"Thought so." And that would be the end of it.

Now, at that time, I myself probably knew even more of the people in the news who hadn't died; but I did not dare to say so to Mr. Jervis (Spear-Servant) Bliss. It would have been boasting, and irrelevant. It was my father whose book he had discovered, and with whom he had the real link.

Of course all this may only be a common human tendency at work. We have an Afghan saying, "two people can become famous only if they boast about each other. Never try to do anything of that kind for yourself." But I could not help feeling that, had I been able to acquire some merit on the strength of my own work, or presence, with Mr. Bliss, we would have got to know one another better. And I wanted to know him better: I have heard (from others, naturally) that he is a most interesting man, once you know him.

Of course, the English are notoriously unaffected, if they feel like it, by name or position. A Victorian statesman, the then Lord Thurlow, being asked when he was going to move into his new house, said, "The Queen has just asked me that impudent question: as I would not tell her, I will not tell you."

Quakers visiting Buckingham Palace, refusing to accord reverence to temporal power, kept their hats on in the presence of the Queen. As the embodiment of the English virtues, she was no respecter of pretension, either, and knew how to deal with such behavior. Sarah Tooley, in *The Personal Life of Queen Victoria*, records that the monarch ordered that a Yeoman of the Guard should uncover each member of the Society of Friends as he entered the royal presence.

There is something quite Oriental about all this; except, of course, that in our country people must keep their hats *on* in the presence of royalty. And Afghanistan has not yet abandoned the option of even more direct action. Russians, as other invaders have learned in the past, stand to lose more than their hats there.

Our Amir Abdur-Rahman Khan, contemporary with Queen Victoria, once received her envoy, who said, alluding to the King's tendency toward violent solutions, "Your Majesty is a very fierce man."

"Yes, sir," said the King, "but I have to rule a strong people."

It is the interplay of conformity and non-conformity, of established behavior and challenges to it, which gives the English some of their piquancy, and adds to their reputation for eccentricity.

Take the Proby Puzzle. P. J. Proby, a famous musical performer, was billed as the top attraction at a Preston nightclub. He is well known for wearing a bow in his hair and splitting his trousers on the stage.

At this appearance, Proby did neither. Members of the audience, convinced in consequence that he might be an impostor, called in the local police. All ended well when Proby was identified – by his autograph.

Some overseas newspapers pretended to see, in this incident, proof that the habitués of the club could not recognize a star by his performance, or even by his face, and were therefore to be laughed at. This might hold true in many countries, but it is not necessarily so in England. The audience could well have been signaling to their guest, "You use these external signs to identify yourself: well, why have you stopped?"

I cannot forget the first words spoken to me by my prospective father-in-law, the poet and author Fredoon Kabraji. He was not English, but virtually his whole life was spent in the English tradition. He said, "I hear you are a very funny man; now say something funny."

A reproach? Absent-mindedness? Literal thinking? A desire to learn or to experience? Mummery? No: an English way of expressing oneself. Perhaps one of the greatest mistakes made by people trying to explain English is to say that it is primarily a medium in which one person communicates information to another.

What really happens, as often as not, is that someone says something, which *acquires meaning* when the other party adds something to it. And the English have a wise saying, "Make yourself into honey and the flies will devour you." Not only the stiff upper lip, but also the mutuality of conversation was summed up by the Earl of Beaconsfield – Disraeli himself – when he advised, "Never complain, never explain."

In establishing oneself, this motto can have useful functions. If a foreigner complains, he is unlikely to be popular anywhere; if he explains, he is seen to be too un English for decent people to take seriously. Playing it by ear may get you anywhere. Take the case of my compatriot Iskandar Salim, a research student of limited means.

He arrived in London off an Aryana Afghan Airlines jet from a sheltered and loving home in Kabul and went to a rooming-house in Swiss Cottage which had been recommended to him. Installed here, he found tea-making equipment, and tea, and thought he would partake of this refreshment. After a few minutes of experiment he realized that he simply did not know how to make tea: this had always been done by the servants. He obviously needed help.

Iskandar went downstairs and out of the door into the uncertainties of Fellows Road, where he approached the first person he saw, a young woman, with the words, "Excuse me, but how do you boil water?" No complaint, you note, and even less explanation.

It worked like a charm. The English lady took him straight to his room, filled the kettle, lit the gas, set out the various things, warmed the pot, and made the tea. The story has a doubly happy ending, for he had not only learned a useful art, but the lady married him. He had established himself.

The real mystery to foreigners is how one does it; how does one establish oneself? I now give you the right answer: one does not do it at all. *They* do the establishing, the English.

"Make them laugh," people say, "show friendliness, admire them, or attack them," and so on. But long experience shows that there are as many ways to become established among the English as there are English people. I can answer best from personal observation.

There was a surly taxi-driver who plainly disliked me as much as I did him. From necessity, I often used his cab.

One day, when he came to the house to pick me up, his face was all smiles.

"Morning. Been readin' about you. See your family comes from BC."

There had been an article on me in a small-circulation magazine, and a copy, he explained, had been left behind by a passenger in his cab. But why should this have changed his attitude? If he had meant, by BC, British Columbia, and had once lived there, I would have understood. Or if there was any advantage to the taxi business in carrying someone who (like most people) was descended from a long line of ancestors, that too. But no.

Even kings and queens seem to have difficulty here, so ancestry is not really the key. George I actually had to pay for what was supposed to be his by virtue of descent, as recorded in J. H. Jesse's *England Under the House of Hanover*: "This is a very odd country," he said, "the first morning after my arrival at St. James's, I looked out of a window and saw a park with walls and a canal, which they told me were mine. The next day Lord Chetwynd, the ranger of my park, sent me a brace of fine carp out of my own canal and I was told that I must give five guineas to Lord Chetwynd's man for bringing me my own carp out of my own canal in my own park."

Eventually the Hanoverians did establish themselves here: but only when they touched the right chord. Trial and error is the method: memorize the phrase. And avoid what the English call Brute Force And Ignorance. You may see English people use BFAI successfully a hundred times as a problem-solving strategy, for every single occasion that *you'll* get away with it; certainly for a good few years of your apprenticeship.

In England, you must not be too contemporary: anything old or outlandish is accepted, if it fits with English assumptions. Ursula Bloom, the writer, once came to the house to write a piece about me for a magazine. After explaining that she had written more books than anyone else alive, and introducing her escorting bluff sailor husband, she asked me about my wife. "I'll have to see her, so you'll waive the Rule of Seclusion, won't you?"

"Seclusion?"

"Yes," she rapped. "She's in complete *purdah*, of course?"

"No, she's as free as anyone else, so far as I know."

"In that case," said the kindly but determined dame, "I think we'll just forget the whole interview. You see, I know what English people want to read. *And* I see you are wearing a very new suit."

A great depth of kindness emanated from that woman. Kindness, yes: but did she have understanding? That, I think, was blocked by assumptions. I hesitate to say that Ursula Bloom knew less about the English than I do. But what was all that seclusion business about?

But we outlanders can always be wrong. I recall an almost sinister observation by J. B. Priestley, in *English Journeys*. Admittedly he was writing about the Great West Road, but note what he thinks about the key word "new," which was used about my clothes by Miss Ursula Bloom:

"The Great West Road," he says, "looked very odd. Being new, it did not look English."

If the newness of my suit was unEnglish, so is another tendency found everywhere else in the world. I refer to the general human desire to seek praise and avoid blame. It is nowadays widely recognized that even blame is better than being ignored: so runs accepted wisdom. As I have extensively argued in other books, this is the phenomenon of desiring attention. Except, that is, among the English. "Marvelous place," they say, returning from vacation, "nobody takes the slightest notice of you."

So, in dealing with What They Are Really Like, we have to admit that the peerless Eric Newby, in *A Traveler's Life*, puts it for all of them. He is writing about his days as Travel Editor of a London newspaper:

> What I liked about the *Observer*, and still do... in all the years I worked for the paper no one ever told me that I was doing badly, just as no one ever told me that I was doing well.

No wonder he got on so well with the Afghans on his *Short Walk in the Hindu Kush*.

28

Thrakintwist and Ciclaton

Not England, but Piddinghoe
The people of the Sussex village of Piddinghoe, near Newhaven, are said to hang ponds out to dry, to dig at night for daylight, and to shoe their magpies. Perhaps these calumnies are a response to the separatism of the Piddinghoeans:
"English men fight, Frenchmen too:
We don't – we live in Piddinghoe!"
    The Traditional Song of Piddinghoe Village

ALTHOUGH THERE IS a lot of it about, the English in general love to fight pretentiousness and snobbery. I can just see those Angles, enrolled by Hengist and Horsa, even laughing at the brothers' putative descent from Wotan. And they wouldn't have been over-impressed by Vortigern, their ultimate employer, either.

Naturally, from time to time, people in the country are swept away by self-importance and its paraphernalia; it never lasts for long. Where are the plumed hats, the monocles, the squires and snotty aristos of the past, and how long an innings did they have? That's the English way: let them fade out. In due course, naturally.

The reason for this is the understanding that posturing is almost always a substitute for something real, not even its symbol. Again, as modern psychologists have discovered (and the English knew long ago) it usually hides uncertainty and lack of confidence. And those are things which the English try to extirpate, even if it means putting you down and not helping you to struggle up again. Indeed, in their (unsystematized) thinking, they are doing you a good turn by preventing you from staggering on in an unreconstructed way.

It is sometimes recounted, always with relish, how a certain English social climber was making his way to his First Class compartment in a train when he recognized a well-known duke sitting in Second. "My Lord Duke," he gasped, "what an honor to meet you!" He could not prevent himself blurting out, though, "But why are you traveling second-class?"

The duke looked at him with great calm and retorted, simply, "Because there is no Third Class accommodation on this train."

It was at a train station that I had a lesson in how the English may seem to be showing off when there is really a deeper reason behind appearances. I arrived at Charing Cross Main Line Station in London one morning with an English friend Aubrey (the name means Elf-Rule), with whom I had traveled from the country. As we were crossing the concourse, I heard the announcement on the public-address system that there was a message for him.

"Better go to the station manager's office," I said, "between platforms five and six."

"No need to do that," Aubrey said, and continued walking toward the exit.

I tried again. "Someone wants to get in touch with you. It may be urgent."

"Shah: it's *not* urgent. Had the message phoned in myself."

I was appalled at such an act of self-advertisement; even if it was worthy of a public relations agent. "So," I said jocularly, "you want the peasants to hear your name, is that it?" I made a mental note of it; a free way to have your name ringing in several thousand ears; an amusing anecdote...

"Not at all," he said, "just making sure that they're on their toes, do you see?"

I was still not quite convinced. "In that case, why don't you just choose a name at random?"

"Matter of fact, I usually do. Knew I was coming up with you this morning, and wanted to see how you'd take it, that's all."

The English have a saying, "If you don't use it, you lose it." This may lie behind their constant, though hidden, curiosity. Again and again I have noticed how the English doggedly experiment, collecting data, sometimes without apparent meaning, which might come in handy one day. Like the shilling, knife and piece of string of that English invention, the Boy Scout.

Mr. Gladstone was at a dinner party, when someone said that it would soon be asparagus time. The Prime Minister remarked that it had already started, "but only the very rich, or the very foolish can enjoy it at present." He then gave the current price of asparagus. His wife, even, was astonished. "How can you possibly know that?" she asked. "I am sure that we have bought none." "No, my dear," Gladstone told her, "but when I see a new thing in the stores I always like to inquire the price, and I went into a store in Piccadilly this morning and asked what the remarkably fine asparagus they had in the window was selling at."

To read some of the English Sunday newspapers, one would think that there is nothing but snobbery and pretension about in the land. All kinds of things are advertised, mostly on the basis that they will make you appear up-to-date, cultured, educated or in a high income bracket. Detailed and well-illustrated articles tell you about the latest herb, or quiche, flight of ceramic ducks for the wall, "antique of tomorrow," motor-car or vacation place. The readers must have endless hours of fun; they must also feel increasingly frantic as they try to keep up with the Joneses (identified in English books as a Celtic, not an English, name). But what of the people who make all the discoveries of unspoiled retreats, rustic ways and the rest for them?

I was in a Somerset village once, and got up early to enjoy the summer air. Another walker and I came upon a native with a long, crooked stick with which he was clearing dead leaves from a hedge.

The other man stopped to talk, and I listened to this exchange:

"Morning, Everard [Boar-Hard]."

"Mornin'."

"What do you call that thing you're working with?"

"Oi calls it a thrakintwist."

"Would you spell that T H R A K I N?"

"Ass royt."

I stayed where I was as the other man walked off down the road. Presently the rustic straightened up and said, "Serve 'im royt oi shouldn't wundar."

"How do you mean?"

"Well," said Everard, "ee write for one o' they Lunnun papers, all about wotswot in the country. I knows 'im well. Ee come round askin' silly questions, so I give 'im silly aansas. One day they'll foynd 'im out. Thrakintwist! Oi aad one, but the wheel came off!"

Not long afterward, I read (guess where?): "As a delightful old countryman confided to me one recent balmy morning in Somersetshire, a 'rake and twist' is locally known as a *thrakintwist*. There is poetry in the word: what immemorial memories are conjured up by the honest simplicity..."

People like that made up the Merrie England legend, which a recent writer speaks of as that "chestnut about the deep underlying bond between cottager and landowner – helotry and tyranny, no more," says Stephen Vaughan (in the *Observer*) referring to a book, *The Long Affray*, in which Harry Hopkins blows the gaff on the legend.

Thrakintwist. It suddenly gave me a clue, or at least a chance for my imagination to start working on an old problem. There is a Persian word *sakarlat*, which means "scarlet cloth": indeed, the English word for this shade of red is traceable to it. So far, so good: there are many Middle Eastern words in English and other Western languages. But I had often wondered how it happened that the Persian sakarlat became the English word for "cloth of gold," and further transmogrified into *Ciclaton*.

The physical route is obvious enough: rare and exotic stuffs for the fashionable of the West, during the Middle Ages, came from the Islamic world, the mysterious East. And the word? Remembering my countryman and his Thrakintwist, I like to think that, centuries ago, some equally sly member of the lower orders – or a trader faced with a sneering aristocrat – said, airily, "That, my Lord, is what you've been asking for, Ciclaton, we call it in the trade."

Either that or the medieval merchant or lackey momentarily forgot what scarlet cloth was: or maybe he didn't have any, and passed off the gold cloth instead.

Practical jokes and telling stories against oneself are excellently successful ploys used by the English, often to the great discomfiture of foreigners. So widespread are these customs that they are used as a sort of ongoing instruction method by the Anglekins.

Lord St. Leonards, Lord Chancellor of England, was the son of a working barber, but this did not exempt him from the suspicion that he might prize his gravity too much. He was going to visit a mental institution – with the Surgeon-General – and someone informed the administration there that a little man who thought he was a judge would be arriving for admission as a patient on that day.

When the Lord Chancellor arrived and announced himself, the doctors humored him and answered all his questions. Then the visitor asked, "Is the Surgeon-General here yet?"

"No, but we expect him soon."

"Then," said the Lord Chancellor, "I shall inspect some of the rooms until he arrives."

"We can't permit that," said one of the keepers.

"Well, then, I shall walk awhile in the garden."

"Can't let you do that, either."

Lord St. Leonards thought that that was too much. "Why, don't you know that I am the Lord Chancellor?" he demanded; only to be told that there were four lord chancellors there already.

He was getting very annoyed when the Surgeon-General made his appearance. "Has the Lord Chancellor arrived?" were his first words.

"Yes, sir," they told him, "we have him safe, but he is by far the most violent person in the house."

And this, of course, became one of the Lord Chancellor's favorite anecdotes.

It is often thought that nothing is sacred in this strange country. The fact is, if you watch carefully, you will find that the people who say that are the ones who think that "sacred" and "pompous" have similar meanings.

The other week I was listening to an active, but oozingly sentimental, charity snob from another country talking to an Englishman about his work and the wonder of helping others. This was the dialogue:

> CHARITY SNOB: We collect money from wonderful human beings, people who are all heart, once you have got through to them. Why, some of them are the highest in the land. I always tell them a little story about self-help. There is a saying, "Give a man a fish and you feed him for a day; teach a man to fish, and he can support himself always." It is so heart-warming, and an old Chinese saying, you know, from their Classics, I believe...
>
> ENGLISHMAN: Yes. A good match to the one I once heard: "Give a man good luck, and you can throw him into the sea!"

I could see that the charity worker was utterly revolted by the heartlessness of the cold-fish Englishman. Yet the latter was only pointing out how nauseating the snob's attitude was, by posing as devil's advocate. That seemingly cold-hearted Englishman would reach into his pocket, but he would like to impart an Anglean lesson at the same time.

One of the warmest-hearted Englishmen I have ever known said, when we first met, "Now look here, you're getting far too much publicity in *The Times*." In fact, I had featured in two articles, and once on the Court page, and had had two letters to the Editor published, in the preceding decade. Had I had less experience of the English, I would have considered him hostile, or envious, or both. Not so. His motive was not to censure me, not to look superior, not to run down *The Times*. He was just playing his part as an unconscious operator of the English training specialization. The phenomenon has no name, so I had to find a term myself: Education Through The Intimidatory Approach, which could be acronymed as ETTIA. The survivors emerge strengthened.

Like most foreigners, I have heard about the Englishman who quit the Foreign Legion because its brutalities seemed too soft after his English Public School; but that is about endurance and what my English technical adviser, Mr. Coggins, calls Saveloy-Fair. What I am talking about is much more positive: and it has a product. It makes you look for something inside you which can't be deflated, can't be harmed, can't be got at. Not by anybody or anything mortal, at any rate.

The process is nothing less than a tribal initiation. It has not been conclusively demonstrated as such only because anthropology is something which English people apply to members of "remote" communities, Native Peoples and all that. Not the other way about.

The analogy is with the Rite of Passage, a ceremony, probably involving shocks, marking such transitions as birth, marriage and death. More intricately, it resembles the long preparation of the warrior, through tests, privations, exercises.

There are slight differences. In the first place, the training is applied by anyone who can get you into the appropriate situation, and is not confined to priests or tribal elders. This gives it tremendous power over you: until you graduate, when you are permitted to apply it to others. That is the point at which the "something inside you" is mature.

This "something inside you" which characterizes Englishry is a protection against a lot of psychological damage. If you commit yourself to something and it is demolished, you may collapse. So, says the typical English person, I'm not really dependent upon anything.

There is a striking parallel, here, with Eastern spiritual teachings, in two fundamental areas. The Sufi, in the words of one sage, adjures you not to value anything "which you could lose in a shipwreck." This is just what the Englishman, with his refusal to be impressed by material things, would advise if he had formulated it in words.

Then comes the second phase. Having divested yourself of attachment to things of the body, you have to get to work on the mind. The Englishman cheerfully and frequently uses the method of self-deprecation. And the Sufi? His slogan, repeated in a hundred texts, is "Revile me as much as you will: for I know myself to be even less worthy than you could imagine."

That which seems to hurt may also sharpen. *The Oxford Dictionary of English Proverbs* preserves this truth as succinctly as any saying from the East:

"The sun which melts wax also hardens clay."

Seen from this viewpoint, the English attitudes have more than an Eastern character. They look like the remnant of habits of thought perhaps injected into the culture in very ancient times.

No circle of wise ones now survives among them, to control the instruction process: the training is diffused among the tribe, and everyone is a teacher of it. So, though there are no exploiting gurus to beware of, no mentors now exist who could pilot the community, or even the individual. Perhaps they will emerge one day.

Johnson's "Patriotism is the last refuge of a scoundrel" had been treated as an intemperate outburst, as a joke, or as a *bon mot*. For me, it means that Johnson sees how easily people can be manipulated, and how they will imprison themselves, with a formula.

I choose patriotism as an example because it combines emotionality and conditioning, and hence is a very powerful force. Now just note how an Englishman, no traitor or even internationalist, can deal with this explosive.

The story goes that one Englishman was saying to another, "I was born an Englishman, I have lived an Englishman, and I shall die an Englishman!"

The reply of his compatriot, believe it or not, was, "My dear chap, have you no ambition?"

Superficially this seems idiotic, anti-patriotic, or just point-scoring. I have heard it said, too, that the English captured the joke from the Scots, and that the answer should have been, "Awa' wi ye, man, hiv ye nae ambeeshun?"

When you know your Englishry, however, you will understand that the true paraphrase of this line is, "You have limited yourself too much, being obsessed by a single idea."

When you know even more, a fresh dimension appears. Brendan Behan, though Irish, may have been privy to some secret English aspiration, when he wrote, in *The Hostage*, "He was born an Englishman and remained one for years."

Perhaps we hear the voice of the Angles once again. They did not remain little Schleswigians, or else there would have been no England as we know it. Their descendants have been observed turning their attention, to put it no higher, to the entire globe.

They have done as much as any other people in studying the world. They have even seemed, at times, to be trying to rule it. Now, when Lord Chesterfield said, "To govern mankind one must not overrate them," I think that he was trying to understand something but hadn't quite got there. With more thought and more time he would have realized that mankind is ungovernable by imposed methods, whether overrating or underrating is involved. In him, I'm pretty sure, the Angle was probing, trying to find the Anglean destiny. Even if that eventually means remaining English only for some years, I am quite persuaded that they are capable of any required transition.

Naturally, the Englishman has to go through the intensive and oft-repeated treatment which has been prescribed by the inner Anglean; that is the regulative mechanism. In the home, in school, among his peers and betters, he is constantly tested for assumptions, falsity, pretension and snobbery. Many English people, as always with any initiation or higher teaching, simply do not make the grade.

The Englishman has to endure the psychological equivalent of the spiritual despair which the Sufi sage Saadi called the *Shab-i-Tarik*, the Dark Night. For him, and you, I give these lines of Al Tughrai, to show that people have known it and survived:

> And why has Death so long delayed
> To wrap me in his friendly shade:
> Left me to wander thus alone
> When all my heart held dear is gone?

A Yugoslavian diplomat, Fuad Azembegitch, once complained to me about English chauvinism. "An Englishman's dog bites a piece out of a foreigner's leg," he said, "and the Englishman's reaction is to hope that this meal does not upset his pet's digestion!"

I am not sure that Fuad believed me when I said: "It's nothing to do with nationality. The English are dog-lovers. They'd be just as concerned for the dog's health if it had bitten a fellow-countryman..."

This esoteric training is what produces the imperturbability associated with the English. It does not succeed with everyone, but even the failures fulfill a function. They are perceived as terrible examples of what one may remain.

The mark of the highest initiate, of course, is to have thrown off attachment to externals, reliance even upon the totems of the tribe. This is the reason behind the apparent paradox of English detachment. It explains how senior military officers (those beyond field-rank, major) can calmly speak of drill and spit and polish as "eyewash." A general, over dinner at the Cavalry Club in London, surprised me, before I had learned this lesson, by observing, "The largest dramatic paintings of the British Army are those commemorating our defeats."

In other societies, it is the petty, the jealous, the inadequate, who knock the Establishment or make fun of the household gods. In Britain, there are indeed such people, but the rest take little notice of them. This is because the artistry with which the real mentors of the culture dismember its sacred cows is recognized as supreme. Its purpose is to free one from the trammels of idolatry, and to ease the candidate's passage into ever higher realms of truth.

Two small examples of the method of high-level debunkery will suffice to fix the process in the mind. One then has a useful benchmark against which to measure many otherwise baffling materials from the English tradition.

For the first we may choose the poet Thackeray, on aspects of life at the venerated Eton College:

> They are proud of it – good heavens! – absolutely vain of it; as what dull barbarians are not proud of their dullness and barbarism? They call it the good old English custom.

The other might be an incident in Alexander Kinglake's classic, *Eothen*. Traveling across the trackless desert, in opposite directions, two Englishmen espy one another. As is usual with this tribe, they confine their contact to a wave in salutation. But, when they have passed one another, and only forty yards separates them, they are forced to stop and have a brief, if almost meaningless, conversation. What makes them do it? Only the fact that their native retainers – and their camels – insist upon the halt. It is the local custom.

Now let us look at how this theme is handled by a more contemporary Englishman. Kinglake died in 1891, but a tale which is remarkably close to his anecdote was told me by the Orientalist (and former Foreign Office minister) C. J. Edmonds. He was a great authority on the Middle East – and a much-respected resident of the Kentish village where I live.

Edmonds served in both World Wars, and the tale he told was set in the Western Desert during the second one. There had been fierce fighting between the Desert Rats and Rommel's Afrika Korps. Separated from their units, two British officers, each mounted on a stolen donkey, were making their way in opposite directions toward where they hoped their comrades might be. Hungry, thirsty, and nearly exhausted, they were in the middle of nowhere.

As they drew abreast, Mr. Edmonds assured me, the following dialogue took place:

"Afternoon."
"Afternoon."
"British?"
"Yes."
"County family?"
"Right."
"Prep school?"
"Yes."
"Public school?"
"Eton."
"University?"
"Oxford."
"Good college?"

"Magdalen."
"Decent regiment?"
"The Guards."
"Homosexual?"
"No."
"Pity."
And each went on his way.

Perfect ammunition, you might think, for a good Marxist to use against the chinless wonders who stand between him and his legitimate aspirations. But Cecil John Edmonds, CMG, the narrator, was himself one of the privileged elite. He was educated at Bedford School, Christ's Hospital and Pembroke College, Cambridge, and was a member of the Athenaeum.

"I notice you mention Oxford, and not Cambridge, your own university," I said.

"Oh, did I? I'll use Cambridge instead, if you think that makes it a better story," he said.

What is the use, many a good anti-capitalist agitator must have thought despairingly, of trying to oppose people who knock themselves for you all the time, and apparently without any unfavorable effect?

What, I wondered, while pondering this phenomenon, is the rationalization by means of which the English so cheerfully repudiate things which others hold sacred? There must be some give-away of their secret, somewhere in their literature.

Leafing through Samuel Butler's *Notebooks*, I came across the leak: "Truth is not in lying, but in knowing when to lie and when not."

This revelation provided the key to many a door of Englishry.

But be warned that this is fairly advanced stuff. If you happen to be one of those foreigners (or English people) still at the stage where you find Mr. Edmonds's self-mocking hard to understand, re-read this chapter only when you are sure that you understand the passage, from *Alice in Wonderland*, in which the young man is questioning old Father William:

> "You are old," said the youth, "one would hardly suppose
> That your eye was as steady as ever:
> Yet you balance an eel on the end of your nose –
> What made you so awfully clever?"

Father William's answer should be carefully studied:

> "I have answered three questions, and that is enough,"
> Said his father; "don't give yourself airs!
> Do you think that I can listen all day to such stuff?
> Be off, or I'll kick you down stairs!"

The self-mockers have no false humility.

29

Watching Them

> *Larceny*
> John [Bull] likes a bit of petty larceny as well as anybody in the world. He likes it, however, with this difference – the iniquity must be made legal.
>
> Douglas Jerrold: *Heads of the People*

PEOPLE ALL OVER the world complain that the English are given, at times, to doing very unBritish things, such as buying land and elephant tusks for a couple of hatchets and a handful of beads. There is to me only one flaw in this claim about colonial exploitation: they do it to one another, too. It is a part of the secret training system. That is why quite a lot of English people feel hurt when accused of imperialist plundering. "Look what we gave you," they say. It's quite touching, really.

For an example of this principle at work, we need look no further than London. I prefer to choose an instance from times past, so as to avoid the suggestion that I am aiming at any present-day person or interest.

Let us take the case of the brothers Lord (William) Stowell and Lord (John) Eldon, in the nineteenth century, when a lot of colonising and the like was going on. The two young men were going to see a play and stopped for dinner at a tavern. They only had a guinea piece between them, and William dropped it. They searched, but in vain; it must, they thought, have disappeared into a crack between the floorboards.

But all was not lost, as John soon proved. Calling the waitress, he said, "We've dropped two golden guinea coins. Try to find them."

She went down on her hands and knees, and soon found the lost coin, which had rolled under the fender in the fireplace.

"That's a very good girl," said John, "and when you find the other one you can keep it for your trouble." These two gentlemen later became distinguished members of the English judiciary.

Duplicity? Certainly not, in Anglean terms. The two were undoubtedly attuned to the very English sentiment encapsulated in Sir Francis Bacon's words:

> It is a certain sign of wise government and proceeding that it can hold men's hearts by hopes when it cannot by satisfaction.

Some say that the English have not yet shaken off the pirate in them, the way of life that brought them here in the first place. But did Sir Walter Raleigh not answer that charge effectively enough when people called him that? "Did you ever hear," he asked, "of any that was counted a pirate for taking *millions*?"

My personal recollection of the controversy is even more explicit. My father was in converse with Winston Churchill, while I took photographs; and the English "pirate" charge was mentioned.

"My dear Sirdar," Churchill rumbled, "we are *reformed pirates* now." I still have my photograph and, oddly enough, the man had adopted a rather piratical pose as he said those words. He went on, "Besides, it ill behooves Afghans to speak of pirates, particularly when they are using a *Soviet* camera." Quick of him to notice that; it was, in fact, one of those twin-lens Russian Lubitels.

And perhaps there is still something of the pirate in them. Maybe it wasn't difficult to get the English out of Schleswig, but is it so easy to get the Schleswig out of the English? See the *Daily Telegraph* for September 24, 1985, under the heading "Motorway Pirates":

> Pirates struck on the M4 yesterday when they unhitched a trailer carrying a £4,000 speedboat from a parked car... and drove off with water-skis, wetsuits and lifejackets.

Those who think that the English were nomads rather than pirates may care to reflect that, as Thomas de Quincey complained, it was only in the nineteenth century that it became illegal to wander abroad in England and sleep out of doors.

Before moving on, I would like to remind my Afghan readers, who may think me too Anglophile, that I know our history as well as they do. The answer to their question is "Yes, I know they came at us with machine-guns, field-artillery and even airplanes, but we dealt with all that; we are a hard people, who already had all the beads, hatchets, and trinkets we needed. In fact we now export them to the Portobello Road, for the English to adorn themselves and their houses."

Knick-knacks, of course, were not the only material resources of the English. Their explorers knew what money was and would use it if necessary. Cecil Rhodes (who was English in sentiment, if South African in other respects) made that clear. He said to General "Chinese" Gordon, "What is the earthly use of having ideas if you haven't the money to carry them out?"

Some of the more sheltered among the English people may imagine that this attitude had been acquired by Rhodes from foreign parts. We can show that it was already alive and well long before his time.

Charles James Fox, the eighteenth-century English statesman, was told by the Duke of Newcastle that he wanted to keep the use of the secret service funds in his own hands. "How," inquired Fox, "could I manage the House of Commons unless I knew who had been bribed and who not?"

We don't know what happened about that, but a further insight comes nearly two centuries later, when Stephen Leacock is contrasting transatlantic with English tendencies: "The difference seems to be that our politicians will do anything for money and the English politicians won't; they just take the money and won't do a thing for it."

The English, you see, know how to do or not to do things, and how to make money while doing them, often throwing in a lesson in the process. Even kings can do it. There is an example in one of the exploits of Henry VIII.

The King was once out hunting in Windsor Forest when night fell. Disguising himself, he approached the Abbey of Reading and was invited to dine. He dug into the sirloin of beef so heartily that the Abbot said, "I would give a hundred pounds to feed as lustily in beef as you do. Alas, my weak and squeasie stomach..."

The King returned, unrecognized, to London. Some weeks later he had the Abbot arrested, clapped into the Tower of London for a time, and fed on bread and water. Then a sirloin of beef was set before him, and "of which the Abbot fed as a farmer of his grange." Out of a hiding-place sprang the King; and demanded his hundred pounds, in gold.

Note the English pattern: observation, application, and profit – for somebody, at least.

All foreigners – and quite a lot of English people – used to puzzle over a formerly much-used slogan which the Government promoted without cease: "British Way and Purpose." I have decoded it. The translation is "adaptability." But you must never actually ask how they do it.

The whole thing is geared to making you learn, not primarily to teaching you. It was not an Englishman who said to me, in another connection, "I taught him perfectly, but he did not learn," but he had learned the phrase in England.

Some English people try to worm information out of others, but even in more mundane matters than Way and Purpose they never get very far. Joseph Chamberlain, the English statesman, had a "regimen of his own" which seemed to give him the secret of perpetual youth. Someone asked him what the method was.

He smiled, and said, "Never walk if you can drive; and of two cigars always choose the longest and the strongest." He has even converted the comparative into the superlative...

They won't even tell each other: so what hope is there for the rest of us? None by that route.

Sometimes you simply can't see what they are driving at, and sometimes even another Englishman is baffled. But there is always a reason.

There is the case of Henry John Temple, Lord Palmerston, whose words during his visit to the office of Herman (Teutonic: "Army Man") Merivale rather mystified the *Gentleman's Magazine*:

> Merivale was Permanent Secretary to the Colonies. As such he was greeted with customary jauntiness by Lord Palmerston – then making his first official

visit to the Office – with the words, "In the first place, Mr. Merivale, where are the Colonies?"

Prime Minister may only mean Chief Servant to the Monarch, but Palmerston's words, surely, have a regal ring.

I should warn you that the revelation of a meaning, in England, can be subject to a delayed-action effect. Sooner or later the reason for that Victorian remark may well surface, perhaps in connection with space-travel or microchips or something.

I say this because the matter of Jenkins's Ear and its time-scale has occupied my attention for some time. Every schoolchild in England knows about it. It fascinates their teachers. On April 9, 1731, a Spanish patrol vessel intercepted the English brig *Rebecca* off Havana. She was boarded and plundered, and the Spaniards, perhaps bullfighters in civilian life, cut off one of Captain Robert Jenkins's ears. He took it back to London (in a leather case) and presented it, with his complaint, to the King.

For ages, nobody took much notice of poor Jenkins; the English were angering slowly, as is their wont. Seven years later, however, the matter was "severely discussed" in Parliament. War with Spain ensued, breaking out on October 23, 1739, getting on for nine years after the incident.

In the meantime the Spaniards, with a false sense of security, must have imagined that they had got away with the amputation. Perhaps they had read the Anglo-Saxon law-books, where only derisory fines for such conduct were detailed. "If an ear be struck off, 12 shillings." The fine for murder was a mere 100 shillings: far short of a declaration of war.

Observation, visual evidence, must never be forgotten, however, in England. The sight of the ear, produced in Parliament (not to mention its being paraded around

London) must have played a part. And, in Parliament, as elsewhere in these islands, sometimes observation alone (or the observation of actions without words) will do the trick.

We need look at only one instance, and readers can observe others, day by day, as they occur. This one concerns the great William Pitt.

It was the occasion of Erskine's first speech in the House, and everyone expected Pitt to reply to his opponent. Indeed, it looked as if he so intended, for he at first took copious notes with pen and paper. But, with every sentence uttered by the unfortunate Erskine, Pitt's attention and manner relaxed. At length, with all eyes now fixed upon him, "he, with a contemptuous smile, dashed the pen through the paper and flung them on the floor."

The rest of the account is predictable:

> Erskine never recovered from this expression of disdain; his voice faltered, he struggled against the remainder of his speech and sank into his seat dispirited and shorn of his fame.

Or, as the *Dictionary of National Biography* puts it more succinctly, "Pitt's by-play crushed Erskine."

With the English, you don't just decline the beads and the hatchets, or fire if they fire at you, or listen to their words: you *watch them as well*.

"You'll watch out for the English," said my grandma. She had that very positive way of talking, and seldom used the conditional form. I never knew whether it was an order or a prophecy, when she put things like that.

"Why?" I asked, for I was only about five at the time. "They watch others, and see how well they have done," she said: and I remember her exact words, even the rest of the speech, which was "That'll do for now. Now run along and wash your feet. They're filthy."

She was, of course, perfectly right (on both counts: I'd just run in, barefoot, from the garden) and I have remembered what she said, sometimes in remarkable circumstances, for over fifty years. She was one of those people who must be right, one felt, because she was always fair with me.

I still find new applications for that "watching." People often say, "Remarkable woman, my grandmother, you know," in England as well as everywhere else. Well, in the case of mine I join them without reserve.

30

Heisenberg Wasn't So Original

> Churchill's V-sign caused some consternation at first. A woman pointed out that the Sign was traditionally used for invoking the Devil, not for victory. This was "communicated to the Prime Minister, but had no effect."
> E. & M. A. Radford:
> *Encyclopedia of Superstitions*

THE HABIT OF analysis, seeking a central theme, assuming that there must be an answer in line with your assumptions, is not an English one. The English *can* do this: but it is not their procedure of choice. Many of them regard those who cannot "taste, chew and digest" as disadvantaged. Their rather Eastern tendency to interpose a time-pause between any question and its answer is illustrated in the constant, and popular, saying of Professor C. E. M. Joad, "It all depends on what you *mean* by..."

I took several dozen books on the English by foreigners, and worked through them to assess this question. The outlanders' conclusion is that the English have no system for most things, but can solve problems admirably when they have to.

The English reaction was summed up by my window-cleaner, whom I faced with this Continental perplexity. "Werl, you're bonkers if you try something which might not work when things work out anyway," he exclaimed, looking at me with amazement. He added: "Is that wot yer do in that there room all the time, thinkin' about things like that?"

My sympathy is with the English, after reading all those foreigners' books, which may inform or entertain, but do not understand. Just look at the tables of contents: religion, love and marriage, commerce and industry, education, town and country, manners and customs, language and class. Neat categories to investigate things which are anything but neat.

There is a fable told in Afghanistan which may help to explain the inevitable despair of all those observers of England:

A small boy once caught a fly. He dismembered it, putting the various parts in neat piles of legs, wings, and so on. When he had finished doing that, he looked around and said, "The parts are here, all right: but where is the *fly?*"

The English go about things in the opposite way. They collect material, move it around, look at it, think a little, and let it settle down until an answer appears.

One of my favorite Press-cuttings is from a review of one of my books, by a Fellow of All Souls, writing in a scholarly journal. "This book," he says, "is to be tasted, chewed and digested slowly."

The English don't jump to conclusions, because they have an idea that just thinking about a thing may have an effect on that thing. What a thing is, for practical purposes, may depend upon what people think about it.

Knowing that, I wonder why the physicist Werner Karl Heisenberg (1901–1976) is credited with the discovery of the

Uncertainty Principle as late as 1927. Briefly, this says that you can't measure the position and momentum of a particle simultaneously. This is because that which you interpose, to examine it, will affect the result. The English have known this instinctively for as long as I can trace their behavior.

At the same time, an Englishman will completely ignore the Operator Effect; perhaps to verify how important it is, for they are always experimenting.

I got back to London after one journey, having lost the filling from a tooth. I found a dentist: one with a very professional manner.

Sitting in the chair, with all kinds of high-tech instruments and a drainage tube in my mouth, almost unable to breathe, there was no way I could have spoken a word, and he must have known it. Yet, as he plied his screaming water-drill, the surgeon shouted into my ear, "How do you like it in this country, then?"

At that moment the drill hit something, and I jumped up, with an anguished "AAARGH!"

"That's good. Glad to hear it," was his reaction, as he firmly pushed me back into the chair.

You can't classify that kind of thing, though for seasoned England-watchers it will be familiar. The unregenerate foreigner will tear his hair, trying to fit it into his pigeon-holes. Does it come under DRILLS, DENTAL? Under COURTESY, or INSENSITIVITY or SADOMASOCHISM, or even under APLOMB? The dentist was probably just checking the Operator Effect.

In this book, of course, it is the English, which is to say the multivious, method which is being followed. Just as, for one celebrated theorist – Herbert Marshall McLuhan – the Medium is the Message, so in England the Method is the Material, and the other way about.

William Joyce, "Lord Haw-Haw," broadcasting from Nazi Germany during the war, must have thought that he had scored a hit by constantly calling the British "The Brutish." He evidently never consulted the *Oxford English Dictionary* for, in the 1933 edition, they'd beaten him to it. Look up BRUTISH and this is what you find:

> BRUTISH: 1 Of or pertaining to the brutes, or lower animals, as opposed to man
> 2 Pertaining to... the brutes
> 3 Rough, rude, savage, brutal
> 4 Brute
> 5 *BRUTISH, obs. form of British*

My italics, of course. So, although obsolete, the term was formerly in use: though for how long the *OED* does not say. Nowadays foreigners tend to call English directness by softer names, such as "tactlessness." Their brusqueness, or tactlessness, call it what you will, is deliberate; paradoxically, it is engendered by the operation of careful purpose.

It is this very word which gave me an early breakthrough in understanding the English, through the wisdom of an Afghan sage, Sufi Abdul-Hamid Khan.

The old Sufi and I were in London. As Master of the Royal Mint in Kabul and a considerable calligrapher, he had the task of supervising the production here of a new issue of high-denomination Afghan banknotes.

We were received with courtesy by the managing director of a large security-printing firm, who asked me to translate for Abdul-Hamid something which, though a pleasantry in English, would have been considered rather coarse in our language.

As I hesitated, the Sufi picked up my thoughts, and said, "He's being tactless, I suppose?"

I said, "Well, he hasn't got your *saliqa*" – the word we use to mean intuition, including a sense of delicacy.

After the meeting, at Abdul-Hamid's hotel, the old man asked me what the English word for "tact" was, and I told him. "And what, exactly, does it mean?"

"It means," I said, "being sensitive to how people are feeling, to things that might hurt or affront, and acting accordingly."

"Aga," said the sage, "although I don't know these people's tongue, and you are a master of it, experiences such as ours today indicates that you cannot be quite right."

"Friend Sufi," I said, "far be it from me to question any of your perceptions, but everyone in this country knows full well exactly what this very common word means, and is thoroughly sensible to its nuances. I admit to including myself in their number."

He was a very gentle kind of man, and he just smiled kindly and asked me to find a good English dictionary. I went out and bought one, the current edition of *Chambers*.

"Now please, if you will, look up that word." He pointed to his note, in perfect Nastaliq phonetics: "*TAKT.*"

I riffled through the book, to page 1122:

"Here you are: '*tact* [pronounced] *takt*, noun. Adroitness in managing the feelings of persons dealt with...'" I put it down and smiled.

He nodded. "Now please see what else it may say under that heading."

Reluctantly, I opened the book again, and read the rest of the sentence:

"'Nice perception in seeing and doing exactly what is best in the circumstances.'"

The Sufi bowed. "Thank you. Now perhaps you see what I mean?"

"Not entirely. I think that man at the printers did lack nice perception."

"Ah," said Abdul-Hamid, "there you have it. I am quite sure that he did not lack it. He had the perception of what kind of effect any words of his might have on us. What he was *doing* was a consequence of what he thought was best – for him – under the circumstances."

Best *for him*. That was the clue. So, when an Englishman says or does something you don't like, ask yourself whether he really is acting against his own interests. He may only be using his assessment to handle the situation. How do you know, for instance, that he doesn't want to ruffle or confuse you? It could be in your own interests to know.

Multiviousness crops up all over the place, and it is often hard to know at the time what the Englishman is aiming for; although it may become clear long after the event. People who don't know this naturally call the English confused, opportunist or deceitful.

Dr. Yusuf Shawarby, an Egyptian professor of Earth sciences, asked an English geographer at an international conference why General C. G. Gordon, and others, followed and mapped the River Nile in 1874–77, and why people in Victorian times were always seeking its source.

The reason for his inquiry, he told me, was that the Nile's source was known in Europe nearly a millennium before the days of the great Victorian explorers. The geographer Abu-Abdullah Al-Idrisi of Ceuta had drawn a map tracing the river and showing where it rose, when working at the Sicilian court of Frederick II, nine centuries before.

The English scholar didn't hesitate for an instant. "Well," he said, "perhaps they just wanted to see for themselves."

What does *that* come under: geography, General Gordon, Nile, evasiveness, fatuousness, careful checking, trying to ruffle your feathers, or failure to research what others had already done?

It could be any of these, omnidirectional, or none. William of Occam, the medieval Englishman and author of the Don't Make a Meal of It theory, would have approved the geographer's solution. The Romans thought that the ancient Britons did things by magic, and even the later, more Teutonic, Anglekins and others had their magic swords and witches. But the magic power resides in the Englishman's finding answers by accumulating information and digesting it, ready to be used when the time is ripe.

Sometimes, though rarely, they will tell you how they do it. At a London train station I jumped into a taxi and gave the name of my club to the driver. Now this club has the same name as a hotel not far away; but the taximan hesitated not at all, neither did he say "Club or Hotel?" He delivered me to the club.

Thinking it over during the short journey, I wondered how he had divined my thoughts. The best way, as Occam would have advised, was to ask him, and I did.

"That's easy, guv," he said. "People who go to posh hotels is always trying to impress someone, unless they're pop stars, and you don't look like one of them. Members of West End clubs don't bovver. I sore your trousers wasn't pressed, so I reckoned you was a Member."

"How did you know I wasn't a rich and famous man, unconcerned about my appearance, or someone up from the country who didn't have to bother?" I asked.

He looked at me appraisingly. "Nar" was all he said, shaking his head.

It's all around you here. Sherlock Holmes, after all, was an Englishman.

This English method, of approaching things from unusual angles, of withholding judgment until there is something to assess, of switching from one category to another (or not accepting categories at all) and, above all, of self-deprecation, may account for the widespread belief that the English are mad.

Even the Danes, close kin of the English ("Denmark – Land of our Ancestors," *Daily Telegraph*, May 4, 1985), seem to believe this. Shakespeare, in *Hamlet*, is my authority:

> FIRST CLOWN: He that is mad, and sent into England.
> HAMLET: Ay, marry; why was he sent into England?
> FIRST CLOWN: Why, because he was mad; he shall recover his wits there; or, if he do not, 'tis no great matter there.
> HAMLET: Why?
> FIRST CLOWN: 'Twill not be seen in him there; there the men are as mad as he.

The usefulness of the English habit of withholding judgment was recently demonstrated, coincidentally, in direct relation to this very example.

A friend, Nicholas Fry, writes to tell me about what happened to him one day in France during a performance of this play.

The line about people in England being mad "was greeted with a roar of laughter from the French audience, which I naturally joined in," he says. "However, one of the party leaned across to my hostess in some agitation and inquired whether I was not offended at this slur on the British character."

This supposed madness is never more in evidence than when the English are imparting information by the method-without-a-system which – to outsiders – is positively Oriental, even metaphysical, in texture.

And from that mysterious witches' brew, through the conflation of material and method, comes something that actually does work. The ordinary educational system itself operates in the same way. Stephen Leacock, himself a professor, says in *My Discovery of England*:

> Oxford trains scholars of the real type better than any place in the world. Its methods are antiquated. It despises science. Its lectures are rotten. It has professors who never teach and students who never learn. It has no order, no arrangement, no system. Its curriculum is unintelligible. It has no president. It has no state legislature to tell it how to teach, and yet – it gets there.

Perhaps to describe this, Shakespeare uses the word multipotent: "having power to do many things." To get closer to the truth, we would have to invoke another English word, omni-form, a sort of opposite to uniform, and signifying "capable of every form."

At the heart of it all is something quite English – and baffling to Europeans, Americans, Australians and others – but not unfamiliar to us in the East. Look at the use of "capable of every form" in the poem of Ibn al-Arabi, the Spanish Sufi of seven centuries ago:

> My heart is capable of every form; varying with the changes of the innermost consciousness. It may have the form of a gazelle meadow, a [Christian] monk's cloister, an idol-temple, the pilgrim's [Islamic] Kaaba, the tablets of the [Jewish] Torah...

Idolatry the English may have: but they use it instead of letting it use them. A fundamental, if unformulated, axiom here is: Nothing is Axiomatic.

People imagine that the English worship externals and tradition. Well, just question this assumption and you can turn the thing on its head. In England, tradition is supposed to be prized. But few people in the country today have anything – language, dress, habits, even food – in common with most of their ancestors.

Social, political, spiritual objectives? They change from time to time. Far from being insular in all senses, the English import their institutions, laws, manners – and traditions – *ad lib*.

They dress their elite troops in bearskin hats taken from the Russians and in Hungarian hussar jackets. These become English, and traditional; but don't bet on them as permanencies. They have imported science, universities, religions, even Iraqi (tabby) cats. They call their own things by foreign names: "Irish" stew is an example if you want one. They call foreign things by their own names. The Solar Helmet, or Topee, has nothing solar about it. It started life as the name of the fiber of the *shola*, Hindi for the hat-plant or Indian papilionaceous *Aeschynomene*.

English adoptions are treated by them like the totems of certain distant ethnic groups: if the rain-idol does not provide rain, as anthropologists and the English know, it can be thrown down or abandoned. But the omniformity moves on.

When the Turk Mohammed the Conqueror stormed Constantinople, confusing the Byzantines by attacking under their own banner, he did something which went into history books. An Englishman would not have seen this as unusual.

English people see no difficulty in adopting anyone's external paraphernalia if they find it useful. Sometimes they go further. A distinguished professor once said to me, "You seem to be making a name for yourself as an exponent of Sufi thought. I have reservations about that: after all, you have only studied it *in the East.*" (My italics, of course: his emphasis was on the word "only.")

Only in the East? The assumption is amazing: at least, it is to an Easterner. I am not ruling out the possibility that the English might acquire (or re-acquire) that philosophy and even return it to the East. They can do anything when they put their mind to it.

But that will only happen when the English have taken the label off the Sufic way of thought and detached the affix invented by a German, F. A. D. Tholuck, in 1821, of Suf(i)-*ism*, and removed it from categorization. Then they will have done to (or for) it what they are pre-eminently capable of doing.

What the English are actually doing, in anthropological terms, may parallel the method adopted by the Tiv of Nigeria, reported on by Laura Bohannon in 1952. I was referred to this analogy by Dr. Peter Wade of Queen's College, Cambridge, after I remarked about the tribal mentality of the British.

The Tiv people had legends to organize their lives and duties which were adapted from time to time to suit circumstances. "Thus, in effect, history was constantly being rewritten in order, as Bohannon puts it, to provide a charter for current social relationships."

Exactly what we find in England. Interestingly enough, however, it was the British who disturbed this flexible and efficient way of ordering life. When they came to administer the Tivs, their influence caused the "facts" to be written down and thus fossilized, creating "tougher disputes about whose version was right."

If the factors which gave rise to the British Empire were chaotic, the Imperial Administration was not, being so bureaucratic and dogmatic as to spoil the dynamic of English pragmatism. The great evolutionary system on which the Brits prided themselves ran into the sand. I think that this is what former colonials mean when they say that the British were one people when at home and another while living in the dependent territories.

The English, more than any people I know, are suspicious of the single answer, the panacea. This makes it difficult for ideologies to make headway among them, except for those who may have been made over-emotional or dependent by manipulation or propaganda.

They go in for strange cults, it is true, but they change them in the process, leaving the original to wither on the vine. A supposed Indian guru with thousands of followers recently roared at an Englishman, "Do you want to hear the truth?"

The Englishman said, "Naturally, I'd prefer to: but don't break the habit of a lifetime just for me."

Again, the English method, testing, probing, being provocative, collecting, digesting, keeping quiet, making up one's own mind.

And how do I know? Well, not long after the incident with the Indian, this same Englishman, unrecognized by the same guru, went up to him as I watched and cried out, "Master: how can I gain enlightenment?"

I said, "Why ever did you do that?"

"Ah," he told me, "they expect it, you know. Just testing."

They have their own ways, you see, these English.

Among the abundant proofs that Englishry, at any given time, is an ongoing activity, or a vehicle which carries its own track with it, like a caterpillar tractor, is this statement in F. E. Halliday's *A Concise History of England* (London 1964):

> We live only at the beginning of history, and the time will come when the story of England, from Stonehenge to the Atomic Age, will be dismissed in a sentence.

They have started the process already. Look how the entire history of the tribe from its beginnings is dismissed in two sentences:

> *Angles,* or *Angli* (Ger. tribe who occupied the dist. of Schleswig-Holstein in the 5th Cent., and settled in E. Anglia, Mercia and Northumbria. From them the name England is derived (Angleland)).

Thus *Everyman's Encyclopaedia,* published in London in 1967.

31

Secret Rituals

Tell Them
If you find yourself surprised or shocked by what they say or think, do not hesitate to tell them so frankly. There is no nation which stands criticism, even severe criticism, so well as the English.

André Maurois: *Three Letters on the English*

"WELL, YOU OLD bastard, stopped beating your wife yet?" I can guarantee that this would be your last conscious observation, if you ventured it in my country. For that matter, even the first four words would end your existence even in parts of the continent of Europe.

In England, however, you have only to utter this phrase and people may punch you, but only with delight. Accompany the remark with a playful, painful poke in the ribs of your victim, and people will show even greater pleasure. It is, in short, a ritual. As specialists will tell you, a ritual is something performed in certain company at places which may be entered only at specific times, with words which have a full meaning for the initiated alone.

That well describes the one we are about to look at. In the buildings dedicated to its ceremonies, you will be greeted with heavy, ritual jocularity by the officiant, and you will be pressed to drink quantities of alcohol, which is considered an honor. You are in one of Britain's seventy thousand pubs: one for every seven or eight hundred souls.

When you have established yourself as something of a wit (I suggest you do this by saying "Watch it, watch it, har, har, har!") you will be allowed to hear, and ultimately to repeat, the other sacred mantram. This underlines, again, the daring interests alluded to in the first. It runs like this: "Well, what've *you* been up to, eh?" The answer is to tap your nose, and the countersign is "Say no more, squire!" This innocent rite is the reason why so many foreigners have gone home and written books complaining that the English are "ridden with vice."

The native customs, like all good traditional mysteries, have a deep meaning, one not immediately penetrable from a mere inspection of signs or translation of words: so I shall not analyze the verbal forms, only observe them.

In England, two things are seen as valuable in maintaining social life: allegations of unusual origins or acts, and humor simulating aggression. Any reference to these, preferably accompanied by body-movements (put out of your mind the calumny that the English never gesticulate), is proof of one's unusual gifts: and/or a thorough awareness of the tribal ways.

I say "unusual," because your popularity will generally be confirmed by shouts of incredulity, such as "Did you hear that? What Indries Sherk just said to Ted, Fred?," and much slapping of thighs. Thigh-slapping to music, remember, is strictly taboo, being associated by the autochthones with the evils of Bavaria and leather shorts.

That the ritual is in fact a religious one involving the hereafter is evidenced, more often than not, by the cry "I could have *died*!" It signifies, of course, an allegorical, not a literal, death.

Naturally, this secret rite has been seriously misunderstood by generations of alien observers. They have rashly concluded that the English are drunken and idiotic. Idiot they may be, but only in the original, Greek, sense of the word, which meant "a private person."

Beginners may find the prospect of entering into native rituals daunting. They will be glad to know that they need not ever enter a public-house to pursue their inquiries.[6] They can be In the World but Not of It, and learn of the ways, feelings and history of England from a superficial inspection of inn-signs.

I have this on high authority. The great Dr. Brewer, in his *Dictionary of Phrase and Fable*, proclaims: "Much of a nation's history, and more of its manners and feelings, may be gleaned from its public-house signs."

Brewer actually lists a number of names of English hostelries and their derivations so that we can taste their essential Englishness, not to mention sentiments and history. They include:

Bag o' Nails/Bacchanals
Bull and Gate/Boulogne Gate
The Chequers/Stuart armorial bearings
Red Dragon/Wales
Spread Eagle/Germany
The Globe/Portugal
Queen of Bohemia
Rose of the Quarter Sessions/La Rose des Quatre Saisons

---

[6] Even if they do enter a pub, they don't have to consume alcohol. Everywhere they will find people eating snacks or even large meals, drinking fruit juices, mineral waters, coffee and dealcoholized beers and even wines... Pubs are not behind other English institutions in frustrating expectation.

How English it all is: apart from the fact that inn-signs are not originally English at all, having been introduced by the Romans in pre-English days, as a solution to illiteracy. What are they really up to, in making such statements as Dr. Brewer's obviously foreign inn-signs, which are alleged to tell us about England? I have worked out one thing about it.

Brewer, whom I must now treat with greater reserve than hitherto, plainly seeks to *prevent* foreigners from entering these places. His theory probably is that, seduced by seeing references to their national arms, royalty, gates, and the like, the aliens will forget and abandon their original mission to penetrate within and observe the secret rituals in their dark interiors. He attempts this by pretending that the names displayed *outside* teach English history, manners and feelings.

Strangely, in the Middle East at least, the very mention of an English drinking-place makes the gorge rise. Pubs are seen as dens of iniquity and immorality, where women dance on tables and drunken men brawl until expelled by the police. The idea is fostered by English films, an arm of disinformation and also of aversion-therapy.

The reality is very different.

Open any English newspaper and you will find complaints about pubs: of poor service, weak beer, horrifying snacks and total boredom. One wonders why people use such places at all. Perhaps because they have been told that suffering is good for the soul.

And perhaps the beer is not as weak as they say. The official Security Commission report, dealing with the drinking habits of security personnel in Britain, said in May 1985 (and this was the lead story in *The Times*):

> Many outstanding and distinguished historical figures have been notoriously heavy drinkers.

London drinking and gambling clubs have flourished on the takings from overseas visitors, especially since the oil price rises of the 1970s. They have no signs outside implying lessons in national manners and feelings. There is precious little of that inside, either, but it can happen, as we shall see in a moment. Hundreds of millions of dollars have been lost in these places by oil magnates from abroad. Few English people can afford to gamble on this scale: one Arab alone lost $10 million in one night's play.

But the English know how to handle things: they don't call an Arab "you old bastard"; they just steer him to the nearest roulette table. And they do not find their guests ungrateful. One moneyed – and titled – Englishman was handed £500 as a tip by a sheikh who mistook him for a cloakroom attendant. He took the money with a cheerful "Thanks, guv," and the story made the newspapers.

One Middle Easterner, who had lost the £10 million which he had brought here only a month before, complained bitterly about the lack of sympathy, as he called it, of an English neighbor at the tables.

"I said," he told me, "'You shouldn't allow places like this, which trap unfortunate visitors into losing fortunes.' And do you know what he said?"

I could not guess.

"Well, he said this: 'It has been historically proved that gambling, known as *Hazard*, was brought here by the Crusaders. Your people taught it to them. It comes from *Az-Zahr*, Arabic for a game of dice. So it's all your people's fault...'"

I expect he poked him playfully in the ribs at the same time: the secret rituals must be kept up. And how many people in, say, Las Vegas, could produce such an instant and erudite connection with a Middle Easterner?

But if gambling, at least with dice, is an innovation in England, introduced at the latest in the thirteenth century, what about beer? Beer is the English drink par excellence, the traditional mainstay of the public-houses: surely the Angles brought it with them from Europe? Not so; the pub may be the focus of English social life for large sections of the population, but beer is a relative newcomer; as the traditional rhyme affirms:

> Greek, heresy, turkey-cocks and beer
> Came into England all in one year.

That was even later than the introduction of dice, a full century after the end of the Crusades. The English took beer to their hearts like the other foreign drinks, coffee, tea and soda, which they adopted later. It became a National Drink, just as the foreign, Roman tavern had become the National Institution, the pub.

"A Nation's history, its manners and feelings, may be gleaned"; quite so. For months the English (and British) nation had been kept on tenterhooks by the mass-circulation Press. Princess Diana (who isn't Princess Diana at all: it should be The Princess of Wales) and Princess Anne (also officially listed, and in *Who's Who*, as Mrs. Mark Phillips) were rumored to have fallen out. Something to do with the choice of godparents for the new Prince, it was supposed. Would the rift heal? How, when and where would the reconciliation take place? Who would be there to set the seal upon the reunification of the Royals?

Thoughts such as these, to judge by the public prints, were coursing through every patriotic vein. Then, just as we had hoped, the headline chuckled: ANNE AND DIANA JUST LAUGH IT OFF. The sisters-in-law, we read, "were seen laughing and joking together." Not only that, but the Queen, Prince Philip and Prince Charles joined them. Not only that, but it was at Sandringham, the Royal Estate. And not only that, but the informal lunch, as befits what the *Express* called a *Public* Reconciliation, took place at – a public house; the King's Head, of course.

See how important the pub is?

32

The Hidden Teaching Method

A Fearfully British Occasion
The mixture of hypocrisy, humanity, grotesque insensitivity, and decent common sense make the Invergordon Mutiny a fearfully (in all senses of the word) British occasion.
John Torode, in the Guardian

WHEN YOU FIND yourself rebuked in England, the matter does not end there. You are expected to take the lesson to heart: but you must not be defeated by it. Some form of rally, even a counter-attack, is not only appreciated but expected: this feedback shows that the process is working, and even how well it is working.

So, when a friend assailed me for being mentioned in *The Times* too often, I was glad of the opportunity to reach into my English-type miscellaneous memory. I answered, "Yes, but of course *The Times* does tend to print what it wants to, in spite of what anyone may say. It is on record that it even commented on Abraham Lincoln's Gettysburg Address without his permission. You will remember its words, 'Anything more dull and commonplace it would not be easy to produce.'"

He came back at me with, "Then maybe they'll have a go at you, one day." That left an opening for me to say, "Yes – when they make me President of the United States, perhaps."

This teaching-situation, usually disguised as anything but that, can take many forms, and can certainly be useful, even as a therapy in grave cases.

I have learned this technique, though I am not such a master of it as the many brilliant exponents of England. Someone wrote me a pretty ridiculous letter of twelve pages (it is not uncommon) and I sent this reply: "I regret to have to inform you that you have not won my monthly prize for the worst garbage I have received in that period."

Now he writes far more sensibly: the quality of his garbage is improving.

There is no doubt in my mind that, whether in letters or in other trials of strength, the English are *experimenting*. They have collected information, they have tentative opinions; and they want to put these to use, to work in the safest possible way; for they are cautious. They might, in short, be following the advice of the great Eastern sage Jabir ibn Hayyan, the Sufi; whom English scholars, of course, call Geber:

> He who does not perform practical work or make experiments will never attain to the lowest degree of mastery. But, O my son, you should experiment to gain knowledge.

Anyone who has been in touch with English people, whether at home or abroad, will recognize the traditional cry, "That'll teach him!" It never refers to anything remotely like a formal lesson. Teaching and learning by unfamiliar means, that is the key to this behavior.

Sometimes you do not even know that the lesson is being given, so elusive is the phrasing, so opaque the intention, of the operator.

Once, in Norfolk, I came across an old countryman, sitting on a log with a pipe in his mouth, gazing at the setting sun. Eager to collect factual information, to match his posture with his meditations, I said, "A penny for your thoughts."

Without hesitation he ticked me off, supplied the information, or initiated a teaching situation; probably all three, with: "I'm wondering how to get hold of a plastic trash can."

"There's none so blind as them as wonna see," goes the saying in these parts; and many foreigners would not have seen that they were being instructed, preferring to think that the old chap was crazy, or that he only wanted to be left alone.

There is a subtle technique they often use. If he wants to be left alone, the Englishman starts to behave really oddly. You may not get the message, but he will achieve his object.

Or he may pretend that he wants to talk: and that works, too, by the Law of Contraries. In England, people don't much like those who want to talk, even if they are lonely. Look like you need a conversation and that's the last thing you'll get.

The same Law may well have prompted the English to teach the Swiss to ski, and the Mediterranean people to sunbathe: when the English have little sun and, usually, less snow. There is a rich discontinuity between their products and their needs. They pioneered the best open-topped sports cars in the world, when their climate called for closed cars, and their roads were simply not up to the standard of, say, the autobahnen. Today they export sand to Saudi Arabia (for water filtration) and weave prayer-mats with built-in Mecca-seeking compasses.

It is the Law of Contraries which probably first ordained that, in England, "Blessed" means "Damned" – as in "this blessed nuisance," and so on. And, of course, in Cockney rhyming slang "Holy Friar" means the opposite: liar.

It is failure to observe the pattern of English thinking which causes such bafflement in otherwise acute students of the English: people who have spent decades trying to understand them. I have been almost embarrassed to read some of their books. Dr. D. J. Renier, that engaging Dutchman who labored so mightily here and produced his highly acclaimed book, *The English: Are They Human?*, says in it: "after a few years I came to the conclusion that the world is inhabited by two species of human beings: mankind and the English." The English bought tens of thousands of copies.

Psychologists noticed many years ago that team games can be regarded as a modified form of battle: a ritual which gives opportunities for both aggressive and courteous behavior, and which provides healthy mental and physical outlets without too much blood-letting. The English have carried this conception further, into daily life. But it is rooted in their Anglean, tribal, heritage.

Once, in Africa, I was entering a large village, when warriors came pouring out of their dwellings, leaping and brandishing their spears in a most threatening way. When I had cowered there for a few minutes, they dispersed and their chief took me to his home. "That was our traditional welcome," he said, "by which we get rid of all the possible hostility which your visit might occasion, in advance."

The unsmiling attitude of the Englishman at the start of a meeting, and the initial heavy weather while getting to know him, seems to me to fulfill a role similar to the events of the sports-field and the African token attack. The Americans' hail-fellow-well-met initial welcome cuts right across this tradition, and must be the cause of the frequent misunderstandings between them and the English.

I caught myself operating the unconscious hostility-through-jocularity, which is another English device, only this afternoon. Our central heating system has been on the blink for weeks, and the repairman has called almost daily, without effecting much change. When I looked up his name in my dictionary, I found that Sylvester meant "Living in the Woods." No wonder his knowledge of electrohydraulics was weak. Today I automatically greeted him with "You'll be moving in permanently, at this rate!"

He immediately replied, "Let's hope I don't have to!" And he set to work, adequately warned, and labored on for nine hours. It is now midnight, and he has just reported that the heating is working perfectly.

The accumulation of information, and the various putting-down gambits, are seldom random. This has to do with the Seeds of Time. The Englishman accumulates ideas and facts as just such seeds. Similarly, he plants words to start conversations, having a shrewd idea of how they will grow. In this, he follows – who else? – Shakespeare:

> If you can look into the seeds of time
> And say which grain will grow and which will not,
> Speak then to me...
> *Macbeth*, I, iii.

It is, of course, the exception which proves the rule. The supposed slowness of the Englishman is because he, rightly, fears emotion's ability to distort understanding and to block time-seed collecting. There are awful warnings in the recorded sayings of those English people who have not learned this lesson.

They are ascribed by foreigners to stupidity, but they often come from clever men.

One such was the pronouncement of Sir Richard (Rule-Hard) Woolley, Astronomer Royal. He said, in the 1950s: "Space-travel is utter bilge."

Examples are always coming up to fulfill the necessary monitory function. The great physicist, Lord Rutherford, delivered himself of this:

> The energy produced by the breaking down of the atom is a very poor kind of thing.

Could he have made a worse mistake? Yes, and he did – in his very next words: "Anyone who expects a source of power from the transformation of these atoms is talking nonsense."

But the educational sparring goes on, notwithstanding. I was once playing chess with an Englishman. Halfway through the game the air-raid warning sounded. I fancied my skill at chess, and so I was surprised when I lost. I said, "I'm sorry I didn't give you a better game."

"Not at all," he said, "you were doing very well until the alert went."

A compatriot of mine, who was watching, hissed to me in our own language that this foreign miscreant was implying that I had been rattled by the possibility of an air attack. I decided to deal with the matter English-fashion.

"You mean that there was an air-raid warning?" I asked the Englishman. "Didn't hear a thing."

"You must have," he insisted, so grumpily that I guessed that I'd probably won that one.

Sometimes you get tales which sound like a mixture of condescension, stressing luck and entertaining the audience, to name but a few. I cannot make up my mind about one case;

though it impressed all the other foreigners at the luncheon where I heard it from an English lady:

> It was in India, my dear – an absolute scream! Some old codger, supposed to be the richest man in the world or something, I don't know, invited Henry and me to dinner. One of the secretaries muddled the message brought by the equerry, do you see, and I thought it was to be fancy dress. So I got myself up outrageously as a Maharani. Well, you'll never believe it, but the old boy thought I was the real thing! He presented me with a very large ruby – apparently it's customary there – and we put little Willie right through Public School on it...

Someone – an Englishman – tried to rally us by intoning, "Oriental rubies are supposed to bring bad luck. I recall..." But few of us were listening.

Sometimes, I admit, foreigners do manage to hit the right stride: but only occasionally, while the English constantly practice the art; you can hear them at it every day.

A distinguished Afghan lady pulled off one coup in my hearing, at a North-West Frontier reception. Madame Siddiqi, wife of the former Governor of the rugged Afghan province of Qataghan and Badakhshan, was talking to a senior British officer in Peshawar, where her husband, Juma Khan, was then Consul-General of our country.

She admired the officer's rows of ribbons, and then said, "What is that decoration for?"

"That," he said, "is a campaign medal. I served in the Third Afghan War."

"What a *good* idea!" she gushed. "Giving medals for wars that you lost. I really must suggest it to His Majesty. You see, we are behind the times. *We* only give them out when we *win* a war."

The officer made an excuse and withdrew, though his flight was not really necessary. Perhaps he had not read the words of Max Beerbohm, another Englishman, whom he could have quoted, from *Mainly on the Air*: "There is much to be said for failure. It is more interesting than success."

Dear Madame Siddiqi. Her memory saved me once, when I was being hard-pressed by a lady missionary who, uncharacteristically, was queening it at an At Home. "Afghanistan?" she said to me, with a note to her voice which brought the whole company to attention. "People there are very *bare*, I suppose?"

I took a deep breath and thought, but at first nothing came: the remark was too far over the top. But the memory of Madame Siddiqi, of Qataghan and Badakhshan, spurred me on. Then I had it. All eyes on me, I answered, graciously, "Oh, yes, so very, very bare. It really should be stopped in case it spreads."

"Spreads?" she asked, falling into my trap.

"Yes," I told her, "it's all due to the increasing numbers of *very bare* English tourists who are flooding the country."

The process is, as I have said, unconscious most of the time. That is not to say that it is unknown. I have a description of how it proceeds without regard to current fashions of thought, how it is not spoken of most of the time, how it can leak out, in the right places. It was no less an authority than Kipling, who wrote, in *The Puzzler*:

> For undemocratic reasons and for motives not of State
> They arrive at their conclusions – largely inarticulate.

> Being void of self-expression they confide their
> views to none;
> But sometimes in a smoking-room,
> One learns why things were done.

Clever stuff, as the English would say.

Anthropologists will perhaps recognize in the story of the Indian ruby a clear echo of characteristic tribal boasting. They may find, in the battle of wits (whether about Abraham Lincoln or bare English tourists), the hint of an earlier, more savage, kind of exchange.

Kurt von Stutterheim, in *Those English!*, recognized the ancient endowment, brought from Schleswig into Albion:

> When the Englishman broke down the bridge that carried him into civilization from his primeval forest, he kept with him this positively animal perceptiveness.

But how did he keep it, and why did others not? My conclusion is that he has kept it in good repair by constantly exercising the modified wildness which we have been examining. The muscles of perception are still in quite good trim. The English proverb says "You can't hide an eel in a sack." True: but one might add that someone who did not know what the devil it was, wriggling in there, might have a hard time guessing its identity.

The modified wildness takes the form of a sort of mild psychological terrorism, designed not to put you down so much as to stimulate you to exertions which will develop your potential, provide something for the community, and earn you appropriate rewards, even honors.

Here and there, if you dig deep enough, or keep your eyes and ears open, you will find both hints and overt statements of the process.

"A sneer pushes you on like anything," says Sir Terence Conran, quoted by William Kay in his *Tycoons*, a book which examines how millionaires in England made it from nothing. The author tells us both the result and the point at which the sneering stops: "A huge personal fortune and a knighthood later, no one is sneering at Sir Terence Conran anymore."

33

Where IS Everybody?

> *Missing*
> Department of Trade figures show that 28,000 people leave Britain to emigrate to the United States annually. American statistics record only 5,000 British immigrants as actually arriving there.
> *Sunday Times Magazine*, February 23, 1986

WHO WERE THE ancient English, and how did they think? If you believe E. P. Dunne's *Mr. Dooley in Peace and War*, the Anglo-Saxon is "a German who's forgotten who was his parents." That's altogether too easy, and too Irish, to cover the whole question.

The Angles not only absorbed the Saxons culturally: some of their descendants taught their children that *the Saxons did not really exist*: there were only Angles. This is very positively spelled out by the best-selling historian Charlotte (feminine diminutive of Manly) M. Yonge, in her *Stories of English History*, for long an important instrument of juvenile education:

> The Britons used to call the blue-eyed men Saxons, but they called themselves Angles, and the country

was called after them Angle-land. Don't you know what it is called now? England itself, and the people English; for these were our forefathers.

The Saxons, at least according to the eagerly read Ms. Yonge, had become non-persons. That disposes, too, of the prehistoric peoples, the Celts, the Phoenicians, the Picts and Scots, the Romans, the Normans and anyone whom they brought here, the Saxons themselves and the Jutes. It abolishes the Jews and the Huguenots, and virtually all the peoples listed by the Venerable Bede; who says of the English, "They are still called Germans by the neighbouring nation of the Britons. Such are the Freesons, the Rugians, Dans, Hunni, Old Saxons and Boructarians."

Somewhere, in all that lot, the Angles were working away, being English. The major early English literary epic is, of course, *Beowulf*. It was brought to England by the Angles themselves. But, as Ifor Evans says in *A Short History of English Literature*: "Though the Angles brought the story to England, it is not even about the Angles." Exactly: just what one would have expected...

Who has not heard an English person, bounding into a roomful of people, cry, "Where *is* everybody?" – or the equally disconcerting, "Nobody here, then?" You see, the Anglean factor does not see things as you and I do. And that unknown, inward thing, is really calling the shots. An Englishman is *not* what he looks like or even what he sounds like. He is within.

Always look at the actions as well as the words: and never forget that English dictionaries include among the meanings of "abroad," the phrases "in a state of mental perplexity," and "wide of the mark, astray." Without careful study you remain abroad, even if you live in England.

Before we cite a case or two of English enigmatic actions, let us look at a few words again. Consider this passage in demotic English:

> A moss-trooper gave a touch of white soup to a Knight of St. Crispin, so he did not dine with Sir Humphrey. A rotten Glasgow Magistrate made him join the majority.

Your understanding is almost certain to be Abroad: wide of the mark, on this one. Reference books, if not all English people, can tell you what it really means. "A thief," it says, "gave a little stolen melted-down silver to a shoemaker, so he did not lack dinner. A rotten salt-herring killed him."

Now we can graduate to ambiguities about ambiguities. One of my favorites is contained in an extract from a report made to a Government inquiry in British India. It was given to me by dear old Lady Evelyn Cobbold. (As she was English, it was with no surprise that I learned she'd made the pilgrimage to Mecca as a Moslem, and published a book on it.) The events described took place not a thousand miles from the Court of my grandfather, the Nawab.

"I agree," runs the Statement from the high official with a patrician English name who is under investigation, "that His Highness the Nawab ordered his Treasurer to give me ropes of pearls as a gift, and that such items were in fact received. I concur that I signed a receipt for His Highness's Treasurer, for twelve (12) 60-inch Ropes of Matched Pearls.

"I agree, furthermore, that my Report states that I received only six (6) Ropes of Matched Pearls 'of considerable value though not yet valued,' which I sent to the Viceroy."

Neither a crook nor an honest man, I would have thought, would be able to get out of that one. He'd knocked off half the pearls, 360 inches of them – thirty feet! But soft:

"I did not conceal, give away, steal or convert to my own purposes, six Ropes of Pearls. I regard the following true explanation as a complete vindication."

When I saw these words, I stopped reading, to speculate as to what possible explanation would account for such an action. Finally I decided that only *force majeure*, actual physical coercion, or insanity, could cover it. I was wrong:

"On the occasion under review, [were there others?] the Treasurer of His Highness the Nawab produced six (6) Ropes of Matched Pearls, all apparently genuine, and also a prewritten receipt for double that quantity, to wit, Twelve Ropes.

"I naturally pointed out the discrepancy. The Treasurer then explained that the Nawab was accustomed to flattery; that it was the royal convention to exaggerate his bounty, as a partial acknowledgment of a gift, and that reasons of state made it desirable to continue the long-standing custom. I accordingly signed the receipt."

But, I wondered, what would HH's Treasurer, let alone the Nawab himself, have to say about the matter? What, in fact, had the Treasurer himself to say? I read on:

"I am aware that verification of the above-stated facts may be difficult or impossible, following the sad demise of both His Highness and the Royal Treasurer in the four years since the event in question: but suggest that I cannot be held personally responsible for this."

Bingo! He was exonerated, of course: but the report notes that he was reminded that he should have reported the shortfall, and the "special circumstances" confidentially, to his superiors at the time.

This labyrinth may contain either deviousness or complete honesty. But ambiguities abound. Was it good or bad luck that His Highness and his Treasurer had both passed on? Was it even chance? What happened to them, in any case? But the inquiry was not concerned with these details. The only action needed, since an appropriate explanation had been forthcoming, was a small slap on the wrist.

"I always tried to avoid ambiguities, my boy," an elderly English judge told me when I spoke of his people's activities overseas. He gave me this example:

"During the British mandate period in Iraq, I heard cases with complete impartiality. Both parties in civil cases would place an exactly similar amount of money on my clerk's table. The loser was invariably refunded his own money, without deductions." Don't ask who got the winner's contribution. Perhaps it went to some deserving charity.

He gave the thumbs-up sign: which in Rome meant "kill him," and in England, of course, indicates that all is well. I expect his little anecdote was designed only to pull my leg.

What may seem ambiguous to you and me is not necessarily so in Darkest England. I have just been looking at *John Bull and His Island*, by Max O'Rell. He seems to find it odd that a north country shipowner "sold his sailing vessels to his sons, and then competed with them with steamers."

But did the sons think it odd? Or, being English, did they perceive any ambiguity at all? *Caveat emptor*, let the buyer beware, may be Latin, but it was in unanimous use here for centuries. If I were English, I would reckon that my father might be selling me his ships for a purpose. The purpose would not necessarily be to give me a smooth ride. Suppose he wanted to stimulate my commercial acumen? The English do not share his assumptions as often as the foreigner might imagine.

Speaking of my father, there is a story about him related by my mother, which shows cultural conflicts and where an Englishman misread the signals because of divergent assumptions.

My mother, when just married, was with my father on a ship bound for England from Bombay. There were many British officers on board, going home on leave. One day, one of these gentlemen swashbuckled up to my father and said, "I say, your wife's a jolly pretty woman, what?"

My father's response was to turn to one of his bodyguards and say, softly, "Just knock him down, will you?"

My mother remarked to me that she didn't know whether to feel flattered or sorry when the gallant hit the deck. But this is not my point. The Englishman might have expected violence, but not so soon. The Afghan did not know that a dog is allowed one bite in the traditions of Englishry; the Englishman did not know that the Afghans, when provoked, behave like the Scots to whom they have often been likened. Readers who require written proof of the long fuses of the English may refer to Henry Miller's *The Wisdom of the Heart*:

> The Englishman, be it noted, seldom resorts to violence; when he is *sufficiently goaded* [my italics] he simply opens up, like the oyster, and devours his adversary.

I do not weep for the supine Englishman, however, and neither has anyone else to whom I have related the story. He was, I am certain, able to bounce back by quoting to himself Byron's reminder: "Adversity is the first path to truth." The tendency to find good in everything is a Christian virtue. Its Anglean adaptation is to find everything in everything.

The ability to rebound like a rubber ball is one of the English talents which have often given their opponents nasty shocks.

An English friend, whose literary agent had submitted his particulars year after year without success to the Editorial Committee of a biographical dictionary, finally referred to the book thus: "It is amazing how *Who's Who* manages to find so many important people whom nobody has ever heard of before. That's what I call skill."

"Damning with faint praise" is one of their terms: but although this technique was known elsewhere before they were heard of, the English have brought it to a fine art and are its best current exponents.

My favorite instance is from a review of one of my books, years ago: before I got the kind of notices which I could show to anyone else. The learned critic said, of me: "He has brought all the power of a considerable talent into the service of an outworn philosophy."

My publishers, not English for nothing, immediately advertised his words as "'considerable talent' – Professor Jones."

I was not as wounded as I might have been. For years I have accepted the dictum of Al-Ghazzali: "Better a public rebuke than to become victim of a secret grievance."

Having recalled those words of *The Book of Counsel for Kings*, I now waited for my critic, Jones, to get his comeuppance from a compatriot. Sure enough, these lines, in print, soon came from – shall we call him – Dr. Smith, whom my critic ("Professor Jones") had unwisely called "Tormented, English coy": "If ignorance is bliss – and I am, indeed, tormented," said Doctor Smith, so English yet so coy, "it's good for both of us, both academics: Professor Jones, demented, is bound to die of joy."

The English are, you have seen, unique; and their singularity is due to a mixture of things. They don't forget or fabricate so much as adapt a story to suit circumstances. They give words several meanings. They take a good deal of time over things. But they are not shy of commenting or speaking straight when they think it appropriate.

And they do all these things to one another, remember: not just to annoy foreigners, who don't really count very much. Professor Jones, demented and due to die of joy because of his ignorance, may gladden the heart of Doctor Smith. But, if you read the delightful autobiography of A. J. P. Taylor (*A Personal History*) you'll find that there is nothing unusual about ignorant professors in England:

> G. N. Clark became the first professor of economic history at Oxford by the simple device of pleading that he knew nothing of economic history and was anxious to learn.

Right. This professor, there to teach economic history, would not be able to do so for some time at least: until he'd learned it. Then, as Dr. Taylor tells us elsewhere in his book, "Few of my college contemporaries were devoted to learning. They regarded Oxford as a place that would give them the necessary social stamp for well-paid jobs in the civil service."

He also says that he had "foolishly assumed that a university was a place devoted to the higher learning."

Instead, people were more interested in "things such as Association football and the drinking of beer."

So another reason for the cry, "Where is Everybody?" becomes clear. The Angles specialize in being elsewhere, or doing otherwise, than might be expected. Hence the need for the inquiry as to where they are: the professor is learning, not teaching, economic history; the lecturer is watching football, the other dons are drinking beer – and so on.

It is not for nothing, some swear, that the word "academic" in English also means "irrelevant" or "only theoretical."

You would have to go a long way before you found anyone more English than J. H. Rivett-Carnac (CIE, VD, FSA). Though no academic, he could write a long, entertaining and detailed book entitled *Many Memories* about his "Life in India, at Home and Abroad." The title-page, in addition to styling him – no doubt correctly: he was a stickler for etiquette – Esquire, gives a potted biography:

> Bengal Civil Service, Colonel Ghazipore Light Horse and Aide-de-Camp to Queen Victoria.

The combination of soldier, administrator and courtier had earned him the letters after his name. J. H. R-C was a Companion of the Order of the Indian Empire. He was also the proud holder of the Victorian Decoration, for services to Her Majesty: the coveted VD. The FSA – Fellowship of the Society of Antiquaries – rounded out his honors.

In spite of his devotion to England, the gallant Colonel reveled in his French ancestry and loved the Germans. And he settled, in his declining years, in Switzerland. Notwithstanding his Continental affinities, his English attitudes are consistent throughout the book. His unstinting service of his country, and his appropriate outlook are unquestionable. So I was not much surprised to come across such passages as this:

> There were a number of scoundrels hanging about the place, natives, or Indians as I see we are now expected to call them.

As he was in India at the time, it was perhaps not so surprising. Yet elsewhere in the book he quotes, with great approval, a long poem which runs, in part:

> Praise to the name Almighty, there is no God
> but One.
> Mohomed is His prophet, and His will shall ever
> be done.
> Ye shall take no care for
> your money, nor your faith for a ransom sell;
> Ye shall make no terms with the infidel, but smite
> his soul to hell.

Why, I wondered, quote the blood-curdling words of an Indian of the kind who, in the time of Queen Victoria, were trying to get such people as J. H. Rivett-Carnac Esquire out of their country? A scoundrel, in fact? Being such a fervent Royalist, had R-C unearthed something written by King John, who is said to have made tentative steps toward becoming a Moslem, centuries ago?

The English king might fit the bill, I thought at first, since the poet's Islamic theology was distinctly unsound. The Koran says that the infidels are to be fought if they oppress the True Believers; but if they cease their oppression, there may be no hostility except to those who continue to practice it.

But then King John seemed too far back. So, was the poem perhaps by some misguided, but yet heroic, Native for whom the gallant Colonel of the Ghazipore Light Horse felt a certain respect?

The King John speculation, I found, was nearer the mark than the Native one. The author was none other than a compatriot of our gallant Royal Aide-de-Camp: the renowned Victorian – and English – scholar, Sir Alfred Lyall.

Well, I thought, at least Rivett-Carnac quoted a fellow Englishman, and not one of those Native scoundrels hanging about the place. I knew there was a consistency in the Anglean mind. All you have to do is to find it.

Having heard, with my own ears, Winston Churchill accept the title of Hereditary Reformed Pirate, I am tempted to interpret Rivett-Carnac's approval of the poem by Lyall. Circumstances alter cases, of course: and J. H. Rivett-Carnac Esquire must have been one kind of Angle when taking part in the Imperial Mission and another at home. As always, I sought authoritative support for this theory. Lord Evans, University of London Professor of English provided it:

> [T]he Angles, Saxons and Jutes came to England in marauding bands and made English history possible. From all accounts they were respectable gentlemen when at home, but they changed their manners when they were looking for Lebensraum.

The Colonel was in India for a good long time, perhaps long enough almost to be able to call it home, and hence to behave like a gentleman there. One reason I can say this is because we used to know him.

Descended from Huguenots, living in the Swiss Priory of Rougemont, ranging around in India, this Esquire remained an Angle. But there was more to him than that. He had some first-rate social contacts, which gained him the post of Opium Agent in Ghazipore, north India, staying in this job until he retired at nearly sixty.

The work involved granting licenses to grow opium poppies, whose congealed sap was sent by the British Government to China in enormous quantities. Not one of the most creditable activities of the British Raj, it was a nice little earner for the Empire, and enabled certain of the less principled Opium Officers to become multi-millionaires.

Rivett-Carnac used to visit Queen Victoria's son, the Duke of Connaught, General of the Meerut Division. My grandfather, the Sayed Amjad Ali Shah, as an Afghan was, like the rest of our compatriots there, not classified as a native scoundrel, as the Indians were. His family were, in fact, the local bigwigs as well as maintaining their position in Afghanistan.

It was considered essential to keep the Russians out of Afghanistan, and intense diplomatic and political activity to this end continued for more than a century. The Afghan kings Abdur-Rahman Khan and Habibullah Khan, for their part, insisted on dealing only with people of similar rank, and that was why the Queen's son, Prince Arthur, Duke of Connaught, was involved. The Ameer of Afghanistan demanded recognition of his country's complete independence, while the British side wanted it to become a protectorate or part of the Empire.

Carnac, in addition to mixing in this august company, was married to a sister of Sir Mortimer Durand, who demarcated the Afghan frontier, and after whom the present boundary, the Durand Line, is named.

Although the Duke, because of his royal descent, could not take any official part in the negotiations with Afghanistan, most of the Durand conversations actually took place under his roof or ours, with our family looking after the Afghan interest, and the Connaughts the British end.

Arriving in England, I thought I'd like to meet the old boy, and collect some reminiscences about the frontier treaty with our King Abdur-Rahman. I might find out something interesting about the opium trade, too. After all, it was one of the strangest things that the Angles had ever been up to.

I signed the Buckingham Palace Visitors' Book and inquired about the Colonel of the Ghazipore Light Horse. Alas, Rivett-Carnac had died in 1923: before I was born – which was perhaps not surprising since he was born in 1838. And his wife had died, in London, aged 92, in November 1935.

I had to make do with another crusty, aggressive old buffer who had known Rivett-Carnac. He'd served on the old North-West Frontier, a huge, wild tribal area, mainly mountains, lopped off Afghan territory for the usual reason (While Pacifying the Tribes) at the time of the British Raj.

We got into the habit of meeting from time to time, and he reminisced a lot about the Great Old Days: though in his telling, the memories were mostly such as to make any Afghan reach for his long Khyber knife. In today's atmosphere many of his exploits would be called atrocities and more. But, one day, chuckling, he recalled something which revealed a more Anglean aspect of his mind.

"Those Afghans of yours," he said, "are real characters. They don't care for judge nor jury. When I was a young subaltern in the Khyber Rifles, one of them came up to me, and said, in very good English, 'What the devil are you fellows doing here, by the way?'

"I said, 'You'd better learn that I've got as much right here as you.'

"'Right to be here?' he said, bold as brass. 'Do you mean to say that you think you're in Peckham, cock?'"

I said, "He must have known London, then, General..."

"More than London," said the old boy, wiping his eyes, "because of what came next. I was a little taken aback, and could only think of saying, 'I'm from Shropshire, I'll have you know, not from the London slums!'

"And what do you think the feller came out with? He actually said, 'Well, the heat's *really* got to your noddle, soldier boy. This isn't Shropshire, either!'"

Fortunately, I was familiar enough with some forms of English tribal jargon to be able to say, "Well, he did have a point, General. It's not really Shropshire up there, is it?"

The old man looked at me over his spectacles, and then, recharging his brandy glass, he cleared his throat. "Where *is* everybody?" he said.

34

Going Native

Take Your Pick
Take care of the pence, the pounds will take care of themselves.

Penny wise, pound foolish.

English proverbs

IF YOU ARE a foreigner, don't allow yourself to feel too well established in England, that's my advice. I admit that this is not based on first-hand experience: so far, nobody's ever told me to go back to my own country. But though you and I may *feel* settled enough, there is documentary evidence to warn us that we may not be as safe as we feel. Especially if we are fashionable, known at Court, have a title, or are becoming too numerous. And that might net almost all of us.

You can look it up, if you like. Just see *Haydn's Dictionary of Dates*, 17th edition, published in London. Look under Aliens (for Haydn at least, they are the same as Foreigners, as he immediately makes plain):

> ALIENS or FOREIGNERS were banished in 1155, being thought too numerous... Baron Geramb, a

fashionable foreigner, known at court, ordered out of England, 6 April 1812.

When I read this, I thought I must delve more deeply, just in case the Baron's misdemeanors might be such as to apply to my case or yours. I discovered that Geramb had sent the War Office a bill, for services rendered, amounting to £5,350. He had been negotiating with the government to supply 24,000 Croatians to serve in the British Army. Alien military and commercial barons should therefore watch their step.

On the other hand, it is quite possible to Go Native. All you need is a deep understanding of what people do and why. This order is less tall than it seems, to adapt a baffling local saying to our purposes. ("A tall order" means "something difficult or impossible to do." "Short order," however, stands for *quickly*. You may care to display your knowledge of countryside talk, by informing your English townee friends that "short un" means "the almost complete absence of tail feathers." Perhaps the feathers went into a proconsul's hat; but be careful not to say this in large country houses, from among whose denizens such functionaries were often obtained.)

All this is not as discursive in intent as it may at first appear; it is preparing you for greater things.

Such impacts are essential before one can go native here to any significant extent. They are useful even if one has no such intention. They make you more malleable.

The English present you with a story – Alfred's Cake, Offa's Dyke, Whittington's Cat and so on. Each inculcates a moral, or provides some other nutrition. Then they take it away, explaining that it is not true, usually citing historical evidence.

King Alfred didn't burn the cakes or start the Royal Navy, they say; King Offa only repaired "his" dyke; Sir Richard

Whittington was a coal merchant: the "cat" was a name of a coal ship, and the story is garbled.

In cases involving babies brought by the stork, the Tooth Fairy or Santa Claus, of course, they simply allow these less powerful tales to wither away, like the state apparatus in the communist dream or the image of the Cheshire Cat.

I have sought and found the reasons for this strange phenomenon: and can reveal that it is nothing less than a part of the secret teaching activity probably handed down by the Angles, and which belongs to the real traditions of the English people as a whole.

To understand the matter properly, we have to make a small *tour d'horizon*.

The English, as we know from observation, history, song and story, are great explorers and experientialists: I have known many such myself, and still do. We all know what they do in the midday sun, in spite of the prevalence of mad dogs, their sole companions on their forays; Noel Coward has recorded that well enough.

They climb mountains in spite of a fair assumption that there is nothing much on the tops ("just about the same as below," one of them has stated). They invent the jet engine and will even accord a Scotsman facilities at St. Mary's to discover penicillin. You get the idea.

But why? Because there is a restlessness about them which, for me, betokens more than just suppressed and rechanneled inquisitiveness or itchy feet. Freudians have sought to explain such behavior as due to parental strictness and promises in infancy: the "you'll know when you're older" kind of thing. But there are other nations almost entirely devoid of explorers and inventors where parents are far stricter – and promise more – than British ones.

The Anglekins are reaching out for something all right. This something is an ideal of theirs which they formerly tried to gain by rougher methods. This mutation of tactics is not in itself unique. More recently the Germans and Japanese have regrouped after trying to beat the hell out of the rest of us, and now charm the pennies out of our pockets instead.

The English used to specialize in getting rid of anything they could lay their hands on. I refer you to an account of their habits (by no less an authority than Professor G. M. Trevelyan, of Cambridge) when they were just out of Schleswig:

> The colonizing energy of the English immigrants, combined with their savage destructiveness, altered the civilization and racial stock far more than any other Nordic invasion of the period... city life. Christian religion and the Romano-Celtic language all disappeared, together with the native tribal areas and Roman administrative boundaries; the sites of the towns and villages were generally, though not universally, changed.

Well, *mutatis mutandis* (with necessary change, Lat.,) the English still do that kind of thing, but nowadays with legends. The overweening desire for change to bring about something better has been transmuted from the physical sphere to the mental: I nearly said the spiritual. Their academics attack one another with a fierceness worthy of their ancestors. I know: some of them have even had a go at me.

The idea (also known in the East, though there it is almost entirely confined to philosophers) is that you can liberate energy and point in a new direction if you break up the assumptions of the past. Once you understand this, you can see why certain kinds of iconoclasm are so rife among the Anglekins.

Take the case of Sir Francis Drake and the Game of Bowls. For a long time it was claimed that he coolly resumed play on receiving word of the Spanish Armada's arrival, because of his aplomb and self-confidence. Then came the denouement. It was revealed that Drake, near Plymouth Hoe, knew that the tide was not yet right for him to attack on it: hence the delay. And he wasn't even the commander of the ships which fought the Spaniards: Lord Howard, High Admiral of England, was. Reason for breaking this news at the time the historians did so? Because the national instinct perceived a need, just then, for timing and perhaps showing heat instead of coolness. That's my theory.

Generations of schoolboys were taught that Sir Walter Raleigh cast his cloak upon the mud, in a gesture of chivalry, for Queen Elizabeth to walk upon. Then the English revealed that this was a common practice in Spain, and even that the tale involving Raleigh had been invented by Thomas Fuller (1606–61), when both Elizabeth and Raleigh had been dead for decades. Perhaps people were getting too courtly or something. There is sure to have been a reason.

The vanishing of Robin Hood is one of the easier ones. "It is doubtful that he ever lived," says Brewer, and there are many others who agree. Though his time was supposed to have been in the twelfth century, the first published ballads did not appear until about 1490. "We are unlikely to adopt a brand-new national hero dating from, say, AD 1600 who was unknown before. We don't read of Robin till he'd been dead for centuries," someone says, to clinch the debunking. No doubt.

But why downgrade Robin and his Merry Men? Perhaps to prevent people getting certain ideas at the wrong time. Such as that they can set up bandit camps, whether in Sherwood Forest or elsewhere, and disturb the quiet of the realm. Or affect the seriousness: for it was also disclosed that "merry" doesn't mean "happy." It meant, in the old days, "active, energetic."

And there may even be metaphysical reasons, though I wish to say little explicitly about this. If there is an evolution from conquest, brute force, to social mores, why should there not be one even beyond that, which this process could advance? Time may tell.

The process of the abrupt reversal of belief, and actions as well, can take place on the living stage of human actions as well as in tradition. I have space for only one illustration of this in the mysterious world of the English, but it is a good one.

John Holt was Chief Justice of England, and lived from 1642 to 1710. He was fond of walking around the countryside, a common English pursuit. One day he arrived hungry at an inn, but had no money. Holt heard that the landlord's daughter was suffering from an ague which had defied the efforts of doctors to cure. So the traveler offered to treat her with a talisman. He wrote some Greek words on a piece of parchment, tied it around the patient's arm – and she recovered at once. The landlady fed him and naturally refused to present a bill, and so all parties were satisfied.

Here we see, in the full light of day, the creation of a myth, a story, a legend, a magic. But the tale does not end here. The Judge was one day trying the case of an old woman brought before him accused of the crime of witchcraft, and of having a written spell in her possession.

When he examined the evidence, Holt found that it consisted of the very same parchment which he had given the girl with the ague all those years before.

The Judge explained matters to the jury, they acquitted the woman, and the myth was broken. No doubt the parchment had been in constant use for the forty years since the Judge had prepared it.

The Edinburgh Review, in noting this strange course of events, added:

> [T]his incident came so opportunely to the discomfiture of ignorance and bigotry as to put a final end to prosecutions for witchcraft in that part of the country.

An Englishman Needs Time: as Eartha Kitt has said – forty years in this case. No doubt the time had come to abandon witchcraft prosecutions. But, when the talisman was written, it had been a time for talismans.

"The freedom of time," said the novelist Jeffrey Archer in an interview, "is the greatest privilege."

I had spent a lot of my life with traditional tales. And it is my opinion that they are not so much invented as based upon just such experiences as that of the English Chief Justice. They come from reality as much as from imagination.

Going Native can be very hazardous indeed, unless – like any interloper in the trackless jungle – you keep a very sharp lookout for native booby-traps. I have a friend who has an immense number of quarterings on his shield. He is a successful industrialist and respected intellectual on the Continent, and his children are all at English public schools. One day he took me to his London club.

We were seated at one of those long, communal tables which are part of English tribal life. If you take your place at one, instead of sitting at a separate table, it means that you are prepared to talk to any other Member who happens along for a midday bite. Two Members came and sat opposite us.

One of the newcomers, after we had nodded our good-days, said to my host, "Don't seem to remember having seen your friend here before."

Now the other man should have said either "No"; or "So-and-so is a Member of the Athenaeum," or something similar like "he farms in Wiltshire." But no: he was a Member of one of England's premier clubs, but he was still a foreigner, albeit one who spoke perfect English.

Instead he said, "Idries Shah has written twenty or thirty books. Some of them are used in honors degree studies at more than a hundred universities."

He had been far too foreign. The Englishman looked straight at him. "How amazing," was all he said. And this man was the head of one of Britain's major universities.

Much more of that kind of thing, and my foreign friend will undoubtedly be asked to resign. When I tackled him later, he showed that he will never understand the English. He said, "I don't understand! I'd reduced the number of universities by three hundred, for purpose of understatement..." But here's an interesting thing. My Continental friend had made a gaffe, but I had not. And I had been embarrassed by that "How amazing." So the English scholar evidently decided to make it up to me, without having to contact me directly.

The upshot was that I received offers of honorary doctorates of law or literature, from one university after another, "in recognition of my work." The only common denominator, in most cases, was that, "among others" (as discreet inquiries revealed) the honor had been proposed by the English academic.

In going native, there are intricate problems even if you have long been in the country and studied it with all your skill. I have a friend who was the ruler of a state in the old North-West Frontier area. I had often visited his court, a model of the courtesy and chivalry of the ancient monarchies of Central Asia. I cannot actually name it, but it is one of those principalities whose rulers' titles (like The Wali of

Pusht-i-Koh or The Akhound of Swat) have always had a romantic appeal for the English.

One day I arrived at the State, to find that the young prince, the heir to the Throne, was finally home after finishing his education at one of the older English universities. Our family is related to theirs, and the old Ruler made me co-host at the celebrations to mark the return of the heir. I let the Court arrange the tent-pegging, the wrestling and the sharpshooting, and the feeding of five thousand warriors, and said that I would take on the arrangements for the main banquet.

"Although you have been in the Land of the Infidels," the old Chief said to me, "there is nothing I would like better than a return to ancient ways; for you know and prize the old values. Let us have a traditional feast, like proper soldiers and princes, before it is all swept away."

What did he mean? I wanted to know.

"I am not sure that I will see another year, even a single further national celebration of any kind. For my dear son, now attached to the ways of the unbeliever, is going to run this state and its ceremonies after the pattern of the Franks."

Such, indeed, as I was informed by the fresh-faced boy, would be his practice. As a youth of noble blood, he had been invited to many ceremonial occasions in England. At each he had tried to learn the advanced social practices of the West, just as he had gone there to acquire its learning. Now, to bring his people into the twentieth century, he was determined to adopt progressive ways. I recorded his words:

"When I first attended English functions at the highest level, I was so naive that I found myself affronted at every turn. I did not know where to look when servants raised their voices in the presence of their masters! Instead of making a silent signal for the chief guest to lead the company into a meal, a man in false white hair shouted, 'Dinner is served!' Instead of maintaining a decorous silence during the meal, all gabbled together. Hence, when a speech was to be made, a lackey in a red coat had to shout, 'Pray silence!' It even started the moment we arrived at the house. A man at the door, instead of knowing your name, as any well-trained domestic should, especially in the case of people of quality, asked you who you were. As soon as you told him, he bawled it out at the top of his voice. Among us, as you know, it is the custom that only inferiors who come to do homage are thus treated."

So why was the young master importing such barbaric habits here, where protocol had been unchanged for fifteen centuries?

"Ah, well you see, after several such experiences, I got quite used to it. After a few more, taking my lead, I suppose, from the other people there, I began to see it as admirable. There must be *something* to it, or people wouldn't stand for it, don't you think?"

The graft did not take. It was reported to me that complications arose the very first time the new regime tried out English ceremonial ways. The first man to arrive was the thirty-third hereditary Khan of a clan with forty thousand fighting men; he also bore the title of King. When he was asked by the doorman at the castle what his name was, he was not best pleased. "Tell thy master, snivelling ape," he snarled, "that if he does not know my name by now, he will hear it from a myriad throats in battle!"

Professor Trevelyan's original Englishmen, fresh from Schleswig, would have understood that reaction. So, in England or elsewhere, make sure you Go Native at the right time, and to the appropriate extent.

As I reminded my young friend, the Anglefied prince, "Your people have a proverb, 'What took a hundred men to build may be thrown down by a single one.'"

You can successfully Go Native in England if you can think just like everyone else here does; though there is no obligation to exclude any other kind of thought. Just don't be ruled by it.

Thinking like them involves having an inner sense of what is right and what is not quite right. I do not say that the inward Anglean command-and-control system is yet perfect. If it were, the community would probably have attained all its objectives. Its effectiveness, however, is attested by the fact that, with less resources and fewer apparent chances of success, the English have got farther than many a country of comparable size and population.

I think that the inward Anglean is still working (sometimes in various directions at once) on the matter of developing the Right Angle, the completed England.

There was, at first, a lot of leeway to make up. Fletcher and Kipling, in their *School History of England*, make no bones about it; they do not look back to a golden age of their progenitors:

> The Saxon Englishman was a savage with the vices and cruelties of an overgrown schoolboy, a drunkard, a gambler and very stupid. But he was a truth-teller, a brave, patient and cool-headed fellow.

The Englishman's high opinion of himself, which is what most foreigners speak and write most critically about, seems to date only from the sixteenth century, and cannot therefore be regarded as a permanent trait. Donald Home, in his *God is an Englishman*, traces this characteristic to the (Welsh) Tudors, observing that "English conceit was born in the anxious but exhilarating nationalism of the founding of the English Church." By Victorian times it was in full flower. But how many English people today would recognize themselves in these inspired words of Joseph Chamberlain?:

> I believe in this race, the greatest governing race the world has ever seen; in this Anglo-Saxon race, so proud-reaching, self-confident and determined, this race, which neither climate nor change can degenerate, which will infallibly be the predominant force of future history and universal civilisation.

Lord Colyton of Farway and Taunton, the distinguished former diplomat, has written of his people's "feeling perhaps that we were already losing ground" toward the end of the Second World War. That gives the English sense of superiority an innings of something like three hundred years. I think that the deeper instinct of the people dates from earlier – and will endure longer.

Many of this community's successes are well known: they include most of the things for which the English are admired or envied. The failures (which point to experimental probing, and perhaps emotion drowning out the "brave, patient, coolheaded fellow" within) are also well documented.

Sometimes the competence of the inner directorate, the guiding role of the group-mind, works well. At other times the higher consciousness may be less stunningly active. That it can come to the surface at the drop of a hat may be seen by anyone who observes the English at calm appraisal.

One day, before I had attuned myself well enough to the thinking-patterns of Joseph Chamberlain's Greatest Governing Race The World Has Ever Seen, I dropped in at the Patent Office with an idea. The staff were very willing to listen to my idea. One official sat inert, eyes closed, as I described the Afghan *sandali*:

In Central Asia we have this warming system. It is a charcoal brazier, burning under the table at which you sit, with thick fabric hanging down all round the table. It keeps you warm in the coldest weather. I would substitute, for economy, ease of use and safety, an electric or other non-flame heater.

He was a large, very Saxon type of man; that is to say, an English one, having shed the vices and cruelties and developed the patience and cool-headedness. I was sure that he was a truth-teller as well. He sat silently for quite a long time. Then he said, "Why not use central heating for the whole room?"

I said, "It's cheaper to heat a small area. It is wasteful to heat, say, a dining-room which is used only a few times a day."

He nodded, and signaled to two other officials. They came to his side. At his behest I repeated the idea. The three of them looked at one another. Then my interlocutor cleared his throat and raised his eyebrows. The others nodded. They knew what he was about to say.

"This device of yours," he said, "we do not feel that this kind of thing is wanted in England." He looked at the faces of the other men. They were already smiling in unison. Right or wrong, they thought as one man.

35

New English Bottles

Kindness
Kindnesses are easily forgotten, but injuries! – what worthy man does not keep those in mind?
      William Makepeace Thackeray: *Lovel the Widower*

THE MARQUIS OF Halifax, talking of England, once said that here, "A man that should call everything by its right name would hardly pass the street without being knocked down as a common enemy." Now this may be why so many strange euphemisms and weird phrases are used by the British aristocracy and others: he had put the word around. "Never call anything by its right name, or you'll be in trouble."

That was my tentative conclusion until one day when, driving a noisy boneshaker through the streets of London, I was stopped by a policeman. "Have you a Haudible Means of Approach?" he asked.

I was about to say, "No, only an old car," when the noble Lord's words came into my mind, and I immediately reversed my earlier opinion of him as only an eccentric adviser to the Quality. Like many other things in England, I reasoned with Afghan cunning, the Marquis had said that because, in the streets to which he referred, people like this policeman had a language of their own. "Audible Means of Approach," while somewhat labored, seemed to describe my car perfectly. Indeed, it was little else.

So I said "Yes, Officer," in my nicest voice. Surely the vehicle could have been heard coming from afar. In view of this, his next question baffled me: "Let's be seein" it, then." Suddenly, to my chagrin, I realized that the original phrase must be quoted from some legal nonsense about Having An Audible Means of *Signaling* One's Approach, as garbled by the constabulary. Audibility itself was not enough. The constable threatened to do me for not having a motor-horn.

Some of my fellow-Afghans swear that English eccentricity is based on nothing more than misunderstandings such as this. But, as they're only Afghans, what would they know?

No, I think that I shall stick with Halifax's explanation, only noting that I do not know the reason for this strange English custom. Perhaps they have harnessed incoherence as a ploy to fool the enemy, or the foreigner. Nothing wrong with that, as the great Henry Root, luminary of English social investigation and author of *The Henry Root Letters* and *The Further Letters of Henry Root*, would put it. No, of course not, Henry, who ever said there was?

The procedure, too, may be a way of catching people out verbally, as people do by physical signaling in England. The standard joke is one about a yokel. A superior young man comes across a countryman sitting with rod and line dangling into a well. He throws him a coin and asks, "Caught many?"

The rustic bares his toothless gums. "Thrave," he says, "you be the fourth today."

This, you will not need to be told, is an authentic English teaching-story, and they all know it. The version I have given here has an extra twist, used in advanced Anglean training. Many ordinary English people imagine that the "thrave" here is the Oxfordshire (and Bucks) version of the word "three." So it can be, but that is not the intention of the instructor. Those who look the word up in a good dictionary will find, of course, that there are still deeper significances. *Thrave* means (naturally, among other things) both "two dozen," or "a good number."

Once you get into dialect, which some English people swear is the Real English, they do something worse than knocking you down in the streets as a common enemy: they almost permanently addle your brain.

I suppose Lord Halifax had not been to the North Country, or he would surely have modified his dictum. There they have a word spelled and pronounced "Rake." This means a track up a pasture, a journey on a track, the amount carried on such a journey, or a string of wagons (which could be on the track and also on the journey) which may or may not be carrying the amount already referred to.

If you don't believe this, and who would blame you, just look it up in a good dictionary. Now translate Standard English into North Country, as follows:

> *There was a rake with a rake running through it. People went for rakes along it, with rakes carrying their rakes, in a rake.*

I was explaining all this to a fellow enthusiast, when he fell to the ground, his face crumpled, an expression of mingled alarm and desperation frozen on his features. At the time we were actually in a North Country village, having confirmed with some locals that they did indeed use the word in the senses given by Chambers.

It has been said, especially by soured priests, that the whole thing, the secret language, is a pagan conspiracy and a special form of anti-clericalism. I must say that there is some possibility of a case being made out for this.

Where the native dialects have it that *Bloody* is "by Our Lady," where "Paul's work" is really "a bungled job," and "Christmas!" is an expletive, yes – there are grounds. If you look up the meanings of "to christen" in an English vernacular dictionary such as Partridge, what do you see? "To soil, chip, damage (something hitherto unmarked)."

Yes, there are grounds: though essentially the English are religious. It's just that they have this proverb, "God comes without a bell."

Changes in religion are matched by changes in outward signs of all kinds. A man wearing a blazer may seem to you to be impeccably dressed for Henley or the like. Just turn back the pages, though, of *Punch*, to 1885, supposedly in an epoch when river-lazing and aristocratic manners were at their height. At that time someone wearing a blazer could be, and was, panned for looking "like a nigger minstrel out for a holiday."

You can seldom predict whether an act is going to be seen as good or bad. Sometimes you may be shocked and feel sympathy for the English, while they pass the whole thing off with a merry laugh. After a television report showing the Union Jack being burned at a demonstration in a Third World country, I heard an Englishman say: "After all, the flag was adopted only as late as January first 1801, after the Union with Ireland. *And* the reporter fella got it wrong: it's called the Union Flag, not the Union Jack at all." Sting completely removed, no after-effects, no scarring.

I should really have expected that: the name of the speaker was Miller. Miller can mean: "A bee, a vicious horse, a white hat, a murderer, a boxer or a burglar." With that sophistication of options in your name alone, a little matter like dealing with flag-burning would be no problem. Although I am disposed to believe that it is lucky that "Jenkins" and "ear" have so few synonyms; otherwise it could have taken more than nine years for the war with Spain to get off the ground.

And English people often delight in hearing that words they think they know really (or additionally) mean something else. Indeed, you can gain instant social success by memorizing some and spouting them at suitable times and in the right places. There is a popular television teaching-event, disguised as a game, which capitalizes on this proclivity.

Mass-circulation journals, with or without crosswords, constantly feature items which connect with the peculiarities of (English) words.

For beginners, I give a few which have not recently been used:

> SCUTTLE (a ship) does not mean to sink it, but to shut or to open. Hence, theoretically, someone could save a ship by scuttling her.
> M'CHUTA (or ME'CHOOTA) is not the name of an African chief but Etonian for "My Tutor."
> MARYLEBONE (pronounced *Marlibun* or *Marrybunn*) is not from Marie la Bonne, but from Mary on the Bourne (boundary).
> SPRUCE (neat) is not from the elegance of the spruce-fir, but from *à la Prusse*, "like a Prussian."

And here is a good clincher. MAID MARIAN is not the girl associated with Robin Hood. In fact it is not a girl at all, having switched sexes at some indeterminate time in the past, through oral transmission problems (or even, since the English are involved, deliberately). It comes from the *morion*, the Moorish-Spanish helmet worn by Morris dancers and brought to England from Iberia, according to English sources. One of the male dancers was known as the *Mad* Morion.

Have fun; but remember, if you are not English, that they have a special skill in this art. We have it on good authority, for a British Prime Minister (and Englishman), Clement Attlee, said: "I think the British have the distinction above all other nations of being able to put new wine into old bottles without bursting them." What kind of wine *does* burst bottles? I expect Attlee could have told you; sometimes these apparently mixed metaphors look like traps to lead you on. This quotation, though it speaks of the British, is found in the Penguin *International Thesaurus of Quotations* under "England and Englishmen." And the book has no section for "Britain and the British." Let the Celts say what they may – if there is any need to keep their end up. I note that it is an Englishman, not a Scot, for instance, who writes:

> Bruce, with grey eyes growing wider,
> Watched a persevering spider.
> Then rose
> And swiped the English on the nose.

Hugh Chesterman's *Kings and Other Things*, published something over fifty years ago in London, puts a lot of new wine into old bottles. It's worth looking for it in a library if you still doubt that the English regard history as something invented for English people to make fun of.

Perhaps that is because, as Halifax said, tell the truth and you may be knocked down as a common enemy.

36

The Solution

Shall We Talk Nonsense?
English offers unparalleled scope for inaccurate and mushy writing. It's a splendid language for talking nonsense in, or for generating verbal fog; it's the ideal language for a politician, it offers wonderful scope for the avoidance of precise and responsible thinking.
                    Christopher Derrick: *Reader's Report*

HAVING ESTABLISHED THAT eclecticism is the basis both of this book and of the English method, it still behooves me to repeat that my assessment of what might help in increasing Anglekin activity (and decreasing the reverse) cannot be mechanically systematic.

In fact, this warning was sparked off, all unknowingly, by Mary MacRoberts. She was quite ancient and from Scotland; and insisted upon becoming my daily help when she bumped into me outside the Maida public house in a part of London now known as Little Venice; having filled her wizened frame, so far as possible, with highland restoratives.

I took her on, and she came, when she felt like it, to clean the apartment, one of a number in the house where I lived at the time.

I was able to follow her accent and meaning well enough: but an English friend, Morris ("Moorish, Dark-Colored") who lived downstairs was not so lucky: in fact he was quite snooty about her. "That's not English," he would snarl, when at a loss to understand her, which was often.

One day I thought that things had gone too far when, perhaps to taunt him, she answered something like this, to his baffled fury: "Wanya ken whee I was last nicht? I'll tell ye. Twas a braw bricht minlicht nicht, ilkit the noo..."

"Speak English!" he roared. I stepped between them, for I had done my homework.

"Morris," I said, "you think that that is Gaelic or something. But I have to tell you that almost every word that Mary uses is pure Anglo-Saxon, and far more English than the words you speak."

There was no more trouble with him after that; he said he'd check up, but I didn't care. The facts were true. Later he even went so far as to confirm that it was pure English that our Irish plumber was speaking when he said "I'll be after seeing you before, so I will," when making an appointment.

I cannot say that we were always able to profit from what Mary was trying to convey, since much of it seemed to contain messages which defied ordinary thought-processes.

One day Mary said something about "Yon Norwegian."

I said, "What Norwegian?"

"Yon Norwegian in the loft."

I knew that the man in the attic was Chinese; in fact I knew him well. His name was Ingram (Raven of Ing) Wu Yang Su, and he came from Canton. But I let it pass, and after that he was referred to between us as "The Norwegian."

Then, one day, as Mary scraped the black marble doorstep with the whitening stone, which she insisted on doing because she had always done that at her ain hoose, I mentioned the Norwegian.

"And wha's he, when he's at hame?"

I translated what I meant into the best lowland dialect I could manage: "Och, ye well ken, Mary, yon Norwegian laddie Ingram wha's in the wee attic."

"Norwegian? He lukes more ilkit a *Chinese* tae me..."

Now for the significance: the application, as the medieval preaching monks called it, torturing a moral from a text which, as often as not, would not bear the interpretation. Mary was giving me the kind of look that the Scotsman in *Dad's Army* assumed when he snarled "We're *doomed*."

I saw it all, in a flash. Mary was using an ancient ploy, perhaps one brought over by the Angles, best encapsulated in the term "the confusion technique." People do it all the time in England; but in its purest form it is found among the Lowland Scots, together with their Teutonic dialect, and they have used it for centuries against the English, who settled in the south and called it England. I emphasize this geography because, of course, there are Angle-descended people in Scotland as well. A Scottish friend recently explained the difference between the two "septs" for me, thus:

> When pushing northward, the acute Angles turned right into Scotland, and the obtuse Angles turned left, into England.

And my point in all this? Simply to say that there are undoubtedly vast treasures of technique and neglected skills, stored up there in Scotland, to which the English are linguistic and gesticulatory heirs. They must, however, clear away their false impression of those Scots who are not Gaels, before they can win through to a share of the common heritage.

One need only quote the national bard, Robert Burns, to be quite sure of both of my points. He uses Anglo-Saxon words almost unsullied by either the Gaelic or the Norman:

> O wad some Pow'r the giftie gie us
> To see oursels as others see us!
> It wad frae mony a blunder free us,
> And foolish notion.

I admit the poem is addressed primarily to a louse, but that point, I feel, would be a quibble if adduced in attempted refutation. Look at the content, as well as the container. Burns is appealing to us all to look and see.

Clear away all the barriers to understanding the Scots, starting with the language, then the Welsh, then the Irish, and you will have a United Kingdom indeed: and perhaps a springboard, like the word "Eureka," to even greater things.

There have been some, upon whom I have tried out this theory, who have suggested that this is not so much a confusion technique as an attempt to muddle through. I believe that such persons, insofar as they have been English (not all of them were) are hoist with their own petard. The very use of the term indicates that they have at least heard of the primary English technique. And what's wrong with that? in the endearing phrase heard throughout the land: the answer to most, if not all, criticisms here.

Others have opined that before such an attempt could be made the English would have to shed the overweening modesty which is one of their chief features. But, as I have reminded them, there are always those who will make the necessary sacrifice in a good enough cause. People who are not afraid to request the Highest Quarters to confound politics and frustrate the knavish tricks for which foreigners are famous will always rise to a challenge and hie forth in the cause of progress.

A recent item in *The Times* supports me. The Civil Service Department asked the public to put names forward for membership of the "List of the Good and the Great," to serve on Royal commissions and the like. More than six hundred people submitted *their own names* in less than three months. Now there's a brave attempt to overcome modesty.

As for the cause of education, this is highly thought of in England in some quarters and interest is increasing. All that is needed for my plans to work are a few minor adjustments. I am not talking about the two million adult illiterates in the country, but of even more interesting questions.

Britain is a land of tradition; so we are told. This may explain the illiterates, for the condition is surely traditional everywhere. But does it explain why one survey, reported in the *Daily Telegraph*, found that books dating from the year 1807 were still being put on the market by educational publishing houses? Some science books dating – it must be admitted – from much later (1887) were still in print. One adventurous educational publication tells children that the motor-car is a "new and useful part of life." No fewer than 127 of the 800 science books available were published before the 1939–45 war.

This state of affairs, I am glad to see, is ascribed to "professional men and women" who "abhor change and will do all they can to avoid it," in the words of Sir James Pitman, obviously a true Englishman.

How long, asks the paper's Education Correspondent, will it take for any good thing to catch on? The answer, as all true English people have known in their bones for quite a time, is just as long as it takes to get rid of the professionals. Was it not an Englishman who penned the immortal lines:

My Auntie May would be alive today –
if the doctors hadn't killed her.

I am aware, of course, that reference books give "false dice" as one meaning of "doctors." But that does not invalidate the fact that "doctoring" means adulterating; and a doctored cat, if questioned, would not agree that it has been improved by the operation.

Mind you, one has to be careful what one tampers with: another good English precept. Perhaps, after all, those hundred-year-old texts actually contain truths which are missing from more recent works. My reason for saying this is that the papers are full of stories about how the experts have found out that cholesterol is bad, and then that it is not; that salt increases blood pressure, and that it does not generally matter; that hot tea does not warm you, and so on. One academic recently proved that people fall off bicycles because they lose their balance; he had spent a lot of money on experiments. Any moment now someone may well refute him. So, don't try to run before you can walk, as we say in England.

I say this because of a reflection about doctors, occasioned by my reference to them a moment ago. Perhaps you had not noticed, or did not know, that doctors in England usually have no doctorate. They are generally Bachelors (even if married) and Fellows (even if female) but not doctors. Except that their name-plates say "doctor." There may be a reason for this. Some researcher – preferably a non-professional one – should look into it.

Then, while on the subject, please observe that these doctors are divided into two types: physicians and surgeons. English physicians, though not surgeons, operate from premises called Surgeries. And, although the surgeons are considered doctors, they must never be called "Doctor," even if they have no doctorate. They are known as Mister. This holds good even when, as is not infrequent, they really do have doctorates.

In order to clarify, though not in any excessive, un English, way, some of these problems, a Commission might be set up. It could be composed of the Great and the Good. Its only requirement would be that it should not function in any sequential or logical way.

Mind you, the Commission may well discover that the doctors behave like that because of the patients. English people, according to a survey by the London Hospital, remembered less than half of what they had been told by a doctor. Of those who did remember, some believed "instructions exactly opposite to those in fact given them."

These, then, are the bare bones of the theory. Though seemingly limited to Scottish dialect, the presence of a Chinese gentleman in Maida (a place in Calabria) Vale, a passing mention of a non-existent Norwegian and a little about education and medicine, I hope that the general argument is as clear as is usual in this country.

37

Nothing of Significance to Say

The English Transgression
We are the children of light, and it is we that sit in darkness. If we are judged, it will not be for the merely intellectual transgression of failing to appreciate other nations, but for the supreme spiritual transgression of failing to appreciate ourselves.
G. K. Chesterton

MY GOOD AND kind friend Robert Cecil, CMG &c., is not only English (and an authority on German history) but has been Head of Cultural Relations at the Foreign Office. He was one of the three people (the others are the Venerable Bede and Beowulf) who made me think deeply about the ultimate origins of the English.

He told me the true story of a learned Englishman who went to give an address in another country. The lecturer began by modestly disclaiming any special knowledge or capacity. He could, he continued, probably not add much to what his distinguished audience already knew. The result was that hardly anyone took any notice of his talk. They were all scholars, it is true: but the visiting authority had said he had little to say, and they took his word for it. The lecture-hall, at a university with a world reputation, nearly emptied almost as soon as he had spoken these first few words.

Now this may have been because these people were accustomed to the hard sell, and could not marshal their attention if they didn't get it. Or perhaps they had too much reverence for authority, and simply believed everything that they were told.

In England, we find almost the exact opposite. After all, there is the case of the English limerick, told me as a warning by Professor Allan Nevins, founder of the Oral History Research Office at Columbia University, and a lifelong friend of our family. I take it not only as humor, but as a warning and even as a teaching-story:

> There was an old fellow called Baird
> Who said, "What I could say if I dared!
> And say it I must – or else I shall bust!"
> So he said it. And nobody cared.

The first, and probably also the last, hurdle for all who would live among the English is "nobody cares." How many times, I wonder, have I heard people from overseas say, "You could fall down dead in Piccadilly Circus and nobody would care!"? Foreigners think that the English just don't bother about anything. In fact they do: but only about things they have decided to care about. The figures show that they are among the most charitable people on earth. Whether you like them or not, you can't deny this, and that virtually every single one of them has been reared on the nursery rhyme, "Don't Care was *made* to Care."

Months can pass without your meeting anyone who thinks he has anything Significant to Say. Silence is important here. The English mystic William Langland, in *The Vision of Piers*

Plowman (fourteenth century), goes back to the Creation to confirm the peerless nature of silence: "Adam, whiles he spak nat, had paradys at wille." The English have internalized, and act quietly upon, ideas which other peoples feel they must express by noisy demonstration. The process is going on all around you if you live here. Sometimes you get startling signs of it, though it is not often fully visible.

At one melancholy period of my life, an English couple helped me to an extent that I would have thought hardly possible. They were prepared to make a considerable sacrifice, had stood by me when they could have lost much more than any reasonable person would expect to do, all for the sake of a stranger.

When the crisis had passed, and all was well, the three of us were sitting in their house, just getting used to the new situation: our escape from the calamity which had come so near, and had brought us close.

I said, "Of course, in spite of everything, I don't know you two very well. Thanks are very little to offer in exchange for your kindness. But I do want to know one thing. What made you offer me such help? I am almost unknown to you, and you have done something that is generally thought of as the action of saints."

They looked at one another for a moment, quietly, and smiled. Then the husband said, "Well, we're not very religious people, if that's what you mean..."

Exactly, I thought. They did not need to think of themselves as religious people. All they had to do was to behave as such people should. Like Mr. Cecil's lecturer, they had "nothing of significance to say."

While I have been in their country, and while working on this book, I have had one sensation again and again.

You can study them usefully only if you are like them. To be like them you must collect material, look, listen, experience, watch. The Anglean heritage distributed among a hundred treasuries.

From Professor Sir Ernest Barker's summing-up to *The Character of England*, that huge and muddled compilation of what the English think, I first discovered that the moment they try to look at themselves, they proceed as fallaciously as foreigners do, and draw equally erratic conclusions. Barker himself says the strangest things. In six years of war, he believes, England,

> isolated from the Continent knew, in its sickness for the sun, and hunger to see different earth and hear different languages and experience different cultures, that the Englishman abroad had been his country's physician, giving it the necessary medicine to relieve its congestion.

Now, who would have imagined an Englishman thinking like that? But there was more:

> The healing wells he had drawn from, France, Germany, Italy, were muddied or had run dry.

Who would have guessed it? The English, pining for their European roots, the land from which they came...

I began to think, reading these words soon after Robert Cecil's anecdote, of another people which I had come across. They prefaced their remarks with "You'll know this already, but..."

They, too, did not seem to care about anything, but were in reality a very caring tribe. They told jokes against themselves, were strong and silent – and they couldn't assess themselves either. No. I dismissed the idea of a connection: it just wasn't possible: there was too much against it. I put the idea out of my mind.

When I read the Venerable Bede, claiming that the English were a part of the Scythian migration from the East, I was slightly surprised that the Angles and Saxons should style themselves thus, but I read up on the Scythians just the same, to follow up every hint.

The Scythians, I found, were a warrior people living in the north of Europe and Asia. They – or some of them – were known to ancient Western writers as the Sacae, and to those of the East as Saka, after some great progenitor. Eventually, they became known as the Saka-Sun, the Sons of Saka.

I looked up the name in the *Cyclopaedia of Names*:

> SACAE, in ancient history a nomadic people dwelling in Central Asia near the sources of the Oxus and Jaxartes.

These Saka people, the Saka-Sun, were no joke to deal with. They descended from Central Asia and defied, or defeated, Darius and Cyrus, the great Persian emperors, who called all Scythians Sakai. They went south and west, plundering the eastern Mediterranean lands. They had, by the time of Herodotus's time, gained an important foothold in Europe.

When they conquered a part of Armenia, they named the country Sakasina after themselves.

Saka-Sun, Saxon; Sakasina, Saxonia... Associations crowd in and bid to rank as conclusions.

The Angle-Saxon conquerors brought so little with them in the way of history – apart from the legend that they migrated from the East – that there seemed no hope of further progress. Then I remembered *Beowulf*, and how an historian had remarked upon its Eastern and other elements. Were there enough of these to seek a locality in the East where a constellation of such beliefs might have been found? A place where the Saxons could have spatchcocked their ideas together before they started westward?

I listed the items isolated by the scholar:

Paganism
Zoroastrianism
Hebrew traditions
Christian stories
Oriental dragons
Indian customs
Greek elements.

Where, I wondered, in the East, did people claim to be descended from the ancient Hebrews, followed Zoroaster and had very ancient Christian bishoprics? Where, in addition, was there a strong Oriental influence, and where in Asia were the farthest centers of Greek civilization?

There is only one such place known to me, and perhaps to anyone, where, to the surprise and delight of archeologists, such culture-mixing had taken place: Afghanistan.

But more specific than just Afghanistan, unlikely though that might be. In its northern part: called Balkh, Bactriana, "Mother of Cities."

Had the Scythians ever been in Bactriana? I knew that the Sakas were there, as is stated in all Afghan history books. I looked up Sharon Turner's *History of the Saxons from the Earliest Times*: the Scythians, were called Saka. They

> ... seized Bactriana and the most fertile part of Armenia... a part of Armenia having been named Sakasina is mentioned by Strabo... and seems to give a geographical locality to our primeval ancestors,

and to account for the Persian words that occur in the Saxon language, as they must have come into Armenia from the northern regions of Persia.

I had been pipped at the post, by over a hundred and fifty years, for Turner had published his book in 1828: and had even found 262 words in Anglo-Saxon which corresponded in sound and meaning, he said, to Persian ones. And that was before the unique combination of Indian, Greek, Oriental and other cultures which flowered in Afghanistan was known to scholars; in 1828 the numerous Sakan relics had not yet been dug up in Afghanistan.

All I could console myself with was that I had, in using *Beowulf*, based my detective work on a different group of ideas, the religious and cultural, rather than upon linguistic analysis.

And the people whom I thought most resembled the English in the East, with their taciturnity and so on, whom I had rejected as impossible candidates for the earliest English? None other than the fair-skinned people of Nuristan, formerly called Kafiristan. These people, talking to an English tycoon friend of mine, had actually spoken of a land in the West with white rocks rising out of the sea. Their legend, he told me, recounted the journey there of some of their people. So he had arrived at a similar conclusion as Turner and me: the three of us each using a different set of criteria.

The Nuristan people are the remnant of an ancient population who lived in Afghanistan when the land was called Aryana. They were displaced, driven into the mountains of the country now called Nuristan, by the likes of us – Arabs, Turks, Iranians and all kinds of others: the Afghans of today.

Like the English, most of our ancestors don't come from the country we live in. And, even if the English did spend a long time in Afghanistan – long enough to absorb into their national epic a whole range of Afghan beliefs – they, like us, originated much farther afield, in High Asia.

Sharon Turner was delighted to find an Eastern land actually named, after his ancestors, Sakasina. But that was only in the interlude before these nomads took to the road again:

> The first scenes of their civil existence, and of their progressive power, were in Asia, to the East of the [River] Araxes.

If the Bactrian theory is correct, then parts of my own country were a homeland for the Angles before they had anything else. On that reckoning, they would have lived longer in my (or our) country than I have lived in theirs. And they were in that very old England before most of my own ancestors, who only arrived in Afghanistan in the ninth century.

That's a turn-up for the book.

And to think that, in between Central Asia and the farthest West, there had been only two Englands. Ethelweard had left it on record that "Old England" was what the Saxons called Schleswig, known by the Danes as Hathaby. There was a still older one, perhaps in Afghanistan, possibly in Armenia. And, as Ethelweard was writing, the newest one was coming into being. Located in Britain it, too, would one day come to be known as Old England.

Salisbury's dictum seems peculiarly appropriate:

> No lesson seems to be so deeply inculcated by the experience of life as that you shall never trust experts.

No, far better than expertise is the more typically English instinctive approach. "What is not wisdom is danger" is an English proverb; and few experts can claim to have wisdom. Inner perception is the technique which gets to the root of things by collecting information, adding sense and avoiding barriers to lucid thought.

The chief features of this procedure are actually in print. Even more interestingly, they were laid down, in four points, by a remarkable Englishman, the thirteenth-century monk Roger Bacon. He was thought eccentric because he lectured in Oxford dressed in Saracen robes: though at that time it was from Moorish Spain that "modern" knowledge had percolated to the West. It is now known that there is a great deal in Bacon's listing of elements which inhibit lucidity:

1. Too much reliance upon mere authority
2. Being enslaved by custom
3. Accepting general beliefs
4. Pretensions to knowledge

Naturally, and largely because of the rigid, Latinate mindset of the scholars of that time, Bacon was persecuted. His monkish superiors felt that he "held dangerous ideas." If he were to return today, he would see both the fruits of his teaching, here in England, and also the problems which exist where he has been disregarded.

All people are in some sense dark ("mysterious; obscure") and the English may well be the darkest. I rather like their own phrase, *a dark horse* – "a horse or person of undisclosed ability." Shall we delve deeper? Very well; reference books show that, in demotic English, "horse" is another word for "holy."

They have another term, too: "As Holy as a Horse." And that means *extremely holy*. The very word *holy* stands for "whole, perfect, healthy." The earliest English greeting, reported to have been used by Hengist to Vortigern, is "Was-Hael!" Be in health.

We Afghans say the same thing: so, Englishpeople: *Salamat bashen*, Peace and health. With characteristic even-headedness, E. H. Whinfield, the Persian scholar, has translated a quatrain of Omar Khayyam which can apply both to the English by their detractors and by the English to them:

> These fools by dint of ignorance most crass,
> Think they in wisdom all mankind surpass;
> And glibly do they damn as infidel
> Each one who is not, like themselves, an ass.

Whether or not the English are, as their historians have insisted, descendants of the Scythians and brought their ways from Asia, we know that they have a strange affinity for the East.

But I would go further.

Have you ever wondered what the factors are which make the East mysterious, interesting and attractive to Westerners? I have isolated twelve points which strike many as characteristic of Eastern peoples:

> They are inscrutable, placid: with deep and
>   concealed emotions;
> They wear strange clothes;
> They have odd customs, including eating unusual
>   foods;
> They have color and pageantry;
> Their languages are extraordinary;

You can't become one of them without very great
   difficulty;
They have (or believe that they have) very ancient
   traditions;
They live in places which are striking, either
   because of the climate or the scenery, or both;
They have unique, or remarkable, religious beliefs;
They have quaint, impressive or mysterious
   buildings;
It can feel very weird to live among them: they
   seem both clever and stupid; and
They have qualities which, like it or not, one must
   admire.

That's the Orientals, from Casablanca to Kamatschka.
And that's the English, too.

A Request

If you enjoyed this book, please review it on Amazon and Goodreads.

Reviews are an author's best friend.

To stay in touch with news on forthcoming editions of Idries Shah works, please sign up for the mailing list:

 http://bit.ly/ISFlist

And to follow him on social media, please go to any of the following links:

 https://twitter.com/idriesshah

 https://www.facebook.com/IdriesShah

 http://www.youtube.com/idriesshah999

 http://www.pinterest.com/idriesshah/

 http://bit.ly/ISgoodreads

 http://idriesshah.tumblr.com

 https://www.instagram.com/idriesshah/

http://idriesshahfoundation.org

www.ingramcontent.com/pod-product-compliance
Lightning Source LLC
Chambersburg PA
CBHW022056090426
42743CB00008B/628